社会科学研究方法 前沿与

Survey Experiment: a New Technique of Causal Study

用问卷做实验：

调查-实验法的概论与操作

任莉颖 著

重庆大学出版社

图书在版编目(CIP)数据

用问卷做实验:调查-实验法的概论与操作 / 任莉颖著. —重庆:重庆大学出版社,2018.11(2023.3 重印)
(万卷方法)
ISBN 978-7-5689-0496-4

Ⅰ.①用… Ⅱ.①任… Ⅲ.①问卷调查 Ⅳ.①C915

中国版本图书馆 CIP 数据核字(2017)第 326304 号

用问卷做实验:
调查-实验法的概论与操作
任莉颖 著

策划编辑:林佳木
责任编辑:陈 力 林佳木 版式设计:林佳木
责任校对:刘志刚 责任印制:张 策
*
重庆大学出版社出版发行
出版人:饶帮华
社址:重庆市沙坪坝区大学城西路 21 号
邮编:401331
电话:(023) 88617190 88617185(中小学)
传真:(023) 88617186 88617166
网址:http://www.cqup.com.cn
邮箱:fxk@cqup.com.cn(营销中心)
全国新华书店经销
重庆市国丰印务有限责任公司印刷
*
开本:940mm×1360mm 1/32 印张:10.375 字数:233 千
2018 年 11 月第 1 版 2023 年 3 月第 2 次印刷
ISBN 978-7-5689-0496-4 定价:49.00 元

总 序

中国当代社会科学各学科的研究方法多由西方舶来,这一事实不可回避。由此亦衍生出不尽如人意的另一个事实,即这些滥觞于西方的科学研究方法在国内学界的传播与应用,并未能像各个学科的一般理论和知识那样,为国内学者或学生广泛习得并恰当使用。归根究底,造成这种现状的原因无外乎如下两点:一是中国社会科学诸学科长期以来重描述的研究范式;二是青年研究者(多为文科生)在初入社科研究领域时就已产生了视数学为畏途的心态。以此为背景的研究或秉承旧有的研究范式,对新的研究方法视而不见,或对西方学界主流的研究方法进行囫囵吞枣、生吞活剥式的使用。这都不利于正在迅速发展的中国社会科学与国际学术界交流。这个世纪开始,随着大批海外学子陆续回国任教,他们给社会科学学科发展带来很大冲击,也从方法上改变了学科研究的范式。

这里说的方法变革所造成的范式转变,并非简单的定量与定性方法之争。此处所谓新的范式是指通过严谨的研究设计,应用科学的方法(定量或定性方法皆属之),采集数据去从事研究。过去数十年国内学界所累积的学科知识,在这个新的研究范式下,已得到验证,甚至有突破性的理论创新。不过,任何转变都不可能一蹴而就，固有研究范式的惯性及其导致的对于科学方法的疏离感，仍然如紧箍咒一般，时刻影响着科学研究方法在国内社会科学学科的发展。

“社会科学研究方法·前沿与应用”丛书的主要目的就是希望拉近学生与科学方法的距离，从而激发他们学习并应用这些方法。2012年暑期，重庆大学出版社雷少波编辑做客清华大学政治学系，言谈间，我提出组编一套介绍社会科学研究方法丛书的想法，有别于坊间同类介绍方法的丛书，这套丛书的最大特色在于将理论背后的“理论”呈现给读者，让初学者知其然，更能够知其所以然；同时使用实际的研究成果，提供最直观的应用案例，让读者了解到这些研究方法如何应用到以中国为主题的研究，通过主题的熟悉感，真正拉近读者与方法之间的距离，提升读者学习的热情，为有志于从事相关领域研究的人士提供扎实、恳切的引导及参考。

这套丛书编写的体例大致分为理论介绍、案例点评和软件实操展示三个部分。第一部分的理论介绍，主要是编写者结合自身学习该方法的历程，用最浅显易懂的方式（尽可能使用最少或最基本的数学），来介绍方法背后的理论与原理，以及应用该方法的场景，并重点介绍该方法的标准操作流程，以及提示该方法在操作上可能遇到的限制，为读者学习理论提供最大的便利。第二部分的案例点评是本书的亮点，编写者选取应用该方法的范文（优先选择以中文撰写和使用中国数据的论文）进行点评。这样选择的目的如前所述,是希望读者通过既有的研究,切实学习到该方法是如何在中国场景下落地的。编写者的点评首先发挥导读的作用,同时亦不会避重就轻,而是无褒贬之忌讳,既点出该方法在范文中使用的准确、巧妙之处,也会点出研究过程中存在的短板,无论是方法操作上的问题,还是研究设计本身的缺陷,抑或是数据上造成的罅隙,这也是编写者希望读者能够在实操过程中尽量避免的部分,毕竟方法的习得容易,但是要用得对、用得好,还是需要熟悉方法、经验丰富的资深使用者指导。此部分的点评就是希望用文字为读者建构一个面对面的学习场景,起到教师与学生一对一现场教学的效果。第三部分的软件实操展示,使用的软件主要还是坊间常用的 SPSS,STATA,R 三个软件。编写者使用数据范本,实际演示该方法通过不同软件的操作步骤,尽可能做到精准、简洁,同时兼顾可读性、可视性。原则上,这部分至少会涵盖两个软件操作展示,未来如读者有需求,我们将在丛书的网页以附录的方式,编写该方法在其他软件的操作步骤。

丛书总序的最后,必须感谢清华大学的张小劲老师、王天夫老师、洪伟老师、孟天广老师,北京大学的严洁老师、任莉颖老师,中国政法大学的卢春龙老师,人民大学的孙龙老师和远赴英国的呼和那日松老师,诸位同仁鼎力相助,为这套丛书的出炉提供了智力和时间上的大力支持。丛书编著过程中,经历了许多波折与挑战,若没有他们的投入,这套丛书的顺利问世几乎是不可想象的。特别感谢重庆大学出版社雷少波编辑的鼎力支持,我当初言谈间大胆的设想方能实现。也特别感谢林佳木编辑、邹荣编辑不厌其烦地催稿，如果说雷编辑是伯乐的话，林、邹两位编辑则是催促着我们前进的鞭子。丛书的完成，这些文字背后的贵人缺一不可。

编著这套丛书，是为试图改进中国社会科学研究对于国际主流方法的使用状况，这也是上述诸位共谋此事背后的雄心壮志，但不积跬步无以至千里，任何实质性的转变都要依靠些微的积累和推进方能实现，落在实处，就是这一本本小书的质量。若能对有需要的读者有所启发，或能由此催生后续研究的跟进，就是编写者最大的心愿。由于编写者学识所限，这套丛书一定还存在诸多不足和有待完善之处，希望读者和相关方法的使用者及时反馈批评意见，以便于我们再版时加以订正和改进。

苏毓淞

于清华园

2016.10.5

序

这本书所讲的调查-实验是当下社会科学研究最理想的研究方法，它是在过去几十年以来社学科学研究基础上发展出来的，要想知道这本书的价值所在，有必要先了解社会科学研究方法的发展历程。

社会科学最原始的研究方法，是对现有文献的综述，或者是对政策文件和决策机构的描述和分析，例如对民主理论的文献综述，对能源部门的组织机构和人员的描述等，这样的博士论文和学术专著虽然现在还不时出现，但已越来越少，起码在美国的学术界是如此。社会科学的发展，对研究方法提出了越来越高的要求，学术研究正在从传统的文献综述和政策文件分析逐渐过渡到经验研究（emprical study，也译实征研究）。

所谓经验研究，就是用证据来证明研究者的结论，早期的社会科学经验研究，主要是集中在个案调查，又称定性研究，以个案为基础的定性研究最大的好处是对研究对象进行详细具体的描述，又称“细描”（thick description，也译深描），从而得出一套能够解释事件发生的理论。但是个案研究在方法论上的问题至少有两个：第一，个案研究的代表性往往较低，其结论不易被应用于其他地区、人群或案例；第二，个案研究在数据收集和解释的过程中受到研究人员主观因素的干扰，其结论的客观性常常受到质疑。

为了克服个案研究的局限性，1960、1970年代以来，以美国为首的社会科学研究人员发展了抽样问卷调查的研究。抽样，就是在目标总体中严格按照概率原则抽取一个样本，如果这个样本的总体特征与目标总体的特征一致，那么对这个样本的表述也就是对总体的描述，这就克服了个案研究不具代表性的局限；问卷调查，就是用同样的问题访问不同的受访者，并对答案用统一的规则进行编码和量化，这样做的目的是不让数据收集的过程受到研究人员主观因素的干扰，从而克服了定性研究不具客观性的局限。

然而，抽样问卷调查也并不是十全十美的，这种方法的一个局限在于它必须依靠复杂的统计分析来得出结论，常常只有受过专门训练的研究人员才能看得懂，对于一般读者来说，定量分析的结果只是一堆枯燥无味的数字和图表，而定性研究对研究对象的"细描"常常可以弥补定量研究的抽象和枯燥无味。

抽样调查还有一个更致命的问题，就是它无法确定事件发生的因果关系。例如，在一个问卷调查中，研究人员可以询问受访者对媒体的使用情况，也可以询问他们对政治的关心程度，然后，研究人员以媒体使用作为自变量，政治兴趣作为因变量，并通过回归分析证明媒体使用让人更关心政治。但是这个因果关系只是基于研究人员的理论假设，问卷调查并不能真正证明这个关系的存在。

大数据的出现似乎能克服抽样调查概率样本的误差，从而给人们带来了新的希望。概率样本无论有多么科学，都不可避免地存在误差，而大数据是关于所有人的信息，不存在抽样问题，因而也不存在误差。但是大数据的问题在于它只能描述已经发生的事情,而无法展示人们的态度和想法以及可能发生的事情,问卷调查则可以根据研究者的需要来收集人们在态度和想法方面的信息,诸如人际信任、民族主义、政治效能感等社会科学研究中的重要理论问题。大数据的另一个问题是,如果两个事件同时出现,它同样无法确切地描述这些事件之间的因果关系,这是大数据和问卷调查共同存在的问题。

要想证明因果关系的存在,必须依靠实验研究,1980年代以来,社会科学特别是经济学、社会学和政治学的研究人员开始借助心理学的方法,在实验室的环境中对受访者进行预先设计好的干预,例如让他们看一段新闻广播,然后再检测他们对政治的兴趣,如果政治兴趣有所提高,研究人员就可以确定是新闻广播的作用,从而确立媒体对政治兴趣的因果关系。

实验研究虽然可以很好地检测因果关系,但它的致命弱点是不具代表性,实验室的环境不能代表现实生活,实验人群不能代表真实的人口,要想解决这一问题,就必须把实验从实验室搬到现实人群的生活中去,也就是说,要把实验植入通过概率抽取的具备一定人口特征的样本中去。

自1990年代以来,在美国,越来越多的社会科学研究者开始尝试将抽样调查和实验研究结合在一起,从而发展出一种比较系统的新方法:调查-实验,也就是任莉颖博士这本新书的主题。

本书系统地阐述了调查-实验方法的基本原理和实际操作的各个环节。本书包括三个部分:第一部分详细讨论了如何设计一个好的调查-实验，例如如何加入3种实验条件（启动效应、虚拟情境、条目列举），如何运用将实验人群分成实验组和控制组的不同方法，以及如何科学地抽取一个有代表性的样本；第二部分介绍了现有文献中应用调查-实验方法的不同实例，包括该方法在经济学、社会学、政治学，以及方法论研究中的具体应用，为不同领域的学者提供了宝贵的参考资料；最后对数据的后期处理做了介绍，包括可供使用的统计软件，以及数据分析的各种统计方法。

调查-实验法大概只有20多年的历史，是一个正在发展、有待完善的方法，但是它却代表着社会科学研究未来的发展方向，本书的出版，无疑会加速该方法在中国的发展和完善，促使中国的社会科学研究人员对该方法的发展做出贡献，改变中国社会科学研究方法在国际上的落后局面。

这是一部高质量的学术专著，作者无论是在学术造诣还是实践经验方面都深具实力，她在美国攻读博士期间曾经受到系统严格的社会科学方法论训练，并长期从事社会科学调查研究，有着负责超大型社会调查项目的宝贵经验，因此无论是理论还是实际操作，作者都有充分的发言权。

本书将成为学习和应用调查-实验方法的必读书。

唐文方

美国爱荷华大学政治学系主任

政治学与国际问题研究斯坦利华夏讲座教授

作者自序

“调查-实验”对应的英文名称是 survey experiment。顾名思义，这是抽样调查和实验两种研究方法的结合。我个人对于调查-实验的发现之旅是从抽样调查开始的。

1995 年，抽样调查在国内社会科学研究领域还是个新鲜事物。那年我是一名大四的本科生，有幸加入北京大学中国国情研究中心做兼职研究助理，从此开启了我的调查方法人生。后来在沈明明和杨明教授的指导下，我在硕士研究生期间参与了多个方法严谨的抽样调查，并基于一项全国环境意识调查的数据撰写了硕士毕业论文《环境保护中的公众参与》。当时国内虽然开始重视经验研究，但由于社会科学研究者多是文科背景，缺乏统计学的知识背景，量化研究方法尚未得到推广和普及，采用调查数据进行分析的研究成果也较为罕见。

后来我到美国继续深造。量化研究方法是国外社会科学研究的主流方法，研究生为数不多的必修课中包括了初级和高级两门量化研究方法的课程。于是，我们这些文科背景的留学生不得不重温数学知识，积极补习统计方面的课程。好在中国学生的数学基础训练较好，经过努力我们在方法课上一般都表现得不错。

同期，国内社会科学界受到国外研究氛围的影响，开始推动量化研究方法的应用。一方面，一些学者通过学术交流的方式到国外参加培训；另一方面，一些科研或教学机构也邀请国外学者来国内讲学。近几年越来越多的国外留学博士回国任教，量化研究方法已成为高校的常规课程，基于调查数据分析的论文发表也呈不断上升趋势，并且在大多数社会科学学科中都有应用。

就在国内学者对抽样调查的热情不断升温的同时，调查-实验方法在国外社会科学界悄然兴起。我第一次听说调查-实验法是在2011年，当时我已来到北京大学中国社会科学调查中心工作，致力于采集高质量的社会抽样调查数据和进行调查方法论方面的研究。我一个在国外某高校任教的朋友，有意与调查中心合作，特别是打算在问卷中加入一组列举实验的问题。从她的介绍中我得知列举实验是一种获取受访者对于敏感问题真实作答的技术。遗憾的是，这次合作未能实现。

当前，调查-实验法已成为国外社会科学研究中用来探讨因果关系的重要方法。该方法的特色首先在于采用了两个“随机”：随机化的样本选取和随机化的样本分配。前者源自社会调查，提升了调查-实验样本的代表性，从而使实验结果的适用性更广；后者借自科学实验，保证了实验组间样本特征（可观测和不可观测）的平衡，可以有效排除系统性因素对于因果推断的混淆。调查-实验的特色在于处理变量及其操纵方法的设计，该设计从根本上决定了一项调查-实验研究的价值，同时也标志着调查-实验在研究方法上的创新。

可能国内大多数学者对调查-实验这个名字还比较陌生，这本书可以帮助他们了解调查-实验的概貌。如果一些学者有抽样调查或实验方面的方法训练，他们理解和接受这个方法就更加容易。对于有抽样调查基础的学者来说，这种方法可以理解为社会抽样调查中搭载了实验设计。抽样调查中的核心技术是抽样和问卷设计，调查-实验就是在这两种技术之外增加实验设计，具体包括随机化分配和处理的操纵设计等。对于有实验背景的学者，调查-实验可以理解为是实验方法的拓展——地点从实验室扩展到实地；被试从少量自愿样本扩展到大量抽选样本；处理手段主要通过调查设计来实现等。因此，具有这两方面经验的学者在阅读本书时完全可以略过一些初级知识。

另外，本书也可以作为调查-实验方法的操作手册使用。书中在简要介绍调查-实验方法的发展历史、学科应用与基本原理后，用较多的篇幅讲述了调查-实验的设计、执行与分析，并且借助实际案例展示了不同形式的调查-实验学术研究及不同分析方法的软件操作。学生阅读本书后有望独立设计并实施简单的调查-实验；对于进行复杂调查-实验的研究者，本书也可以作为参考。

当然，本书作为调查-实验方法的第一本中文专著，肯定存在一些疏漏甚至谬误之处。恳请读者如有发现及时反馈给编辑部，我将认真吸取大家的意见和建议，在本书再版时给予更正。

本书成书的艰难是我始料未及的。在这过程中我非常感谢重庆大学出版社编辑们的督促和耐心，特别感谢林佳木编辑对书名的雕琢和对文字的编订。我也要感谢学界朋友们的鼓励和扶持，本丛书中清华大学苏毓淞老师和北京大学严洁老师的书稿都对我有很多的启发。同时感谢恩师北京大学的沈明明教授、杨明教授、美国爱荷华大学唐文方教授对我学术和职业上的引导。最后，我由衷感谢家人的陪伴和支持，让我体会到生命中的喜乐与满足。

任莉颖
于燕园
2017.1.20

目 录

/ 第1章 /

调查-实验概论

1940 年 3 月，正值第二次世界大战，时任美国国务卿萨姆纳·韦尔斯将被派往欧洲寻求和平解决方案之事在公众中引起了争议。著名的市场研究和民意调查专家埃尔莫·罗珀针对这个事件做了一次民意调查。他对两个问题分别设计了两种提问用语。第一个问题是关于韦尔斯出访欧洲，一个版本提及了罗斯福总统的名字，另一个版本则没有。第二个问题是关于美国援助英国和法国，一个版本提及了希特勒的名字，另一个版本则没有。具体如下：

1(a)你赞同萨姆纳·韦尔斯出访欧洲吗？

1(b)你赞同罗斯福总统派遣萨姆纳·韦尔斯出访欧洲吗？

2(a)你认为美国是否应该比目前更多援助英国和法国？

2(b)你认为美国是否应该比目前更多援助英国和法国抗击希特勒？

罗珀抽选了两个代表性样本，每组样本大约 1550 人。第一组样本选用 1(a)和 2(b)问题，第二组样本选用 1(b)和 2(a)。调查结果发现提及罗斯福总统的名字没有影响到赞同韦尔斯访问的比例(均为 43%)，然而不赞同的比例由 25%上升到 31%，没有观点的比例相应降低了 6 个百分点，意味着一些人因为听到罗斯福总统的名字从没有观点转变为不赞同。

第二个问题的结果也很有趣。对于是否该更多援助英法两国，两组均有 12%的人表示没有观点，然而当提及希特勒的名字时，支持率从 13%上升到 22%，反对的比例相应下降。这样，对于第一个问题，提问用语的改变使一些人从没有观点到有观点(不赞同)，而第二个问题中把希特勒当成共同敌人的认知，使一些人的观点从反对改变为支持。

上例就是一个简单的调查-实验。在调查-实验中，研究者通过改变问卷的某个或某些元素,如问题的用语、顺序、格式等,模拟类似实验中的操纵,然后借助社会调查的抽样方法,并采用实验中随机分配的研究设计,获取两个或多个特征相近的样本组,从而将实验环境从封闭的实验室迁到开放的实地。

早期的调查-实验主要用于调查方法论的研究,近年来由于这种方法在应用性研究领域取得了重要的成果而引起社会科学研究者的重视。本章从三个方面概括介绍这一新方法:第一,为什么要做调查-实验?第二,调查-实验是如何产生并发展的?第三,调查-实验的基本原理是什么?调查-实验产生的直接动力在于因果分析在社会科学研究中的重要性,于是本章第 1 节概要介绍了因果关系的定义及因果推断的相关理论。然后在第 2 节讲述了调查-实验产生的基础,即实验和调查作为两种独立的研究方法在社会科学研究中的应用及效度分析。第 3 和第 4 节描述了调查-实验的发展历程和国内外应用状况。最后在第 5 节归纳了调查-实验的基本概念和原理。

1.1　因果研究

社会科学研究的使命有三:发现问题、解释问题和解决问题,其中解释问题是关键。发现了问题,人们自然而然地就会追问“为什么”;而要解决问题,首先要去理解问题发生的原因和结果。因果分析是解释问题的核心,也是调查-实验产生的直接动力。那么因果关系是什么?该如何根据经验证据推断因果关系?要掌握调查-实验方法首先应对此有清晰的理解。

1.1.1 因果关系的定义

探究因果关系首先要明白什么是因果关系，哲学家们对此多有贡献。早在18世纪，哲学家休谟就提出了因果关系的三层含义：

第一是原因和结果事件之间在时空上毗连(contiguity)，时空连接是因果关系的先决条件。如果两个时空相距很远的物体产生了因果作用，那么其间必然存在某种因果链条的衔接。第二是时间顺序(succession)，即因先果后。第三是必然联系(necessary connection)，即因果现象相伴而生，有其因必有其果。(Hume, 2005/1739:61-65，转引自彭玉生 2011:3)。

这三条被认为是因果关系的"金律"。然而休谟认识到这三条只是判定因果关系的必要条件，于是在此基础上他又补充了五条：

①同样的原因永远产生同样的结果，同样的结果也永远只能发生于同样的原因。②当若干不同的对象产生了同样的结果时，那一定是借着我们所发现的它们的某种共同性质。③两个相似对象结果中的差异，必然是由它们互相差异的那一点而来。④当任何对象随着它的原因的增减而增减时，那个对象就应该被认为是一个复合的结果，是由原因中几个不同部分所发生的几个不同结果联合而生。⑤如果一个对象完整地存在于任何一个时期，而却没有产生任何结果，那么它便不是那个结果的唯一原因，而还需要被其他可以推进它的影响和作用的某种原则。(转引自陈晓平，2003:24)。

请注意，补充的这五条中有几个关键词汇："同样""差异""共同”“增减”。这些关键词汇成为后人从经验角度验证因果关系的指导。

一个世纪后的英国哲学家密尔在其名著《逻辑体系:推理和归纳》中系统地阐述了他的归纳逻辑和因果理论,其中包括五种“实验研究方法”(Methods of Experimental Inquiry)①。这五种方法也被人们称为“探求因果关系的方法”或“密尔方法”,其中包括契合法、差异法、契合差异并用法、共变法和剩余法。这五个方法中契合、差异和共变是最基础的归纳方法。

有关文献中一般都用图示来帮助理解密尔方法,这里借用陈晓平(2008)的图表来介绍契合法、差异法和共变法的逻辑。

表 1.1　密尔“契合法”示意

场合	有关的先行(或后继)现象	被研究现象
(1)	A、B、C	a
(2)	A、B、D	a
(3)	A、C、E	a
⋮		
所以,A 是 a 的原因或(结果)		

契合法,用密尔的话就是指“如果两个或更多的包含被研究现象的事例中仅有一个情况(circumstance)是共同的,那么,那个独自地(alone)使所有事例契合的情况就是所说现象的原因(或结

① 密尔在著作中的章名为“实验研究的四种方法”,但其内容却列出五种方法,其中“契合差异并用法”是对契合法或差异法的某种扩展,未被列入四种方法中。密尔把这种方法又称为“间接归纳法”,而把其他四种方法叫作“直接归纳法”。

果)”(转引自陈晓平,2008:3)。如表1.1所示,对于被研究对象a来说,在不同的场合下都存在A这样一个共同的现象。依照契合法逻辑,如果A在时间顺序上先于a,则A是a的原因,如果迟于a,则A是a的结果。

表1.2 密尔“差异法”示意

场合	有关的先行(或后继)现象	被研究现象
(1)	A、B、C	a
(2)	—、B、C	—
所以,A是a的原因或(结果)		

密尔对差异法的解释是:“如果被研究现象出现于其中的一个事例和它不出现于其中的另一个事例,这两个事例除一个情况不同外其他所有情况都相同,那唯一的情况仅仅出现于前一事例;那么,那个独自地使两个事例有所不同的情况就是那个现象的结果或原因,或原因中不可缺少的部分”(转引自陈晓平,2008:3)。表1.2的场合(1)中,a出现,其先行或后继现象中A也出现;在场合(2)中,a没有出现,其他和场合(1)同样有先行或后继现象出现,但A没有出现,这时可以认为A是a的原因或(结果)。

表1.3 密尔“共变法”示意

场合	有关的先行(或后继)现象	被研究现象
(1)	A_1、B、C、D	a_1
(2)	A_2、B、C、D	a_2
(3)	A_3、B、C、D	a_3
⋮		
所以,A是a的原因或(结果)		

契合法和差异法是基于对现象的静态观察,而共变法则通过动态观测来确定因果关系,密尔将其总结为:"当某一现象以某种特定(some particular)方式变化时,另一现象则以任何(any)方式变化,那么,后者是前者的一个原因或一个结果,或通过因果关系的某个因素与它相联系"(转引自陈晓平,2008:3)。可以发现,表1.3 和表 1.1 相比只有一些小的差异,这些差异就意味着对于现象 a 和 A 的观测出现了量的变化,而基于这些变化的共同性归纳出 A 和 a 的因果关系。

密尔的因果逻辑是社会科学比较研究方法的基础,特别适用于小样本的个案比较。如斯考切波(Skocpol)在其著作《国家与社会革命》中比较分析了法国、俄国和中国三个国家革命发生的原因(斯考切波, 2007)。这三个国家在历史、文化和发展进程上有诸多差异,但有一个共同点,就是都发生了大规模的社会革命。作者从这一研究对象入手,采用共变法的逻辑,排除先行现象中的差异,最终发现这些国家在发生革命前存在着三个共同的机制,一是国家当时面临巨大的外部压力;二是国家内部存在一个掌握土地的上层阶级;三是使得农民组织起来参与革命成为可能的社会环境。斯考切波也应用了差异法比较了中国和日本,两国都面临国际压力,都存在掌握土地的上层阶级,但日本天皇成功地推行了自上而下的改革,而中国当时的社会环境下土地改革却十分困难,最终中国发生了革命,日本则平稳过渡。

1.1.2 因果推断

确定了因果关系的定义及逻辑,那么实际研究中该如何根据这些知识来推断自然或社会现象间的因果关系呢?接力棒传到了统计学家们的手上。

在密尔差异法逻辑的基础上诞生了现代实验研究。一个理想的差异法实验首先要控制因和果的发生顺序，以满足休谟提到的第一和第二原则，然后挑选两个在各方面完全相同的个体，对其中一个个体实施处理，导致某一个特征改变；而对另一个个体不实施任何处理，也就是没有引起该特征改变。这样，两个个体之间只存在一个不同的特征，最后观测实验结果是否会出现不同，从而得出该特征与实验结果之间的因果关系。

大多数自然科学实验可以比较容易地选择相同特征的前测个体，并且有效控制实验室的环境，使实验过程免受其他外界因素的影响。然而在社会科学研究中，这个理想的实验过程在现实中是不可能实现的，因为没有两个社会个体能够满足除了一个且仅有一个不同的特征而在其他方面完全相同，而是会有许多特征未被观测或控制，其中每一个特征都有可能是原因。

英国统计学家费舍（Fisher）的随机化分配推进了实验方法的发展。在其 1935 年出版的著作《实验设计》一书中，费舍通过一个真实的“女士品茶”故事论证了随机分配（random assignment）的方法。故事发生在伦敦郊外一个沙龙派对上，一位女士宣称她可以分辨出奶茶是先放的茶还是先放的奶，这引起了绅士们的争论，最后决定要做个实验来验证这位女士是否具有这项能力。在这本书中，费舍讨论了这个实验的各种细节及可能结果，如应该为那位女士奉上多少杯茶？这些茶应该按什么样的顺序奉上？对所奉各杯茶的顺序应该告诉那位女士多少信息？依据那位女士判断的对错与否，费舍还计算出各种不同结果的概率。

后人在费舍随机分配的理论基础上发展出了随机组实验，其逻辑是:虽然在现实世界中不能找到两个完全相同的理想个体,但是可以找到两个或多个统计上具有相同特征的群体。实验过程中把实验对象按照随机分配的方法分成两个或多个组,每个组在处理操作前具有相同的统计特征,即使观察到差异,也是由于随机分配产生的偶然因素所导致。这样因果关系的论证从必然改为可能(或概率),实验对象也从个体转变为群体。

无论是寻求特征完全相同的个体,还是使用统计特征相似的群体,实验研究隐含的逻辑可以通过潜在结果框架(Potential Outcomes Framework)来理解。什么是潜在结果?比如某英语培训机构推出一门快速记忆英语单词的课程,我可以选择参加或者不参加。如果参加了这门培训课程,我的词汇量会增加到 10 000 个,如果不参加,我的词汇量是 5 000 个。参加与不参加培训班可以理解为实验中的处理(treatment),词汇量的增长就是处理的潜在结果。之所以称为潜在结果是因为在一个个体上最终只有一个结果会出现并被观察到,也就是和个体所接受的处理(比如参加培训)相对应的那个结果。另外的结果是观察不到的,是假定另外一种处理(比如不参加培训)带来的潜在结果。

潜在结果的概念最早由统计学的泰斗奈曼(Neyman)在其 1923 年的博士论文中提出,但由于该论文用波兰文撰写,直至 1990 年有学者将该论文翻译成英文后人们才知道奈曼早期的重要贡献。美国统计学家罗宾(Donald Rubin)在 1974—1980 年发表的一系列文章论述了潜在结果的框架及其分析方法,后被其同事命名为罗宾因果模型(Rubin Causal Model)。

罗宾因果模型基于潜在结果的概念将因果效应定义为潜在结果之间的差异,如上例中比较我词汇量的增长就能知道培训班对我词汇量的因果效应。这一定义有两点需要注意：第一，因果效应是对同一个体在事后同一时间潜在结果的比较，对同一个体事前事后不同时间的比较不符合此定义；第二，因果效应仅和潜在结果有关，而与哪种潜在结果被观察到无关，也就是说潜在结果是稳定的，不会因是否被观察到而变化。

这一定义显然只具有理论意义，不具有操作意义。对因果效应的估计必须依赖能够观察到的潜在结果，然而潜在结果在现实中不可能全都被观察到，从定义出发无法获知因果效应的大小。罗宾因果模型通过实验设计和数据分析来应对这一问题。首先该模型将因果效应的估计从个体层面上升到群体层面，通过比较组间的平均处理效应来推断因果关系。比如选择两组人参与实验，一组人参加培训班，一组人不参加培训班，然后比较两组人的平均词汇量来证明培训班的作用。由于参与实验的不是同一个体，而是一个群体，这样就必须引入一个假设，称为个体处理稳定性假设（Stable-Unit-Treatment-Value Assumption，SUTVA），其含义是参加实验的个体之间不存在相互干扰或互动，也就是每一个体观察到的结果不会受到参与实验的其他个体的影响。比如我参加培训班和不参加培训班对我的词汇量的影响是稳定的，不会因为其他人是否参加培训班而发生改变。只有在个体处理稳定性假设满足的情况下罗宾因果模型才有效。

此外，罗宾将不能观察到的潜在结果理解为数据缺失，因此要进行因果分析，就要把缺失的潜在结果填补上。罗宾因果模型会利用一些个体的背景变量（协变量）来进行缺失潜在结果的预测。协变量必须满足一个条件，即不能因个体是否得到处理而受到影响，因此多选个体永久性特征或发生在处理之前的变量。协变量可以使估计更加精确,最重要的是控制混淆因素的影响。比如对英语感兴趣的人更愿意参加培训班,同时对英语感兴趣的人词汇量也较大。如果直接比较参加培训班与不参加培训班人员的平均词汇量就会高估培训班的作用。这时将对英语的兴趣作为模型的协变量就可以避免这种混淆。

罗宾因果模型中分配机制至关重要。分配机制是决定哪些个体得到处理,从而哪些潜在结果可以被观察到的过程。是否得到处理本身就是个协变量。在费舍的随机分配机制下,这个协变量能非常有效地排除混淆因素的影响,使模型分析变得简单,分析结果更为精确。比如通过随机分配,参加培训班和不参加培训班的两组人在对英语的兴趣上没有组间差异就排除了这一因素对培训班效果的影响,如果不能实现随机分配,必须加入其他协变量力求获得组间各项特征的平衡,这只得借助更为复杂的分析方法,更脱离现实的假定来实现。

1.1.3　实验与实验推理

实验是因果推断理论的应用。维基百科中对于实验的定义是:

"实验是一个验证、反驳或确认假设的过程。实验探究因果效应的方式是证实当某个特定的因素被操纵时会导致什么相应的结果。实验在目标和规模上各有不同,但都基于可重复的程序和对结果的逻辑分析。"

这个定义中包含了实验的几个重要特征:第一,实验是关乎一个因果效应的假设,实验的目的就是去"验证、反驳或确认"这个假设。第二,实验过程中要基于因果推断的逻辑证实因果效应的存在，包括操纵原因、控制干扰和观察结果等。第三，实验是可以重复操作的，同样的操作环境和步骤应能复制出同样的结果。

因此，实验的首个判断标准是因果假设中的“因”在实验中是否可被研究者操纵，如果是，则为实验，如果否，则不能属于实验。第二个标准是样本是否可被随机分组，如果是，则为标准的实验，如果否，则成为准实验（quasi-experiment），也就是不太标准的实验。

随机对照实验（Randomized Controlled Trial，RCT）是一种最为标准的实验形式。在这种实验中，实验对象被随机分配到实验组和对照组，研究者对实验组和对照组的成员施以不同的处理或干预，以达到操纵原因的目的，然后比较实验组和对照组在结果上的差异，从而获取因果效应的证据。

准实验是基于实验推理（experimental reasoning）。这类实验不是研究者主动设计并实施的，他们往往不知道分配机制是怎样的，或者无法对分配机制进行控制，而是通过经验判断来说明所获数据类似（as-if）实验数据。如自然实验（natural experiment），研究者没有直接参与分配机制的设计与控制，但是有其他方，如政策执行者，甚至社会事件和自然现象将参加实验的个体实现分组，而且分配机制近似随机。

也可以基于实验推理，利用辅助的证据和推论来改造观察数据，进行因果分析。如倾向值匹配，研究者并不知道分配机制是怎样的，而是通过选取一些协变量预测实验个体接受某种实验处理的可能性，从而模拟一种随机分配机制，进而获取组间平均处理效应的差值。

常用的回归模型也是借用实验推理来分析观察数据。具体地说,其基本逻辑是将数据分割为系统模型和随机残项。系统模型是理论解释部分,不可解释的部分归为随机残项。模型部分由核心自变量和控制自变量组成。核心自变量类似实验设计中的处理,控制自变量中统计显著的变量类似实验设计中的条件控制(如物理实验中对于温度和密度的控制等),统计不显著的控制变量则纳入残项,并且残项假定完全随机,类似实验设计的随机分组(彭玉生,2011)。

因此有学者感叹道,“最有用的方法论问题,就我们的观点而言,不是一项研究是否具有实验性,而是在于具有多少实验性并且在哪些方面具有实验性。”(Gerring and McDermott, 2007:698)由此可见,在社会科学研究中因果关系一直以其特有的魅力吸引着研究者们。

1.2　实验与调查

实验和调查是实证研究的两个重要方法。实验的优势是因果推断,应用到社会科学研究中可以更有效地揭示某一社会现象发生的原因和机制。调查的长处则在于归纳,通过对凭借问卷调查采集到的大量数据信息进行统计分析,可以概括出某一社会现象的现状。所以严格地讲,调查属于观察性研究方法,而实验则属于探究因果的研究方法。两种方法各有其长,也各有其短,而调查-实验作为二者的结合,在一定程度上达到了取长补短的效果。

1.2.1 实验与社会科学研究

实验曾是自然科学所独有的研究方法，因为实验的一个重要条件是实验对象或实验环境可以接受研究者的有意控制或操纵。如物理学首先成为实验研究的受益者，因为在实验室里可以有效地控制温度、密度、压力、浮力等条件。

实验研究方法向社会科学领域的推广始于心理学，最早的心理学实验室于1879年创建于德国的莱比锡，创建者是Wilhem Wundt。Wundt早年受训于药学专业，他把实验的方法引入到心理学的研究中，从而促使心理学从哲学中剥离。Wundt本人著作等身，其学生更是继承了其实验心理学的衣钵，成为各国心理学研究的领军人物。如他的学生Stanley Hall是美国心理协会的创始人和第一任主席，也是《美国心理学杂志》（*American Journal of Psychology*）的创办者之一。Wundt的老师中多有学界精英，其中包括提出需求层次理论的马斯洛。当心理学的研究对象从意识转向行为时，实验在心理学研究中更是有了用武之地，甚至成为主流研究方法（McDermott，2013）。

社会心理学作为心理学和社会学的交叉学科也较早采用了实验方法。1898年Triplett在《美国心理学杂志》上发表了第一篇实验性的社会心理学文章，研究自行车竞赛中赛车手是独自匀速还是在与别人竞争的情形下可以产生更好的成绩，该现象成为社会助长（social facilitation）理论的早期证据。Triplett的文章被后人认为是社会心理学发展史的分水岭，标志着该学科进入实证研究时代（Jackson and Cox，2013）。实验方法也进入社会学研究的其他领域，两个领军人物是Ernest Greenwood和Stuart Chapin，他们分别于 1945 年和 1947 年出版了《实验社会学》(*Experimental Sociology*)和《社会学研究中的实验设计》(*Experimental Designs in Sociological Research*)。1966 年 Donald Campbell and Julian Stanley 出版了《研究中的实验和准实验设计》(*Experimental and Quasi-experimental Designs for Research*),该书成为社会研究的经典教科书,堪比费舍的《实验设计》对于医学研究的贡献(Oakley,1998)。

政治学和经济学研究者们对实验的应用最初持保留态度。因为这些学者认为他们研究的对象是真实的世界,在实验室里是不可能营造的。正如 1909 年美国政治学会主席劳伦斯·罗威尔(Lawrence Lowell)在年会致辞中所提:“我们的局限是不可能进行实验研究,政治是观察式的,而非实验式的科学……”(Lowell,1910:7,转引自 Druckman et al,2006:627)。这些反对持续了许多年,直至 20 世纪 40 年代行为主义兴起,才有力地推动了实验方法和社会科学研究的结合(Jackson and Cox,2013)。

一般认为 1944 年冯·诺伊曼和摩根斯顿《博弈论和经济行为》的出版标志着实验经济学的诞生。1953 年 Maurice Allais 基于实验证据,在 *Econometica* 上发表文章首次质疑了预期效用理论,是早期实验经济学的重要成果。同期,Vernon Smith 也开始在经济学研究中引入实验的方法,并得到了诸多心理学家的响应,如在 2002 年和 Smith 一起获得诺贝尔经济学奖的 Kahneman,二人基于实验方法推动了行为经济学的发展。在 20 世纪 90 年代,实验在经济学研究领域实现了突破,其代表就是《实验经济学手册》和其他几本相关教材的出版。此后接连有几位获得诺贝尔奖的经济学家在自己的研究中采用了实验研究的方法(McDermott,2013)。

实验在政治学领域的“渗透”归功于 20 世纪的行为主义革命,

在此之前，只有零星数篇政治学研究文章声称使用实验方法，其中最为著名的是 Harold Gosnell 在 20 年代芝加哥选举时的实地实验（field experiment），然而该研究由于未使用随机分组的方法，所以不属于严格意义上的实验（Morton and Williams，2010；Bositis and Steinel，1987）。1956 年，美国著名政治学期刊《美国政治学评论》（*American Political Science Review*）刊登了 Elderveld 在密歇根州安娜堡市选举期间关于宣传和投票的实地实验的研究论文，这是政治学实验研究的论文第一次被主流学术期刊接收。然而 10 年后该期刊上才出现第二篇实验政治学的文章（Druckman et al，2006）。在 20 世纪 50—60 年代，国际关系领域开始涌现了大批实验研究用来评估博弈论，其成果多发表在 1957 年创刊的《冲突解决研究》（*Journal of Conflict Resolution*）。在 20 世纪 70 年代，一批政治学实验室在美国几所著名高校，如纽约州立大学石溪分校、耶鲁大学、密歇根大学、加州大学洛杉矶分校等创建，并培训了大批政治学实验研究者。同期，政治学实验研究有了自己的专业期刊《政治实验研究》（*The Experimental Study of Politics*），但几年后该期刊就停办了。停刊的一个主要原因可能是政治学主流期刊开始逐渐接纳实验研究的论文。的确，从 20 世纪 80 年代起，美国几大顶级政治学期刊，如《美国政治学评论》（*American Political Science Review*），《美国政治学期刊》（*American Journal of Political Science*），《政治期刊》（*Journal of Politics*）上发表的应用实验研究的文章逐年增加，进入 21 世纪后甚至出现激增状态（Morton and Williams，2010；Druckman et al，2006）。

实验方法在经济学、社会学和政治学研究上方兴未艾，然而在公共政策和行政管理领域却呈现相反的趋势。1960 到 1980 年代在美国曾经出现“评估的黄金时代”，许多公共政策项目都采用了随机实验的方法来评估实施效果，甚至政府规定社会项目预算的1%必须用来做评估。然而在过去几十年里实验评估的热情出现降温，一方面是因为一些评估项目的干预手段不但无效甚至有破坏作用；另一方面也是因为决策者对于评估失去耐心，希望尽快将政策付诸实施（Oakley，1998）。行政管理领域也有学者呼吁应用实验方法，如 20 多年前 Bozeman 等在《行政管理研究与理论期刊》（*Journal of Public Administration Research and Theory*）上发表一系列文章支持实验研究（Bozeman and Scott，1992；Bozeman，1992），然而这一努力并没有得到领域内其他学者的响应和接续，实验研究方面的文章很快断档。随着实验方法在其他社会科学领域应用的普及，近年来行政管理研究者再次发声，倡导本领域研究方法上的革新（Blom-Hansen，Morton and Serritzlew，2015；Margetts，2011）。

综上所述，实验方法自 19 世纪末起从心理学发端，逐渐应用到社会学、经济学、政治学等社会科学领域。20 世纪中期的行为主义革命大大推动了实验方法在社会科学研究的普及，近几年实验方法已得到越来越多学者的青睐和推崇。

1.2.2　调查与社会科学研究

调查在社会科学研究上的应用可以追溯到 19 世纪末英国的社会学家 Charles Booth 有关伦敦贫民的研究。Booth 利用访谈的方式采集了大量数据来了解贫民的情况，探究贫困的原因，并且在 1889 到 1903 年出版了 17 卷巨著《伦敦人民的生活与劳动》（*Life and Labour of the People in London*）。除了研究社会问题，一些新闻记者和市场研究者也开始采用调查的方法来了解人们的想法。新闻记者关心的是人们对于政治领导人的态度和总统大选的选举倾向，而市场研究者们则想知道人们对于某种特定的产品和服务的评价，因此这些需求推动了抽样调查作为一种研究方法的发展（Groves，2009）。

首先是问卷的标准化。早期的社会研究者们大多亲自访谈，他们不太关心问题的语句，认为有经验的访谈员会知道该如何提问。而市场研究和民意调查机构由于调查的人数众多，需要雇佣人去访谈，这时就有必要精心设计问题以保证每个访员的提问内容和方式相同。后来，问卷设计也引起了学术界的重视，并且发展出了一些特定的测量方式，如瑟斯顿量表（Thurstone Scale）和李克特量表（Likert Scale）。

然后是抽样方法的科学化。在现代科学抽样技术出现以前，对于社会的研究要么是基于政府普查，要么是基于对可得样本的调查（straw polling）。比如，20 世纪初美国著名的杂志《文摘周刊》（*Literary Digest*）在 1916 到 1932 年的每届总统大选前，它总会在它的百万读者中调查他们的投票倾向，每次都成功地预测了获胜当选的总统。在 1936 年总统大选前，这本杂志根据同样方法预测共和党人兰登将击败寻求连任的罗斯福总统。而盖洛普等民意调查专家却基于少量样本的调查预测罗斯福总统会获得连任。选举结果证实了盖洛普的预测，后来盖洛普选取样本所用的配额抽样方法在民意调查界得到了广泛的推广应用。

与此同时，概率抽样在农业研究上取得了突破性发展，标志着现代抽样调查的诞生。其核心就是通过调查总体中的一部分来获知总体的特征，就好像从人体里取一滴血来化验就可以知道全身血液的状况。当时正值经济大萧条和第二次世界大战爆发,美国政府不得不削减用于普查的资金,于是将概率抽样应用在 1940 年美国十年一次的人口普查中。1948 年总统选举前,一些学术研究者采用概率抽样的方法预测杜鲁门会获胜,而当时享有盛誉的盖洛普等民意调查公司仍然采用配额抽样的方法预言杜威必胜。这次盖洛普的预测失败了,这使民意调查的抽样手段从非概率的配额抽样转向概率抽样。民意调查历史上这两个里程碑式的事件使社会科学研究者在感性上认识到抽样调查的魅力。

1930 年代末,一些高校开始建立抽样调查研究机构,如普林斯顿大学的民意研究室(Office of Public Opinion Research);起初在丹佛大学,后移至芝加哥大学的国家民意研究中心(National Opinion Research Center);密歇根大学的调查研究中心(Survey Research Center),等等。第二次世界大战结束后,大批原本服务于美国政府的调查专家进入学术界,抽样调查方法迅速普及到社会学、政治学、教育学、公共卫生、经济学及其他社会科学领域的研究中。到 1960 年代后期,抽样调查已成为社会科学研究数据采集的主要方法,许多大型的历时追踪调查和跨国调查得到资助,并且在密歇根大学创建了美国高校校际政治与社会研究联盟(Inter-university Consortium for Political and Social Research, ICPSR)来共享调查数据,促进了调查数据的再利用(Marsden and Wright, 2010)。

基于抽样调查数据的著述不胜枚举。以政治学领域为例,Brady (2000)列出了多个跨国比较的研究,如:

- 五国公民文化研究(Almond and Verba, 1963)
- 七国政治参与和平等研究(Verba, Nie and Kim, 1978)

- 八国政治行动研究(Barnes and Kaase, 1979; Jennings and van Deth, 1989)
- 三国政治参与研究(Verba, Schlozman and Brady, 1995; Kaplan and Brady, 1997)
- 欧洲晴雨表调查(Inglehart, 1977)
- 世界价值观调查(Inglehart, Basanez and Moreno, 1988)。

Brady甚至宣称,正如望远镜之于天文学,显微镜之于生物学,地震、天气和环境探测仪之于地理科学,抽样调查是社会科学中一个根本的数据采集方法(2000:47)。他在同篇文章中再次强调,抽样调查对于政治科学和社会学尤为重要。因为人口学和经济学可以从普查局、劳动统计局、农业部或其他地方获取昂贵而丰富的数据资源,而政治科学和社会学却往往只能靠学者们自己来采集数据。在政治科学领域,抽样调查广泛应用在国家比较、趋势分析及面向人群和机构的研究上。此外,借助复杂的数据分析技术,抽样调查在理论连接、概念丰富化、理论验证能力,以及政策相关等方面对于政治科学的发展都有重要贡献。

总之,在社会科学量化研究趋势的推动下,社会调查,特别是概率抽样的调查,已成为社会科学各学科重要的研究方法而得到广泛应用。

1.2.3 实验和调查的效度

评价一种研究方法的优劣多采用效度分析。效度,简单地说,就是指研究的有效性,一般分为内部效度(internal validity)和外部效度(external validity)。所谓内部效度,就是研究发现在多大程度上符合研究对象的真实情况。外部效度则是指研究发现在多大程度上符合其他总体或其他环境的真实情况。有学者将内部效度进一步分解为三种:建构效度、因果效度和统计效度(Blom-Hansen, Morton and Serritzlew,2015)。建构效度就是“在理论验证的实验中从数据中得到的推论是否对于所要评估的理论是有效的”;因果效度是指“研究者在目标总体中发现的关联是否为因果关系”;统计效度是指“研究者关注的变量间的共变关系是否统计显著以及是否相当大”(第 256 页)。这种分类方法中统计效度和因果效度存在交叉。依据休谟的“金律”,即因先果后、因果共变、真实相关,因果效度中包括变量间的共变关系,而统计效度就是为了验证这种关系的真实性和强度,包括选用正确的统计模型、准确地估计参数、控制实验设计中无控制因素的影响等。同时统计效度还包括另外一种效度,可以称为总体效度,即统计分析的结果是否可以推论到目标总体。在社会科学研究中,研究者们非常关注总体效度,以确认研究发现的适用广度。因此笔者在原有的分类方法上做了改进,将统计效度中的共变关系检测归于因果效度,同时将总体效度分离出来,这样,建构效度、因果效度、总体效度和外部效度共同作为对研究方法评价的维度。

建构效度、因果效度、总体效度和外部效度的依存关系可以用图 1.1 中的同心圆来表示,每一个外层的圆都要以内层的圆为核心。首先,建构效度是任何一个理论导向研究的基石,没有建构效度,整个研究是无效的。第二,因果效度要基于良好的建构效度,同时也是总体效度的前提条件。第三,只有因果关系为真,才能推断是否适用于整个目标总体。第四,外部效度要以前三种效度为基础,不存在没有内部效度的外部效度。

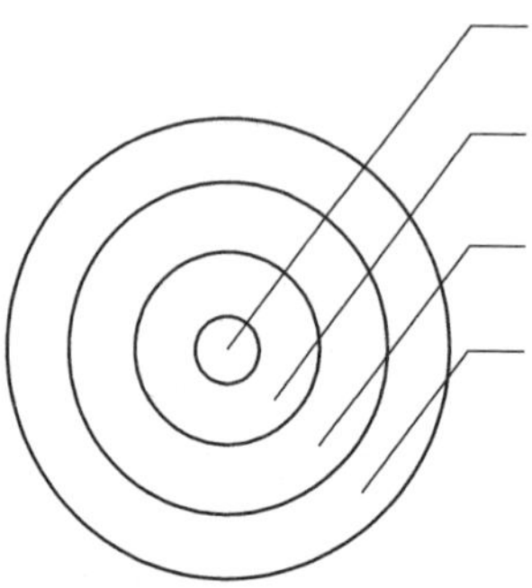

图 1.1　研究效度示意图

和调查相比,实验具有较好的因果效度,这是广泛认可的,但其总体效度和外部效度却受到诸多质疑。第一,实验室里人为营造出来的实验情境在多大程度上符合社会现实？换句话说,实验的控制条件是人为设置的,没有理由认为人们在实验情境外也会遇到相似条件。第二,和自然科学的实验对象不同,社会科学的实验对象是人,而人有自我意识。当实验对象知道自己在参与实验被观察时,会对行为产生实在而未知的影响。第三,社会科学的实验对象往往是出于便利而招募的自愿样本,其代表的总体定义不清,因此实验结论推广到更大的总体存在逻辑上的漏洞。第四,实验对象的数量因受到实验环境的限制而相对较少,对实验结果进行分析时会因为小样本的缘故而降低统计功效。

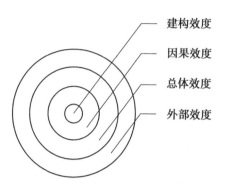

调查如果仅作为观察问题的手段,不对因果关系进行探究,因果效度就不适用。但是正如前文所提到的,研究者们总是企图利用调查数据进行因果推断,于是就产生了问题。首先就是休谟提出的时间原则,即先因后果。因为调查数据多是横截面上的观察数据,在社会现象发生的时间顺序上不能明确把握,而且现象之间可能存在互为因果的情形,也就是所谓的内生性问题

(endogeneity)。虽然社会调查也通过跟踪调查或面板数据来厘清事件的发生顺序,但跟踪调查的难度大,时间间隔长,而且往往需要多期的跟踪数据才能进行时间序列等复杂的统计分析。第二就是休谟提出的必然性原则,即有其因必有其果。对调查数据的分析可以比较容易地发现两个现象之间的相关性,但要确定为因果必然性则要排除虚假相关的可能。一个经典的例子是消防车的数量和火灾毁坏程度的关系成正比,即消防车越多,火灾造成的损失越大。二者看似高度相关,实际上是因为它们都是一个共同原因的结果,也就是火势的大小,而不是消防车的多少影响到火灾的严重程度。因此,调查在因果效度上具有明显的弱点。但是概率抽样的应用,使调查可以具有实验所无法具有的总体效度,基于小样本调查数据分析得到的结果可以推论到更大的研究总体。

所以,对于调查和实验两种方法无从评价孰优孰劣,二者在应用上也长期处于隔离状态。就像锤头和绣花针各有各的用途,不能评价哪个工具更好。如果用绣花针去敲钉子,用锤头去绣花,只能说明使用者有问题。然而,从上述的效度分析可以发现二者结合的亮光。因果效度重在实验设计,而总体效度的关键是样本选取,二者并非水火不容,而是完全有可能兼容并蓄。

1.3　调查-实验的历史

事实显示实验设计早已应用到调查中。如本章开始介绍的有关韦尔斯出访欧洲的民意调查,就采用了实验方法中分组和处理的手段。纵观调查-实验的发展历程,可以发现两条主线:一个是技术的不断创新,另一个是应用领域的拓展。实验处理手段最初主要是对问题语句和顺序的操纵,后来发展了应对敏感问题的各种询问技术和多因子混合的析因调查-实验。调查执行的方式也从纸版问卷的邮寄自填或访员面访,发展到计算机辅助电话访问、个人访问和网络自填。调查实验最初主要应用于调查方法研究,现在已在社会科学研究的各个领域都有所使用。本节将简要介绍调查-实验的发展历程。

1.3.1 技术创新

早期的调查-实验包括几个环节:首先是要选取一个影响因子,该因子一般具有两个取值(如是否提及罗斯福总统的名字),然后根据该因子的取值设计一个问题的两个版本;第二,要将调查样本随机地分为两组,以保证两组受访人具有相同的属性;第三,请两组受访人分别回答两个不同版本的问题;第四,在分析时比较来自两个样本的应答结果的差异。*Public Opinion Quarterly* 的创办者之一 Hadley Cantril 称这种调查和实验相结合的设计为“分投选票(split-ballot)”(Rosen, 1973)。

基于分投选票法的研究一方面给民意研究者们带来了启示,发现通过改变问卷上的提问用语,可以间接捕捉到一些重要的公众态度(Kamin, 1958; Jaros and Mason, 1969)。比如研究政治人物对于公众意见的影响,调查中可以向随机分成的两组受访人提出相同的问题,只是其中一组提及该政治人物的观点,另一组则没有提及。在分析调查结果时,这两组人在该问题上应答的区别可以直接归因于该政治人物对公众意见的影响,而且可以测量其影响强度及对不同特征受访人的影响效果(Rosen, 1973)。然而这种方法也给民意调查本身带来了阴影，因为学者们发现问卷上的一点改动就可能影响到受访者的应答，这意味着民意会很容易被不同的问卷设计所操纵。

分投选票法的设计和执行都相对比较简单，很容易在纸版访问的调查中实现，以至于调查-实验在很长时期内是采用随机分为两组的形式。然而由于分投选票法只适用于双选项单因子变量的研究，开始并没有吸引社会科学实质性研究的学者，而主要应用在抽样调查的方法研究上。这方面研究成果最为丰硕的是霍华德·舒曼(Howard Schuman)，他利用分投选票法设计做了一系列调查-实验，如问题顺序(Schuman, Presser and Ludwig, 1981)，是否采用开放或封闭选项(Schuman and Presser, 1979)，无态度问题(Schuman and Presser, 1979b; Schuman and Presser, 1980)，态度问题中设立中间选项对应答的影响(Presser and Schuman, 1980)等。其他学者在方法上的研究涉及了访员种族对访问的影响(Cotter, Cohen and Coulter, 1982)，问题形式对于收入数据采集的影响(Locander and Burdon, 1976)，以及题干中是否该提及议题的两个方面等(Hedge, 1979; Bishop, Oldendick and Tuchfarber, 1982).

调查-实验没有满足于简单的结合，而是竭力在新的结合体的基础上发展新的处理技术。这方面的成果集中表现在两个方面，一个是对社会期许影响的问题，或敏感问题信息的获取，另一个是从单因子变量分析向多因子变量分析拓展。

敏感问题测量

在社会调查发展早期，受访者应答过程中的社会期许行为已经引起了研究者的关注。所谓社会期许，就是指受访者在回答问题时倾向于给出迎合别人或社会规范的答案。比如对于一些社会道德不认可的行为,受访者会有意识地不报告或低报;对于社会舆论支持的行为则会高报。社会期许在面对面的访问中尤为严重。一般认为,受访者不愿意真实地回答敏感问题,主要是缺乏对访员的信任。如果受访者的答案可以对访员保密,就可以打消受访者的顾虑,得到真实的应答。在此理念上 Warner (1965) 提出了“随机应答”的采访技术(Randomized Response Techique, RRT)。这种方法将一个敏感问题设计为两种相反的提问方式,然后通过随机选择的机制决定受访者回答哪个问题,访员可以得到受访者的答案,但并不明确知道受访者回答的是哪道题。例如想询问受访者是否属于 A 组织,可以设计为以下两个问题:

(1) 我是 A 组织的会员;

(2) 我不是 A 组织的会员。

访员指导受访者投一个硬币,规定如果正面向上就回答问题(1)是否正确,如果背面向上就回答问题(2)。然后受访者背着访员投硬币,根据规定回答问题。访员不知道硬币是正面还是背面向上,所以他并不知道受访者到底回答的是哪个问题。在分析数据时,由于知道回答每个问题的概率,可以通过数学推导计算出 A 组织会员的比例。

随机应答技术在接下来的十几年里得到了不断改进。

Abul-Ela 等(1967)提出两种提问方式不一定要完全对立(是或否),也可以根据应答类别设计 3 个或更多的问题,只要保证至少其中一个问题不会让受访者觉得敏感就可以了。这样,当受访者认识到自己抽选到敏感问题来回答的概率降低时,会更愿意合作。Greenberg 等(1969)在此基础上提出,其中的非敏感问题不一定要和调查中的敏感问题相关,这样会使受访者感受到更小的压力。但是要在同一个调查中对非敏感问题单独提问,以获取其分布情况。Moors(1971)考虑到再次提出非敏感问题时会引起受访者一定的警觉,于是他提出采用对半样本的方法,将受访者随机分为两组,对第一组受访人采用随机问答方法在敏感问题和不相关的非敏感问题中随机选择问题回答,而在第二组受访者中直接询问非敏感问题。这样就引入了调查-实验的设计来收集敏感问题的应答数据。Folsom 等(1973)又将这一方法进一步完善,建议在两个对半样本组中交替使用两个非敏感问题。具体地说,在第一个样本组中受访者随机选择回答敏感问题还是非敏感问题 A,然后直接回答非敏感问题 B;在第二个样本组中受访者随机选择回答敏感问题还是非敏感问题 B,然后直接回答非敏感问题 A。这样,就可以通过一种更隐蔽的方式使受访者更放心地对敏感问题给出真实答案。

针对需要了解频次或数量的敏感问题,或累计应答(aggregated response),Warner (1971)建议可让受访者在答案上秘密加上一个随机数,Boruch 和 Cecil(1979)应用调查-实验的方法提出了新思路。这个方法将受访者随机分为两组,除了所要了解的敏感问题外,还设计其他一个辅助的连续测量问题。一个组的受访者提供这两个问题答案之和,另一组的受访者提供这两个问题答案之差。当合并这两组问题答案的均值时,就可以比较容易地算出两个问题应答的均值:

$$Mean(X+Y)+Mean(X-Y)=(\overline{X}+\overline{Y})+(\overline{X}-\overline{Y})=2\overline{X}$$

或

$$Mean(X+Y)-Mean(X-Y)=(\overline{X}+\overline{Y})-(\overline{X}-\overline{Y})=2\overline{Y}$$

Reinmuth 和 Geurts(1975)提出了两阶段随机应答模型(two-stage random response model),并且应用在购物中心偷窃行为的研究中。这种方法不仅可以估计出敏感行为发生的比例,还可以估算出这种敏感行为发生的频率。

同时,在随机化工具的采用上也有许多变化。如 Takahasi 和 Sakasegawa(1977)提出了不用随机化工具,而采用辅助问题的实验方法。辅助问题可以是一个很简单的两值选择,如"你是喜欢春天还是秋天"?受访者想好答案,但不告诉访员。接下来受访者需要按照一定的规则来回答敏感问题。如果受访者对辅助问题心中的答案是"春天",并且发生过这种敏感行为,则受访者报告给访员"0",如果没有发生过,则报告"1"。如果受访者对辅助问题心中的答案是"秋天",并且发生过这种敏感行为,则受访者报告给访员"1",如果没有发生过,则报告"0"。Fox 和 Tracy(1986)的实验中则采用两个骰子作为随机化工具。受访者抛出骰子后,不能让访员知道骰子的点数。如果两个骰子的点数之和为 2、3、4,受访者必须回答"是";如果点数总和为 11 或 12,受访者必须回答"否";如果是其他情况则受访者被要求给出真实的回答。这种方法又称为强制应答方法(force response method)(Edgell, Himmelfarb and Duchan, 1982)。而 Kuk(1990)在随机化应答实验中把扑克牌作为工具。在这种方法中,扑克牌被分为两堆,每堆所包括的红色扑克牌的比例是预知的,如 20%和 80%。受访者从每一堆扑克牌中各抽取一张牌,扑克牌的颜色对访员保密。如果受访者对问题的回答是"是",那就报告自己从左边一堆中抽取的扑克牌颜色;如果回答是"否",则报告从右边一堆中抽取的扑克牌颜色。访员不知道受访者报告的颜色是来自哪一堆,所以也就无从得知受访者的答案是什么。

随机应答技术的目的就在于让受访者认为访员或研究者并不知道自己的答案是什么。然而这种技术比直接问答的难度要大,对访员和受访者的要求也比较高。第一,访员要能够非常清晰地讲解并指导受访者使用随机化工具或辅助问题,以及如何按照随机结果来回答问题;第二,受访者要能够理解和掌握整个随机应答技术的过程和具体要求;第三,受访者要信任这种方法,相信自己的答案不会被外人得知(Landsheer, Van der Heijden and Van Gils, 1999)。

列举实验(list experiment)或称条目计数法(Item Count Technique,ICT)则巧妙地避免了随机应答技术遇到的难题。1984年,Miller 首先在他的博士论文中提出并论证了这个方法(Droitcour et al, 1991)。这种方法也是将问卷分为两个版本,并把受访者随机分为两组,分别回答不同版本的问卷。一个版本的问卷中包括一组有关事实或行为的问题,另一个版本的问卷中包括同样一组问题,但多出一条关于敏感行为的问题。例如种族歧视在美国是一个敏感话题,如果在公开场合询问美国白人对黑人的态度往往会得到社会期许的应答, 1991 年美国的“全国种族与政治调查(National Race and Politics Survey)”中就应用了列举实验来研究种族歧视问题(Kuklinski, Cobb and Gilens, 1997)。问卷中采用以下两种问题设计:

版本 A：	版本 B：
现在我要读出三件事,这三件事有时会让人感到气愤或不安。当我读完所有三件事后,请告诉我有多少件事情让你感到不安。(我不想知道具体哪件事情,只需要知道有多少件。)	现在我要读出四件事,这四件事有时会让人感到气愤或不安。当我读完所有四件事后,请告诉我有多少件事情让你感到不安。(我不想知道具体哪件事情,只需要知道有多少件。)
1. 联邦政府提高了汽油税	1. 联邦政府提高了汽油税
2. 职业运动员得到百万美元以上的工资	2. 职业运动员得到百万美元以上的工资
3. 大企业集团污染环境	3. 大企业集团污染环境
	4. 一个黑人家庭搬到你家隔壁
这些事中有几件事会让你感到不安?	这些事中有几件事会让你感到不安?

在版本 A 的问题中列出了 3 个条目,而在版本 B 的问题中含有 4 个条目,其中第 4 个条目是新增加的,同时也是研究者所关注的敏感问题。因为受访者不必具体指明哪几件事情让自己不安,在一定程度上会感到自己的隐私受到保护,这样可能会给出真实的应答。虽然这种方法不能确切得知受访者是否选择了版本 B 问题中的第 4 个条目,但通过比较两组受访者对这两个版本问题的应答,就可以计算出选择这个选项的人数比例 $\hat{p}$,即

$$\hat{p} = \overline{X}_B - \overline{X}_A$$

其中 $\overline{X}_A$ 是受访者对版本 A 问题的应答均值, $\overline{X}_B$ 是受访者对版本 B 问题的应答均值。

条目计数法的一个缺陷就是估计方差会过高,为了降低估计

方差，这种方法被升级为“双列举”版本（double-lists version of item count）。这种方法要设计两套列举条目单，第一套如上所述，用X_A和X_B表示，此外还需要再编制一套类似的列举条目，用Y_A和Y_B表示，也是一组包括感兴趣的选项，另外一组不包括这个选项。受访者也是随机分为两组，一组回答X_A和X_B，另一组回答Y_A和Y_B。分析时首先分别估计每套根据条目计数法得到的估计值，然后再将两个估计值取平均数。具体如下：

$$\hat{p} = \frac{1}{2}[(\bar{X}_B - \bar{X}_A) + (\bar{Y}_B - \bar{Y}_A)]$$

条目计数法的另一个缺陷是只适用于应答为“是”或“否”的二分变量，针对连续型变量，Trappmann 等（2014）在条目计数法的基础上又发展了条目求和法（item sum technique）。这种方法也是先将受访者随机分为两组，一组人要回答一道敏感问题和一道非敏感的辅助问题，另外一组人则只回答那道辅助问题。辅助问题和敏感问题都是连续型变量，并且最好用同样尺度测量。第一组受访者报告两道问题答案的总和，第二组人则只需报告辅助问题的答案。例如，在美国为了偷税漏税，有人会故意隐瞒自己的某份工作。如果直接询问，很可能得不到真实的回答。这种情况下可以采用条目求和法，设计如下两个问题：

1. 上周你看了多少小时的电视？

2. 在你隐瞒未报的工作上，你每周平均要干多少小时？

第一组受访者被提问两个问题，只需报告看电视和工作的小时数之和；第二组受访者只需报告第一个问题的答案。这样做是期望受访者能够认识到自己的隐私被保护，从而提供真实答案。

对条目求和法调查结果的分析也比较直接，只需计算两组应答平均值的差就可以算出受访样本在隐瞒工作上所用的平均小时数。

由此可见，调查-实验在应对社会期许心理、降低敏感问题的应答误差上有着重要的贡献。

析因调查-实验技术

当用问卷调查来采集人们的态度和判断时，研究者们还会遇到另外的问题。一是问题太抽象，以至于受访者只能根据个人的理解来回答；二是有些评价的问题涉及基于多个指标的综合判断，但调查过程中却不得不将这些指标分解开来单独评分。应对这种需求，调查和实验结合后有了另一个突破性创新，就是析因调查-实验（factorial survey）。

简单的分投选票法在分析上有很大限制，如一般只有一个处理变量（或自变量），而且变量的取值一般只能有两个。析因调查-实验技术突破了这个限制，可将处理变量扩展到几个，而变量的取值也可以有多个。具体地说，析因调查-实验中研究者会根据自变量的个数和取值水平编制一套假设的情境或对象，称为虚拟案例。虚拟案例就是这个调查-实验的处理手段，它们会被随机分配给受访者进行判断，判断结果就是研究的因变量。

析因调查-实验技术的开创者是 Rossi 和他的同事们（Rossi et al，1974；Jasso and Rossi，1977；Nock and Rossi，1979；Rossi and Nock，1982）。他们在对社会地位的研究中采用了这样的新方法（Rossi et al，1974）。他们认为社会分层应该以家庭为单位来评估，而且一个家庭的地位取决于其所在社会体系对其身份的集体评价。在这个研究中,他们选取了三个自变量:家庭角色(丈夫或妻子),教育程度(小学毕业、中学毕业、大学毕业及以上),以及职业(分为 12 类)。在每一个编制的虚拟案例中都包括一对夫妻,他们有着不同的职业和教育水平,这样总共可以组成 1296 个虚拟案例。作者们对这些案例做了精心挑选,排除掉了现实中不太可能的组合,如高中或小学毕业的医生,总统丈夫的妻子做旅馆服务员等,最后选定 664 个虚拟案例。他们把这 664 个案例采用系统抽样的方式分为 7 组,每个受访者会对 95 个虚拟案例中设定家户的社会地位进行评分。这次调查-实验采用修正后的区域概率抽样方法(modified area probability sampling methods),受访者从美国巴尔的摩市居住在私人住宅的 18 岁以上的白人中选取。但是对于这项研究的结论,作者们认为只有探索意义,因为样本来源是出于方便而选择了附近地区,同时用在虚拟案例中的家庭成员特征过于简单化,还应该包括更多的特征维度。Nock 和 Rossi(1979)继续了这项研究,调查样本仍来自巴尔的摩市,但虚拟案例的维度从三个上升为六个,除了以上三个变量,还加入了婚姻状态、年龄和孩子个数。这样,虚拟案例的总体个数增加至 36000 个,他们从中选取了 2400 个案例,分为 40 组样本,每组包括 60 个虚拟案例,每组样本随机分配给 15 个受访者打分。析因调查-实验技术也被 Jasso 和 Rossi(1977)用于分配公平的研究,并基于调查-实验数据提出了自然对数形式的个体分配公平评价函数(Jasso, 1978)。

如果说 Rossi 等人 1974 年的文章只是析因调查-实验法的最初的果子,那么 1982 年 Rossi 和 Nock 合编的《社会判断测量》(*Measuring Social Judgments*)则标志着析因调查-实验法走向成熟。这本书详细而系统地向更广泛的研究界介绍了析因调查-实验法的原则，成为析因调查-实验方法发展的一个里程碑。Wallander(2009)总结了这以后到2006年间发表在社会学核心期刊上的使用析因调查-实验技术的学术文章。她发现这20余年间，析因调查-实验技术被应用到许多不同形式的判断中，如规范性的判断、实证性的信念，以及个人的感觉、想法和行为倾向等。在案例的设计上丰富多样，在维度的数量和取值水平的数量上也各不相同。然而，发表数量并不是很多，平均每年也就是4篇多。作者也主要来自美国，而且集中在几个特定的研究者。Wallander认为这不是析因调查-实验技术本身的局限，而是在于因应用条件的限制而对这种技术缺乏有效的推广。

析因调查-实验技术近年来越来越引起学者们的重视(Sniderman and Grob, 1996; Nock and Guterbock, 2010; Mutz, 2011)，这和计算机辅助调查模式的兴起是分不开的，具体将在下节介绍。

1.3.2　领域拓展

在纸笔模式的传统抽样调查中搭载实验是一件比较困难的事情，研究者需要将问卷印刷成不同的版本，在执行时也要保证能够把不同版本的问卷随机地发放给受访者。这些困难曾经在很大程度上限制了调查-实验的发展，直到计算机辅助调查模式广泛应用之后，调查-实验的设计和执行才不再因琐碎繁重而难以控制。

首先，在计算机辅助下，问卷不需要事先打印，而是成为一个计算机程序。在这个程序里可以非常容易地实现问题用语、格式或顺序的变换。比如上面提到的Rossi等(1974)的析因调查-实验，仅三个自变量就衍生出7个版本的问卷，1 296个虚拟案例的设计。这无论对研究者还是访员都是件费时费力的事情。然而使用计算机辅助技术,全部虚拟案例可以瞬间生成,并且能够随机分成若干组。

其次,在计算机辅助模式下,受访者的随机分组也成为易事。技术人员可以根据研究要求编制随机分配的程序,访问前受访者会被自动分配到某一组,避免了纸版问卷现场分组的麻烦。于是,调查-实验也不再局限于分投选票法,复杂的随机化分组设计也被更多地应用(如 Tourangeau and Smith,1996)。

除了访员执行方便,计算机辅助模式下的调查-实验的第三个好处是实验处理对于受访者也相对隐蔽。访员不必仔细考虑该用哪个版本的问卷,计算机已经自动选好,访员只需照着提问就可以了。受访者只接触到自己的问卷,不会意识到自己的问卷和别人的问卷有什么不同,从而也在一定程度上降低了其对实验的紧张心理。

计算机辅助调查技术为调查-实验开辟了一条轻省的捷径,但调查-实验的广泛应用和研究者们的推动是分不开的。这方面不能不提的是 Paul Sniderman 教授和他加州大学伯克利分校抽样调查研究中心的同事们(Sniderman, 2011)。

Sniderman 起初对调查-实验并不感兴趣,他一方面认为当时常用的分投选票法过于强求一致,另一方面也是因为自己的研究兴趣是实质性问题而非方法论。然而 1983 年的一天,他在办公楼的咖啡机前偶遇一位同事,这位同事刚在计算机辅助调查技术开发上取得了实质性进展,和这位同事聊天时 Sniderman 首次听到这个新的调查技术,但很快也就忘掉了。一年以后,在一次意外的假期中,他联想起自己儿时参加夏令营时一次关于偏见(prejudice)

和歧视(discrimination)的课程，于是想到这个调查技术，并且产生了新的研究想法。作为一个社会抽样调查研究者，Sniderman 可以通过问卷调查了解到人们的态度(如偏见)，却无法获知其行动(如歧视)。在计算机辅助的抽样调查中加载一个随机实验，在技术上是件简单的事情，然而对于研究来说却是意义重大。他当时的研究想法是询问一组随机选择的受访者："对一个失业但正在寻找工作的美国白人，政府应该给多少帮助?"询问另一组受访者同样的问题，只是把"白人"改为"黑人"。如果应答者中较多的白人支持给失业的白人帮助，那么就不仅可以知道美国白人对黑人的态度，还知道了他们如何对待黑人。

于是 Sniderman 和 Tom Piazza 一起实现了这个研究想法，在美国加州的湾区做了这个调查-实验，根据调查结果出版了《种族的疤痕》(*The Scar of Race*)(Sniderman and Piazza, 1993)。Sniderman 做的其他两个实验也获得了重要的学术成果(如 Sniderman et al, 1996；Sniderman and Carmines, 1997，等)。

Sniderman 注意到在一个计算机辅助调查中进行一个随机实验的用时很短，于是又产生了一个调查搭载多个研究者的多个实验的念头，这样可以大幅度降低调查-实验的成本，使调查-实验方法更为可行。为此他到多所大学"兜售"这个想法，邀请研究者们撰写调查-实验的研究计划，创建多研究者合作项目(Multi-Investigator Project)。后来他又成功地申请到美国自然科学基金(NSF)的赞助，创建了社会科学分时实验室(Time-sharing Experiments in the Social Sciences, TESS)。TESS 主要使用计算机辅助的网络调查模式(Computer-Assisted Web Interviewing, CAWI)，基于全国代表性样本进行调查-实验数据的采集。CAWI 不仅可以在问题语句、形式和顺序上产生不同版本的问卷,也可以在调查中使用图片、音频、影像等,使实验处理手段更为丰富。TESS 的创建和运转无论在研究资金还是在操作执行上都大大推动了调查-实验在学术研究上的应用。

Sniderman 对于调查-实验发展的贡献不仅在于对计算机辅助调查模式的应用,更重要的是在他的努力下,调查-实验被应用到更广阔的实质性主题研究,并且开辟了多研究者合作的模式,降低了单个调查-实验的成本,使这一方法可以被更广泛的研究群体所使用。

1.4　调查-实验的应用

调查-实验的出现至今已有七十多年的历史,本节将对 21 世纪以来国内外调查-实验的应用领域和特点进行综述分析。

1.4.1　调查方法学研究

调查-实验用于社会调查方法的研究历史已久,研究成果众多,研究对象多样,但概括来说主要围绕两大主题,即应答样本的代表性和问题测量的有效性(Groves and Lyberg, 2010; Biemer, 2010)。在这两大主题下,如何降低各种误差是研究的重要目的。抽样调查在样本代表性方面需要首先确定推论总体,抽样过程中要确定目标总体,建立抽样框,然后从中选取调查样本。在这一过程中会出现覆盖误差,即在建立抽样框时包括了不该包括的对象,或没有包括应该包括在内的对象。也会存在抽样误差,即从抽样框中选取调查样本时会因为不同的抽样设计而导致的推论误差。在实地调查过程中，会出现部分样本没有参与调查的无应答现象，这就造成了无应答误差。

在问题测量的工作流程中，首先要对研究的概念操作化，使之从抽象的概念转为具体的问卷问题。如果问卷问题没有准确地反映出概念的实质，那么就会产生效度问题或设定误差。在实地调查过程中，受访者的应答会受到多种因素的影响，比如个人的态度、采访的环境、访员的特征、调查的方式等，这样就会产生测量误差。在访问结束后对数据进行整理和加工时还会出现处理误差。

研究者常常借助调查-实验来寻求降低无应答误差和测量误差的有效手段。因为这两种误差都是在调查过程中产生的，受外界因素影响比较大，而要证明手段有效，就需要排除其他混淆因素的干扰，发现真实的因果关系。因此调查-实验是实现这一研究目的的最合适的研究方法。

一般认为，降低无应答误差的主要手段就是降低无应答率，在此方面研究者有多种尝试。如受访者酬金方面，调查-实验研究证明酬金金额的多少和应答比例正相关（Zagorsky and Rhoton, 2008; Pforr et al, 2015），酬金采用现金的形式要优于彩票或慈善捐献（Warriner et al, 1996; Pforr et al, 2015; Laguilles, Williams and Saunders, 2011），预付酬金的方式效果要更好（Wetzels et al, 2008; Singer, Van Hoewyk and Maher, 2000）等。

也有调查-实验用来测试调查模式对于应答率的影响。如 Wagner 等（2014）比较了面访和邮寄问卷的混合调查模式与单纯面访模式的效果。他们将受访者分为三组，控制组仅采用面访的方式，一个实验组采取先邮寄问卷然后补充面访的混合模式，另一个实验组采取先面访然后补充邮寄问卷的相反顺序的混合模式。实验结果发现两种混合模式降低了调查的成本,但并没有降低应答率。同时两种混合模式的模式顺序对应答率也没有显著影响。Miller 和 Dillman(2011)的调查-实验是为了提高网络调查的应答率。他们发现和邮寄问卷的调查方式相比,在网络访问和邮寄问卷的混合模式调查中,同时请受访者选择调查模式不能有效提高应答率,但如果先提供受访者网络访问模式,再提供邮寄问卷的方式时,可以有效提高应答率。

和受访者的联系信函对于应答率的影响也可以通过调查-实验来检验。如 Fumagalli 等(2013) 通过调查-实验来研究降低跟踪调查样本损失的办法。他们发现,在两波调查之间邮寄地址变更的卡片要比邮寄地址确认卡片或不邮寄任何卡片的方式更容易提高样本被再次访到的可能性。另一个调查-实验发现为年轻人和繁忙人士特制的报告文书相比统一标准的报告文书在提高这部分人的应答率上作用微小。

根据受访者的特点定制不同的采访计划也用来提高应答样本的代表性。Luiten 和 Schouten (2013) 的调查-实验首先基于并行数据判断调查样本能够联系上或成功访问的倾向,然后根据这个倾向来选择混合模式的初始模式。对于初始模式的网络或邮件访问中的无应答者,再采用计算机辅助电话追访。在追访时,对于前一模式没有联系成功的样本,通过调整电话联系的时机、间隔和优先等方法来处理;对于前一模式中联系成功但遭到拒访的样本,则通过指派特定访员的方法来处理。调查-实验的结果证明这种定制的采访计划可以在保持成本不变的情况下成功地提高样本的代表性。

调查-实验也大量应用在对测量误差的甄别和判定上。影响测量误差的因素多种多样，可以源自问卷设计、受访者本人、采访员、采访过程，以及数据采集方式等，并且多用调查-实验的方法来比较不同状况下对应答的影响（Biemer et al, 2011）。传统的对于测量误差的研究主题，如问题用词、问题顺序、问题形式（开放式或封闭式提问）、选项设计、访员效应、社会期许等的调查-实验仍然存在，但随着调查技术的创新，近年的调查-实验比较关注新的调查技术或不同调查模式对应答的影响。如欧洲社会调查（European Social Survey, ESS）在 2002 年启动时一直采用面访模式，在 2012 年决定向混合模式过渡，当时研究者们面临的一个问题就是不同调查模式下采集的数据是否具有和面访模式下相同的质量。Revilla（2015）在爱沙尼亚和英国的 ESS 调查中对这个问题采用调查-实验的方法来检验。实验结果发现在测量的概念和观测到的应答关系上，单一面访模式和多模式下的数据质量很相似，证明了多模式调查方式的转换没有影响到数据的可比性。

调查成本的升高和计算机技术的发展使网络调查越来越受到调查者们的青睐，然而网络调查问卷除了存在纸版问卷就存在的问题外，网络问卷的展示方式也会影响到受访者的应答。一系列调查-实验研究在这方面有若干发现。比如受访者在填写网络问卷时会通过视觉来判断量表的中间位置，而非根据选项的具体内容，这样如果不对一些非实质性选项，如“不知道”或“没想法”以下画线或间距的方式区分开来，受访者会找错参考用的中间点。此外，实验还发现如果选项中间的间距分配不均，量表两端采用的阴影颜色不同等都可能会造成受访者对参考中间点的判断错位

(Tourangeau, Couper and Conrad, 2004; Tourangeau, Couper and Conrad, 2007)。对于网络问卷中图片的使用,Couper, Conrad and Tourangeau(2007) 的调查-实验发现受访者对于自身健康状况的评价会受到影响。如果给受访者展现的是一张健康女性锻炼的图片,他们的自我评价会偏低;如果展现的是一张女性躺在病床上的图片,他们的自我评价会偏高。

受访者本人由于社会期许或个人隐私等原因会在接受调查时撒谎或避而不答,从而造成测量误差。调查方法研究者们不仅会开发新的调查-实验处理技术或调查模式来应对这个问题,他们也通过调查-实验的方法来检验这些方法的效果。比如随机应答技术和列举实验本身就是借助调查-实验来获知受访者的真实状况或想法,这些方法和直接提问相比是否有明显帮助也需要通过调查-实验来验证(Tsuchiya, Hirai and Ono, 2007; Holbrook and Krosnick, 2010)。在敏感问题应答的数据采集中,也有一些新的方法,如三角模型或交叉模型(Yu, Tian and Tang, 2008),也有一些新的调查模式,如计算机辅助语音自助访问(ACASI)或计算机辅助电话语音自助访问(T-ACASI),这些新方法新模式的效果也是通过调查-实验的方法来检验的(Villarroel et al, 2006; Harmon et al, 2009; Jann, Jerke and Krumpal, 2012)。

总而言之,调查-实验是抽样调查方法研究的一个重要工具,特别是在调查技术不断创新,调查难度也逐渐提高的环境下,调查-实验不仅可以用来评估各种调查误差,也可以被用来考察新方法、新技术的效果和作用。

1.4.2　社会科学主题研究

近年来实验的方法在社会科学研究上的应用不断增多。有学者对美国经济学、政治学和社会学领域六个顶尖期刊(*American Economic Review*,*Econometrica*,*American Journal of Political Science*,*American Political Science Review*,*American Journal of Sociology*,*American Sociological Review*)上发表的文章进行文本分析,统计了自 1990 年以来各年采用实验设计的文章篇数及所占比例(Jackson and Cox, 2013)。

他们发现实验方法在社会科学上的应用有整体上升的趋势,但也存在着明显的学科差异。1990—2004 年,六个期刊上发表的实验设计的文章比例不相上下,但从 2004 年起经济学的两个刊物开始领跑,基于实验设计的文章比例骤然上升,政治学的两个刊物从 2005 年起也出现迅速增长的态势,而社会学的两个刊物则没有表现出显著的变化。到 2010 年六个期刊中基于实验设计的文章比例出现明显差距,经济学期刊 *American Economic Review* 上约有 18%的文章采用了实验研究的方法,政治学的两个期刊的比例在 10%左右,而社会学的两个期刊的比例基本低于 5%。

上述纳入统计的文章采用的实验方法包括实验室实验、田野实验和调查-实验,而调查-实验在社会科学中的应用无疑是相关文章迅猛增长的主要原因。调查-实验中多种多样的处理手段都可以应用到社会科学的主题研究中。

首先,调查-实验最简单的处理手段就是在不同的问卷版本中使用不同的问题语句,这种实验设计虽然看似简单,但可以直接用来检测社会科学中的一些理论。如在移民研究中发现本国公民会出于一些经济上的考虑从而反对外国移民。对于这种经济考虑理论界中存在两种解释:一种解释从市场竞争的角度,认为外国移民会挤占本国公民的就业机会,增加本国公民的就业难度;另一种解释则从公共服务的角度,认为外国移民交税少,却和本国公民享受同样的社会福利支持,增加了本国公民的财政负担。为了验证这两个理论,Hainmueller 和 Hiscox(2010)设计了两个调查-实验。他们首先假定出于市场竞争的考虑,本国公民会更加反对有较高劳动技能的外国移民;而出于财政负担的考虑,本国公民会更加反对劳动技能较低的外国移民。于是设计了两个问卷版本,分别询问受访者在多大程度上同意美国应该允许更多高技能(低技能)的外国移民迁居到这里。第一个调查-实验采用"分投选票"的方法,将受访者随机分为实验组和控制组,分别采用这两个问卷版本。第二个调查-实验基于组内设计的原则,随机抽选第一个实验的部分受访者参加,并在第一个实验结束的两周后进行。这些受访者再次被随机分为两组,一组使用和上次相同的问卷版本访问,另一组则使用不同的问卷版本访问。两个调查-实验的结果一致,证明这两个出于经济原因的理论都不能充分解释本国公民反对外国移民的原因,而一些非经济因素,如民族优越感,则有着不容忽视的影响(Hainmueller and Hiscox, 2010)。

调查-实验另一常用的处理手段是设计相同的问题,但采用不同的问题顺序。方法学研究者们早已发现受访者的应答会受到问卷中问题顺序的影响,这被称为"顺序效应(order effect)",是造成测量误差的原因之一。而社会科学研究者们称之为"启动效应(priming effect)",认为问卷问题的顺序实际上营造了受访者应答的一个情境,而这种情境会影响到受访者的应答结果,通过对应答结果的分析可以挖掘出受访者真实的态度或观点。Sniderman 关于种族研究的很多调查-实验都是基于启动效应的。近十几年来，对启动效应的研究仍然是调查-实验的一个主要应用目的。如美国 2008 年总统初选前六周的一次电话调查，其中有两个调查问卷版本，一个版本是在调查开始就询问受访者一组对于国家发展方向、布什总统，以及伊拉克战争方面的态度问题，然后才请受访者回答支持的候选人；另一个版本则在调查结束前才提问这组问题。受访者被随机分为两组，分别使用这两个问卷版本提问。结果发现使用第一个问卷版本的受访者（实验组）中支持民主党人奥巴马的人数几乎是另一组（对照组）支持比例的两倍，证明了启动效应的存在，说明选民投票时如果被提醒伊拉克战争事件，就会严重影响到他的投票结果，布什所属的共和党就处于不利境地（Cassino and Erisen, 2010）。这种调查-实验的研究对于两党竞选时的宣传动员有现实指导意义。

除了问题的顺序，调查-实验中激发启动效应的处理手段有多种形式。如在一项有关日本选举的调查-实验中，为了考察竞选信息对于选民投票决定的影响，研究者设计了四种激发启用效应的处理手段：①只查看自民党官方网站；②只查看民主党官方网站；③先查看民主党网站，后访问自民党网站；④先查看自民党网站，后访问民主党网站。受访者随机分为四组，被指引在回答研究问题前先去查看这些网站上关于养老金改革方面的信息，从而查看这些网站信息对于受访者应答的影响（Horiuchi, Imai and Taniguchi, 2007b）。在另一项在阿根廷进行的关于人们对收入再分配倾向的研究中，研究者用来激发启动效应的是外部研究信息。这项研究将受访者随机分为对照组和实验组，当实验组的受访者回答了家户信息、实际收入水平和他对自己收入地位的认知问题后，访问员会根据研究者提供的信息告诉受访者他对收入地位的认知和实际相比估计得过高、适中还是过低。然后访问员会继续询问受访者对于当时一些收入再分配具体政策的态度。研究结果发现，那些过高估计了自己的收入地位并且被告知真实情况的人在后来更倾向于支持收入再分配的政策（Cruces, Perez-Truglia and Tetaz, 2013）。

为了获取受访者对敏感问题或社会期许问题的真实应答，调查-实验还发展了如随机应答技术和列举实验等处理手段。对于这些敏感问题的有效测量也促进并深化了对诸多社会问题的研究，如种族歧视、移民、毒品使用、性行为、选民投票等。如在美国 2008 年总统大选时期，女性总统候选人的出现成为热门话题。民主党方面，前第一夫人、时任国会议员希拉里 · 克林顿在民意调查中一直领先于党内其他候选人；共和党方面，国务卿赖斯也被认为是理想的总统候选人。盖洛普和美国著名社会调查“社会综合调查（General Social Survey, GSS）”的调查结果显示有大约 90%的美国人愿意投票支持称职的女性总统候选人。然而也有人质疑：在民意调查直接提问的情况下，受访者未必表达的是真实的想法，而可能是为了不违背社会主流规范而做出的虚假回答。Streb 等（2008）证实了这一质疑，他们发现当采用列举实验的方法来调查美国公众对于女性总统的支持时，有大约 26%的受访者会对女性担任总统表示“愤怒或沮丧”，而且这种态度和一些人口特征相关。

虚拟案例也是调查-实验的一种重要的处理手段，基于这种处理手段的调查-实验又称析因调查-实验，主要适用于社会科学研究中关于信念、决策和判断方面的主题研究(Taylor, 2006; Jasso, 2006)。如在美国存在着严重的种族居住隔离的现象,白人和黑人都形成了自己的聚居区。在一般情况下,居民在购买住房时除了房屋本身的特征,还会考虑多种因素,如房产价值、犯罪率和邻居的情况等。然而,这些因素并不是相互独立的,例如常见的现象是美国黑人比例较高的社区社会治安较差,从而影响到房产的价值。那么如何知道美国白人在选择住所的时候是出于纯粹的种族隔离,还是出于一些其他的实际考虑? Emerson 等采用了析因调查-实验的方法来研究这个问题。他们发现白人会因为单纯的种族原因不愿意搬到和黑人混居的地方,这种居住偏好造成的后果就是黑人后代和白人后代的事实上的隔离(Emerson, Chai and Yancey, 2001)。

Wallander (2009)对 1982—2006 年发表的 106 篇基于析因调查-实验的社会学领域的研究文章进行了分析,发现这些文章的研究主题最多集中在法律、犯罪或偏常行为的研究上,其次是家庭、社会福利、社会分化。在 2012 年该作者再次撰文,指导在测量社会工作者的专业判断上如何应用析因调查-实验的方法(Wallander, 2012)。近年来调查-实验广泛应用在一些专业人士的判断研究上,如社会工作者对于儿童保护、青少年吸毒及老年人受虐事件上的判断(Killick and Taylor, 2012; Astrom et al, 2013; Stokes and Schmidt, 2012),医护人员在病人护理、病人家属介入方面的决定等(Brenner et al, 2015; Davis et al, 2014; Lauder, Scott and Whyte, 2001; Mueller-Engelmann et al, 2013; Rattray et al, 2011; Schwappach, Frank and Davis, 2013)。析因调查-实验也应用在人们的态度和行为的研究上,如影响人们报案的因素研究

(Tolsma, Blaauw and Grotenhuis, 2012),流产决定的情境研究(Hans and Kimberly, 2014)等。

由上述可见,调查-实验可以在社会科学主题研究中得到广泛应用。这些应用不仅提供全新的研究视角,有效的概念测量手段,也可以提升社会科学中因果推断和多元分析的合理推论。

1.4.3　国内应用现状

调查-实验方法在国内社会科学研究上的应用正处于萌芽阶段,只在近两年国内外学术期刊上才开始出现国内学者的研究成果。

2014 年国内期刊《国际安全研究》上首次刊登基于调查-实验方法的文章,《支持还是反对军事冲突?——日本与邻国争端中民意的调查-实验分析》。这是北京大学和清华大学两位硕士研究生利用暑期在日本研修期间实施的析因调查-实验,旨在分析当日本与邻国发生领土争端时,日本民众是否以及在什么情况下会支持政府发生军事冲突(陈然,于朔, 2014)。这个调查-实验虽然在设计上存在不足,调查方式上采用街头拦访,一定程度上损害了调查-实验的随机性,但对于国内在国际关系的研究中引入实验研究的方法还是具有拓荒的意义。

同年,国内青年学者孟天广与合作者在美国学术期刊《比较政治研究》(*Comparative Political Studies*)上发表文章探究地方决策中政府官员在什么样的条件下会回应公民意见(Meng et al, 2014)。中国当代政治文化一直倡导干部要勤政为民,重视民意,当地方政府官员被问及是否会在制定和民生相关的地方政策时回应公众意见,受访者可能会出于社会期许的原因而隐藏自己的真实观点,给出肯定的回答。于是这项研究采用了列举实验的方法来获取受访者的真实态度，并且由于研究中要区分正规渠道和网络渠道传递的民意，问卷中设计了两个列举实验，这样共有三个问卷版本。调查采用配额抽样的办法选取了1800个样本，最终完成访问1377个。受访者被随机分为控制组和两个实验组，每个组采用一种版本的问卷进行调查。作者们对实验结果进行分析发现地方官员对于本地公众意见是否回应受公众意见反映的渠道和其对地方性干群关系感受的影响。如果认为地方性干群关系正常，地方官员一般愿意回应各种渠道反映上来的民意；如果关系紧张，地方官员则倾向于回应正规渠道反映的民意，而对网络渠道反映的民意不太理会。这项研究中调查-实验的设计、实施和分析都比较严谨，并且在文章中有详细介绍，本书第3章将对此文重点评析。

孟天广另一篇采用调查-实验方法的文章发表在2015年《公共管理学报》上。在这篇文章中，他与合作者延续地方政府回应性的主题，采用析因调查-实验的方法考察了经济发展和民生福利两个政策领域上级政府和本地公民意见对地方财政决策的影响（孟天广、杨平、苏政，2015）。调查-实验由一个控制状态和四个处理状态构成。实验结果表明，上级政府意见和本地公民意见对地方财政决策选择的影响均只存在于“经济发展支出”领域，而在“民生福利支出”领域没有显著影响。在影响幅度上，上级政府意见对地方财政决策的影响略强于本地公民的相应意见。

2015年在China Quarterly上也发表了一篇采用调查-实验方法的研究文章（Tai and Truex，2015）。中国政府为吸引海外优秀人才回国采取了一系列优惠政策，这项研究想了解人们对于海归及吸引海归的这些政策的看法和态度。作者们以网民为调查对象,通过随机分组的方法考察网民们对于不同身份(学生/教授/企业人士)的海归,以及对不同级别的优惠政策的支持程度。调查-实验结果发现网民们的态度与其收入水平相关,收入水平高的受访者表现得更为支持海外优秀人才回国,而收入水平低的受访者则有一定的抵触,并且随着政策中优惠幅度的增加,普遍的支持率呈下降趋势。

1.5　调查-实验的基本原理

调查-实验的发展具有实践先行的特点。虽然应用历史已有几十年,应用领域也越来越广泛,但现有文献对其基本原理还没有进行系统的梳理,甚至在其名称和定义上也多有争议。

1.5.1　定义

来自调查和实验训练背景的研究者们对调查-实验有不同的称呼。如从事社会调查研究的学者会认为调查-实验本质上就是社会调查,只不过搭载了实验设计,称其为内嵌实验的社会调查(experiment-embedded survey)。而以实验研究为主的学者们则认为这个方法的研究思路就是实验,只不过实验场所从传统的实验室扩展到社会调查可及的实地,而且实验对象从少量自愿参与的被试扩展到有代表性的随机样本,称其为基于调查的实验(survey-based experiment)。于是一个折中的方法就是直接将两个词并列,称为调查-实验(survey experiment)。这一名称目前得到了最为广泛的应用。

同样，对于调查-实验的定义，不同背景的学者有不同的关注点。Nock 和 Guterbock(2010)认为，“调查-实验是跨对象地、系统地改变调查的一个或多个要素，并且评估这种改变对于一个或多个测量结果的作用”(p838)。在这个定义中，作者们关注的是调查-实验中的处理手段的操纵，以及和测量结果的共变关系。他们在说明中强调调查过程或调查协议的任何方面都可以被操纵，不仅包括问卷设计，也包括抽样方法、数据采集模式、受访者酬金等。然而这个定义没有限定调查-实验的样本必须是“大量的，基于概率的，或者是有广泛代表性的”(p839)，对于那些使用方便样本或少量预调查样本的，只要是调查的一些方面受到跨对象操纵，就可以认定为调查-实验。

Morton 和 Williams(2010)将调查-实验定义为“内嵌于调查中的个人决策实验”(p279)，强调调查-实验是借助调查实施的以个人为对象的实验，并且在这个实验中调查对象之间没有互动。作者也认为调查-实验作为一种个人决策实验，可以在实验室，也可以在实地或网络上操作，所以这个定义中也没有对调查对象的构成给予限制。

Mutz(2011)认为“调查-实验”的名称容易产生误导，因为其中的“调查(survey)”在现代社会科学研究中已专指抽样调查。她于是对调查-实验这个名称做了限定，提出“基于总体的调查-实验(population-based survey experiment)”的概念。简单地说，基于总体的调查-实验就是在代表性的总体样本中所施行的实验，所以这个定义的侧重点在调查对象的选取上，特别强调的是采用概率抽样的方法从理论相关的目标总体中选取代表性样本作为调查(实验)对象。

由此可见,学者们的共识是调查-实验具有实验的属性同时采用调查的形式。因此,调查-实验可以理解为内嵌在抽样调查中,并且以调查手段为干预的随机对照实验。调查-实验的核心是随机对照实验,就必须要遵循标准实验的逻辑,这是不容置疑的。然而在调查形式的运用上学者们存在着分歧。调查背景的学者强调样本的代表性及实施的分散性,而实验背景的学者则对此不以为意。

严格地讲,调查-实验既然借助社会调查手段来实施,就应在最大程度上采用社会调查的常用方式。具体包括:①采用概率或非概率抽样的方式选取调查对象;②采用结构化提问的问卷方式采集实验数据;③采用实地面访、电话访问、邮寄问卷自填、网络问卷自填等执行方式;④研究人员不直接接触实验对象。因此一些实验室中的实验,虽然采用了问卷的形式获取被试的一些信息或了解被试前后的变化,但这些实验不属于调查-实验。

1.5.2　概念

调查-实验涉及的概念涵盖调查和实验两种方法的术语,部分术语在前文中已有提及,在这里有必要对这些概念给予明确界定。

首先调查-实验是一个**数据生成过程**(Data Generating Process),人们可以通过这一过程获取有关目标总体的数据。

所谓**目标总体**(target population),就是研究者有意观察的群体。具体到调查-实验,就是通过调查-实验数据分析所了解到的群体。社会科学研究活动的目的是产生、发展或借助理论来理解或解释社会现象,因此研究者们关注的往往是一个较大的群体,如所有中国人,所有中国家庭,或所有国内社会组织等。然而由于客观限制,研究者们不可能对每一个中国人、家庭或社会组织进行研究,而只能选取其中部分作为接触对象。这些被选取的接触对象被称为**样本**(sample)或**实验单元**(experimental unit)[①]。调查-实验要对这些样本进行**观测**(observational measure),并且将观测数据的分析结果推论到目标总体。

调查-实验同时也具有实验属性。实验可以理解为研究者介入数据生成过程,并且有目的地操纵数据生成过程中的元素。**操纵**(manipulation)包括两方面的含义:一是改变,也是狭义上的操纵;二是保持不变,一般称为**控制**(control)。改变的目的是形成不同的实验**处理**(treatment),进而观察是否会导致不同的结果。控制的目的是排除**混淆**(confunding),也就是避免处理以外因素对于结果的影响,以确认实验处理和实验结果的一一对应。

因此,调查-实验主要包括三大类变量:

(1)处理变量(treatment variable):研究者关注问题的原因,是调查-实验中要改变的变量,也是数据分析中的自变量。处理变量的每个水平构成实验中的不同处理,因此处理变量必须能被研究者操纵,并可以根据研究需要改变处理水平,具体可包括物理上的、生理上的、心理上的操纵,或上述操纵的组合。

(2)结果变量(outcome variable):研究者寻求解释的问题或现象,也就是要建立因果关系中的"果",或数据分析中的因变量。结果变量须是可观测的,可采用自己报告、行为测验或生理测量等方式获得数据信息。

(3)混淆变量(confunding variable):对结果变量有影响作用,会干扰研究者欲得到的数据生成过程,但不是研究者关注的变量。

---

① 本书中样本和实验单元两个概念含义等同,可交互替换使用。

混淆变量分为两类：一类是情境变量（setting variable），具体可包括社会、制度、生态或时间等；另一类是个体变量（unit variable），包括个体层面的人口学属性、认知能力、个性、情绪、价值观或社会态度等。混淆变量有些是可观测的，有些是不可观测的；有些能够受到研究者的控制，有些则不能被控制（如性别、年龄等）。

在调查-实验的设计和操作中，有三个重要的机制：

（1）变量操纵机制：指研究者出于研究需要有意地改变处理变量。该机制是区分实验设计和非实验设计的根本标志。

（2）样本分配机制：指的是如何在实验单元间分配实验处理。该机制主要用于区分实验设计和准实验设计，前者对实验单元进行随机分配，后者则由于各种原因未能实现随机化。

（3）样本选取机制：指的是如何选取实验单元。该机制可区分调查-实验和其他类型实验。调查-实验采用概率或非概率随机抽样的方式来选取，其他类型实验一般招募自愿或方便样本作为实验单元。

因此，如图 1.2 所示，处理变量的操纵，样本的随机分配和样本的随机抽选构成调查-实验的三个核心机制。

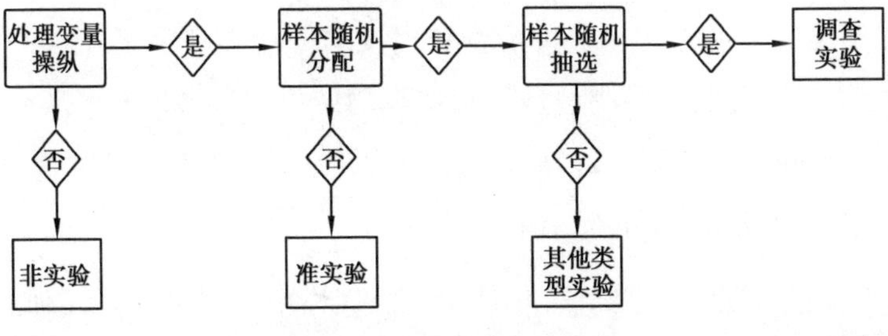

图 1.2　调查-实验核心机制

1.5.3 效度

前面提到，实验在总体效度上有缺憾，调查则在因果效度上有不足。那么，调查-实验应该如何在建构效度、因果效度、总体效度和外部效度四个维度上接受检验呢？

先讨论建构效度和外部效度。首先，调查-实验是一种理论验证的研究，其实验的设计和操作要具有建构效度。具体地说，如果理论中解释了为什么 A 的变化导致了 B 的变化，那么在调查-实验中需要用实验处理 T 来测量 A，同时用实验结果 Y 来测量 B，并且理论中的前提假定要得到满足，理论上恒定的条件要得到控制，实验对象要来自理论所适用的目标总体。也就是说，理论中涉及的概念和条件要在实验中得到很好的再现，其中，对于概念的有效测量是影响建构效度的一个重要因素，社会调查研究者对此多有探讨（如 Marsden and Wright，2010；Lyberg，1997，等）。

外部效度是指调查-实验在不同的群体或情境中重复执行时，可以得到一致稳定的调查结果。具体可以包括四个方面：第一，调查-实验的参与者是否和现实遇到这些影响因素的人相似；第二，调查-实验的情境是否和研究现象现实发生的情境相似；第三，调查-实验所采用的处理手段是否和现实的一些影响因素相似；第四，调查-实验的结果测量是否和实际的结果相似（Shadish，Cook and Campbell，2002）。因此，对外部效度最适宜的评估方法是实验复制，以此来验证实验结果的适用性。

调查-实验的研究目的就是要验证理论中的因果关系，因此，因果效度是评价调查-实验的一个重要维度。同时，总体效度也是调查-实验追求的目标之一，为的是能将基于样本实验发现的结果有效推论到目标总体。然而,因果效度和总体效度会因调查-实验设计的严谨程度而有不同的表现。

首先,调查-实验中因果效度表现为在设计中实验处理 T 先于实验结果 Y 发生,而后在统计分析中发现实验数据之间的相关关系显著并且真实,没有受到其他混淆因素的影响。如图 1.2 所示,调查-实验的因果效度始于对处理变量的操纵,如果研究者没有对处理变量进行操纵,就成为普通的观察式社会调查,无从做出因果效度的评价。其次就是样本的随机分配。随机分配是调查-实验控制混淆变量的重要手段,就是随机将调查对象分为实验组和对照组,这样可以平衡实验组和对照组样本的情境变量和个体变量的属性,从而确认两组实验结果的不同是实验处理产生的效果,而非其他原因。显然,严格遵守随机化原则分配样本的调查-实验在因果效度上最好,而采用准实验设计的调查-实验则在因果效度上打了折扣。

其次,调查对象是否具有代表性会直接影响到调查-实验的总体效度。调查的抽样手段一般分为概率抽样和非概率抽样:概率抽样就是按照一定的概率从目标总体中随机抽选一定数量的样本作为调查对象,总体中每一个元素都有一定的机会被抽中且它们被抽中的概率是已知的;而在非概率抽样中,总体中元素的入选概率不知,而且存在一些元素没有机会入选的情形。随机抽样是提高总体效度的重要手段,因此,采用概率抽样的调查-实验在总体效度上要优于采用非概率抽样的调查-实验。对总体效度的评估除了对样本选取方法的随机性进行判断外,也可以采用统计复制(statistical replication)的方法,即对同一个理论进行验证时,采用同一目标总体的不同随机样本作为调查对象,判断得出统计分析的结果是否相似(Blom-Hansen, Morton and Serritzlew, 2015)。

调查-实验虽然在理论上可以获得较好的内部效度和外部效度,但在实际应用中也面临质疑,其中比较重要的是关于实验效应的持续性。调查-实验研究者们的一个基本共识是调查-实验中发现的因果效应,在现实世界中也会同样存在。比如在调查-实验中发现一个政治广告片会影响到受访者的投票意愿,那么在现实中也会这样。然而,研究者们忽略了一个问题,就是实验效应的持续性。如果一个实验效应只持续了 10 分钟,在调查-实验中可以捕捉到这种效应,然而在实践中这种效应基本是没有意义的。比如一个人在投票之前在餐馆里看到这个政治广告片,影响到他当时的投票意愿,但在从餐馆去投票亭的路上他很可能就忘记了这个广告片,或者在有了深入思考后又恢复了原来的投票意愿,这个广告片的影响就是暂时的,这个调查-实验的外部效度就存在不足。

Barabas 和 Jerit (2010) 比较了同一主题的三个调查-实验和同期进行的自然实验的结果,他们发现在调查-实验中提供新的信息会改变受访者的政治知识和态度,然而在现实世界中同样的政府公告却几乎没有什么作用。经过分析,他们认为这种矛盾主要由三个原因造成:①在现实世界中关于这两个政府公告的报道没有得到国内媒体的广泛覆盖,客观上造成处理力度的不足;②调查-实验中信息的提供是强迫性的,而在现实中,人们在信息的接收上是有选择的,两种研究的实验对象在实验处理上反应的不同也会导致实验效应上的矛盾;③现实世界除了研究中的处理因素外,不可避免地会受到其他因素的影响,这也会影响到实验结果。而且 Barabas 和 Jerit 发现在调查-实验中,受访者会根据收到的信息来调整他们的知识和态度,而在现实世界中,却只会增长知识,很难改变态度。因此,调查-实验的外部效度会受到复杂的现实世界的挑战。

1.6　小结

本章介绍了调查-实验研究方法的产生背景,发展简史和应用现状,并简要论述了调查-实验的基本原理,期望借此使读者对调查-实验有初步了解。

人们对于社会现象间因果关系的探究推动学者们去寻求有效的研究方法。休谟关于因果关系的"金律",密尔的实验逻辑,费舍的随机分配,罗宾的因果模型都为现代实验研究奠定了基础。然而实验方法应用到社会科学研究中经历了一个漫长的过程,从最早期的心理学上的应用,到近年来在经济学、政治学和社会学中的推崇,再到公共政策和行政管理领域的倡导,实验方法已经越来越为社会科学研究者所接受。同时调查方法得益于统计理论的突破,从早期的方便样本,到非概率抽样,再到概率抽样,已逐渐发展成为一个规范的社会科学研究方法,是社会科学量化研究的重要数据来源。实验和调查在因果关系的探究上各有缺憾,这使得二者的结合具有重要的意义。调查-实验的发展经历了技术的不断创新和应用领域的拓展。早期调查-实验较多采用"分投选票"的方法,实验处理手段比较简单,主要是改变问题的语句和顺序,实施上也只能选择纸版问卷一种方式。为了应对受访者应答过程中的社会期许行为,研究者们首先基于实验随机分组的方法开发了随机应答技术,并对此不断完善。然而这种技术操作复杂,对访员和受访者的要求比较高。继而出现的列举调查-实验则避免了随机应答技术遇到的困难,该方法利用实验组和控制组应答条目计数上的差异来获取对敏感条目的认同比例,并逐渐成为调查-实验中获取敏感问题真实应答的主流技术。同时,调查-实验还发展了虚拟案例的处理手段,被命名为析因调查-实验。这种方法将因果模型中的多个影响因子,通过人为操纵其因子水平,形成虚拟案例,请受访者基于案例中描述的情形,回答模型中果变量对应的问卷问题。这种调查-实验技术更接近于人们在现实中做决定或判断的体验,在多因子作用模式的分析上也具有优势。

现代计算机和通信技术与社会调查的结合产生了计算机辅助调查技术,这种技术简化了调查-实验的操作,并能降低调查-实验的成本,使得调查-实验首先在调查方法学领域得到广泛的应用,并且逐渐向社会科学领域扩展。在调查方法学方面,调查-实验主要围绕两大主题,即应答样本的代表性和问题测量的有效性;在社会科学实证领域,则在种族、选举、移民、收入分配、社会公正、社会分化等主题上多有应用。

在国内进行的调查-实验,或者国内学者基于调查-实验数据的研究都还比较少,主要原因可能是国内学者对于调查-实验不甚了解,因此有必要在国内普及调查-实验的知识,推动调查-实验的开展。

实践先行,理论在即。调查-实验可以理解为内嵌在抽样调查中,并且以调查手段为干预的随机对照实验。调查-实验同时具有调查和实验的属性,其核心机制包括处理变量的操纵、样本的随机分配和样本的随机抽选。调查-实验可以从建构效度、因果效度、总体效度和外部效度四方面来评价。建构效度是指调查-实验对所要评估的理论的有效性;因果效度是指调查-实验中构建的因果关系的有效性;总体效度是指调查-实验中发现的因果关系对研究总体的有效性;而外部效度是指调查-实验得出的因果结论对其他总体和其他环境条件的有效性。一项好的调查-实验要能够达到这四个效度上的基本要求,从而提升研究价值。

/ 第 2 章 /

调查-实验操作

实施一项调查-实验，前期都要做好哪些准备？处理操纵、随机分配和样本选取都有哪些方法？该如何操作？调查执行中该注意些什么？数据分析时该用哪种方法？以及如何分析？本章就这些问题分享调查-实验操作的经验，目的在于使读者了解相关的实务知识和注意事项，从而设计并实施自己感兴趣的研究课题。

2.1 调查-实验的准备

任何一项研究工作都需要精心准备，调查-实验也不例外，而且因为调查-实验的目的是得出因果关系的推断，这就使得前期准备尤为重要。如果准备得充分合理，不仅可以得出有效、可靠并且有价值的结论，而且可以节省金钱、时间和精力；相反，如果准备不够，则有可能造成不可弥补的缺陷，影响结论的科学性，造成各种资源的浪费。因此，在调查-实验项目的最初非常有必要花时间和精力认真准备。

调查-实验的准备阶段需要研究者认真思考以下问题并做出决定：这项研究①是否该使用调查-实验的方法？如果是，②该选用哪种实验处理操纵技术？③该采用哪种样本分配设计？④该如何选取调查样本？⑤该如何实地采集数据？以及⑥数据分析时该选用哪种统计分析手段？这几个问题环环相扣，研究者需要从研究的内容和目的，调查-实验的规范，以及财力、物力和人力的限制等诸多方面考虑。

2.1.1　该使用调查-实验的方法吗?

如前所述,调查-实验的方法在调查方法和社会科学主题研究上都有应用。一般来说,调查-实验对于具有以下特征的研究尤为适用。

(1)验证效果一致。调查-实验可以采用随机分配的方法比较两种或多种处理的效果是否一致。比如在进行跟踪调查的问卷修订时,需要验证新的问题用语、选项设置或问题顺序是否可以得到和往年调查一致的应答结果,以保证追踪调查数据的价值。另外,在多模式调查中,也需要采用调查-实验的方法来评估不同模式对于应答的影响以保证数据的匹配。在种族态度的研究上调查-实验的方法可以通过检验应答结果是否一致来验证启动效应是否有效。

(2)验证前因后果。因果推论的一个重要原则就是要因在前果在后,但一些社会政治现象的研究却很难从现实中判断出因果。比如在政治学领域里,很难判断是民意影响了政府决策,还是政府决策塑造了民意。再如人际信任被认为是一种重要的社会资本,但也很难说是人际信任带来国家或地区的经济和政治的发展,还是经济或政治发展较好的国家或地区培育了人们之间的彼此信任。在单纯的社会调查数据的分析中,因果的先后关系一般通过理论来解释,而调查-实验则可以通过设计来确定。

(3)验证真实相关。一种社会现象的出现会受到多种因素的影响,要想分辨出真实原因或判断某种原因的作用大小时首先需要建立一些假定。如果假定不成立,研究成果就是无效的;如果假定不现实,研究成果也往往无用。一些统计方法通过模型的构造来企图控制一些因素的影响，但常常会出现在模型中遗漏重要控制变量的情况，重要控制变量没有测量或不可测，或不知变量的影响的情况，从而得出错误结论。调查-实验则可以通过随机分配的方法排除自变量以外混淆因素的影响，从而可以更加准确地观测到自变量真实的作用方向和效果。

(4)特别需求。调查-实验还有助于获取敏感问题的真实应答。如采用随机分组的方法比较敏感问题设计上不同的用语对于应答的影响；不同调查模式在降低受访者应答顾虑上的效果；采用特别的随机应答技术及列举调查-实验的方法来测算应答的真实分布，等等。此外，一些稀有事件或是伦理上很难执行的实验，也可以通过调查-实验中虚拟案例的方法来获得受访者的决定或判断，并且发现影响这项决断的因素。

2.1.2 该选用哪种实验处理操纵手段?

调查-实验处理操纵手段的选择要与研究需求相匹配。如在调查方法的研究上，问题设计、问题顺序、数据采集模式、访员特征、酬金水平等都可以作为实验处理来操纵，以考察这些处理对于受访者应答的影响。而在学科主题研究上，处理的操纵手段也是多种多样，并且各有其适用对象，较为常用的有常规调查-实验、启动效应实验、析因调查-实验和列举调查-实验。

(1)常规调查-实验。常规调查-实验是指采用传统的实验处理操纵手段而实施的调查-实验，如比较不同的问题用语、问题顺序、选项设计、技术手段、激励方法、执行模式等对受访者应答的影响。这类实验多用于调查方法的改进或问卷修订的比较上。

(2)启动效应实验。这类调查-实验的目的是考察处理手段如何影响受访者对研究问题的应答,适用于那些存在互倚态度或“视情况而定”类似态度的社会问题或现象的研究,可以帮助研究者识别影响人们态度的因素及作用方式。启动效应实验的设计是建立在理论假设之上,因此需要有较强的理论指导。

(3)析因调查-实验。析因调查-实验主要适用于需要得知受访者的决策、判断或评价结果的研究项目,特别是对于以下研究情形尤为有用:一是受访者用来做决策、判断或评价的依据不是相互独立的,而是存在错综复杂的交互关系。这种情况用传统模型分析中交互项来表达会十分复杂,建模容易出错,或因交互项过多而影响统计效率。析因调查-实验可以将这些交互关系“打包”整合在不同的虚拟案例中,使影响因素的作用是整体的,而非分割的。另一种情形就是研究对象是对稀少事件的态度,比如在政治学研究中,抗议示威游行等事件有实际经验的人很少,但如果想了解在何种情形下人们会采用这种方式,就可以借助析因调查-实验的方法。还有一种研究情形是了解或评价专业人员在工作中的处理决断,有些工作情况由于伦理原因不能模拟或复制,所以需要采用虚拟案例的方式通过析因调查-实验来考察。

(4)列举调查-实验。列举调查-实验适用于敏感问题的研究,主要目的是避免受访者在应答时出于个人隐私的保护或社会期许的压力而给出不真实的应答。对于敏感问题得到真实应答是一方面,而列举调查-实验相对于随机应答技术在设计和操作上更为简单,因而更为研究者所青睐,这是另一方面。

另外,选择调查-实验的处理手段时也要考虑实施的限制。比如在网络调查-实验中可以使用图像、音频或视频作为处理手段,在计算机辅助调查中可以很容易生成几百个虚拟案例,而在纸版问卷的调查-实验中实现这些都比较困难。

2.1.3 该采用哪种样本分配设计?

调查-实验的样本分配设计主要有三大类：主体间设计(between—subjects design),主体内设计(within—subjects design),以及主体间主体内的混合设计(mixed research design)。主体间设计又称为独立组设计,或组间设计,是把实验单元分配到处理变量的不同水平上,每个实验单元在实验中只接受其中的一种处理。主体内设计又叫重复测量设计,或组内设计。在这种设计下,每个或每组实验单元接受所有的实验处理,然后比较在不同实验处理条件下的行为变化。混合设计则在调查-实验中同时采用了主体间和主体内的设计形式,如析因调查-实验中常见的形式是一个受访者要回答多个虚拟案例的问题,同时,一个虚拟案例的问题也会让不同的受访者来回答。

主体间设计的优势是一种处理不会影响另一种处理,因为每个实验单元只对一种处理做反应。但缺点是个体间的差异可能会影响到结果的有效性,而且需要的实验单元数量大。主体内设计则消除了实验单元的个别差异对实验的影响,而且需要的实验单元数量较少,但其缺点是一种实验处理下的操作将会影响另一种实验处理下的操作,即实验顺序会给实验结果制造麻烦。为减轻这些负向影响,主体间设计一般采取随机化方式进行分组,主体内设计一般采用随机化方式来平衡处理。

这三类研究设计中,主体间设计在调查-实验中应用最为广泛,特别是其中的简单随机化设计(Simple Randomzied Design)、随机化析因设计(Randomized Factorial Design)、区组随机化设计

（Block Randomized Design）和分层随机化设计（Stratified Randomized Design）。简单随机化设计适用于一个处理变量，没有其他关于实验单元的信息，或者不存在其他已知的对实验结果有显著影响的背景变量。随机化析因设计适用于两个以上处理变量，并且处理变量间存在交互作用。二者都属于无限制的随机化分配。区组随机化设计和分层随机化设计也是适用于一个处理变量，但首先基于实验单元的背景变量，如性别、年龄、地区等对实验单元进行分组或分层，所以又称为有限制的随机化。这两种设计可以降低实验组内的异质性，更好地控制混淆变量对实验结果的影响。

2.1.4　该如何选取调查对象?

这个阶段研究者需要考虑的是调查-实验对象的样本选取方法和样本量的多少。样本的选取方法主要有概率抽样和非概率抽样两种。概率抽样方法需要对调查总体有准确的界定，并且可以获取完整的样本框，这样才能保证每一个选中的样本都有一个确定的非零的入选概率，使调查-实验的结果能推论到研究总体。但是，概率抽样执行相对耗时，同时对人力、物力和财力的要求较高。如果不能满足这些条件，调查-实验就只能采用非概率抽样的方法，如配额抽样、受访者辅助抽样，但是应尽量避免自愿样本或方便样本的使用。

另外，样本量也需要研究者认真考虑权衡。决定样本量的因素很多，不同的抽样方法均有计算样本量的公式，同时也要考虑处理操纵的设计、样本分配设计及成本等因素。对发生率较低的现象需要较大的样本量，主体内设计可以使用较少的调查对象，处理变量较多的析因调查-实验需要更多的样本来分配虚拟案例。如果实验处理的成本过高，也需要考虑降低样本的数量。

2.1.5 该如何实地采集数据?

当完成调查-实验的设计工作后，下一步就是要到实地采集数据。数据采集的模式多种多样。除了传统的纸版邮寄问卷、纸版面访问卷模式外，计算机辅助模式下的调查正是方兴未艾。计算机辅助调查模式一般包括计算机辅助面访(Computer-Assisted Personal Interviewing, CAPI)、计算机辅助电访(Computer-Assisted Telephone Interviewing, CATI)、计算机辅助网络访问(Computer-Assisted Web Interviewing, CAWI)、计算机辅助录音访问(Computer-Assisted Record Interviewing, CARI)、计算机辅助语音自助访问(Audio Computer-Assisted Self Interviewing, ACASI)，等。

对于调查-实验来说，数据采集模式的选择要考虑执行的方便、处理的可控，以及成本和时效等。总的来看，计算机辅助问卷调查具有纸版问卷调查不可比拟的优势。首先计算机辅助调查可以在调查过程中通过计算机程序自动控制样本分配，无须在调查前设定。其次，计算机辅助调查可以自动生成不同版本的问卷形式，特别是在多变量的析因调查-实验需要生成几百个虚拟案例时尤为方便。第三，计算机辅助调查可以搭载多种形式的处理手段，如图片、音频、视频等。在网络调查中还可以直接链接外部网站资源。第四，计算机辅助调查可以通过调查过程中记录下的并行数据，如键盘敲击痕迹数据、视线跟踪数据等更好地了解到受访者对处理的接收情况。第五，从成本和时效来看，除计算机辅助面访(CAPI)调查成本较高外，其他计算机辅助调查模式都可以节省大笔经费,并且具有很好的时效性。

为确保调查-实验数据的采集质量,研究者有必要考虑在正式执行前有充分的预调查阶段,并认真准备预调查要测试的问题,如处理的合理设计、处理的操纵效果及时机等。此外,在调查执行过程中,也有必要对调查过程及处理的实施情况进行监控和调整。

2.1.6　该选用哪种统计分析手段?

选择调查-实验结果的分析方法既要根据研究设计,同时也要考虑实验数据的特征。常用的分析方法有方差分析(Analysis of Variance, ANOVA)、因子水平均值分析(Analysis of Factor Level Means)、协方差分析(Analysis of Covariance, ANCOVA)和回归分析(Regression Analysis),等等。

方差分析方法在实验研究中应用最广,主要用于两个及两个以上样本均数差别的显著性检验。对于完全随机设计的调查-实验,应选用单因素方差分析;而对于一个分组(层)变量的区组或分层随机化设计的调查-实验,应选用两因素方差分析。方差分析模型的自变量可以是定性变量,且自变量和因变量之间不必假定有某种统计关系(如线性关系),但适用于方差分析的调查-实验数据需满足三个假定:①各样本的观测值相互独立;②对于因素的每一个水平,其观察值是来自服从正态分布总体的简单随机样本;③各个总体的方差相同。

当方差分析结果证明实验组和对照组的均值存在显著差异时,就有必要进行因子均值分析,因此其适用条件和方差分析方法相同,可以用于单因素或多因素的分析。因子均值分析方法包括估计和检验两个过程,一方面估计出均值的差异,同时也对这个差异进行统计检验,从而可以判断调查-实验处理作用的方向和大小。

在调查-实验中可能存在一些控制变量是连续型变量,不能简单地按照分类变量来对待,这时有必要选用协方差分析方法。协方差分析是实验研究中控制混杂因素影响的重要手段之一,然而对于协变量(covariate)的选取有以下几个注意事项:

(1)协变量应在调查-实验前已观测到,如在调查-实验过程中观测到,应确保其观测值没有受到处理变量的影响。

(2)协变量和处理变量之间不存在交互关系。

(3)协变量和因变量的线性关系在各组均成立,而且不同组间的总体回归系数应相等。

(4)协变量的取值范围在各组间不宜相差太大。

有时会面临两个选择:①采用完全随机设计,然后用协方差分析的方法来降低实验误差;或是②采用区组或分层随机化设计,用协变量的区间来划分区组或层。一般来说,后一种方法更好一些,因为区组或分层随机设计不必假定协变量和因变量的关系类型,而协方差分析则假定协变量和因变量存在线性关系,如果违背了这一假定,区组或分层随机化设计更为有效。

回归分析是处理两个及两个以上变量间线性依存关系的统计方法,其主要用途是描述、解释或预测。当回归分析应用到调查-实验研究时还可以有效地推断因果关系。此外,在调查-实验研究中,当存在多个处理变量,或者处理变量间存在交互关系时,如析因设计,此时回归分析是一种适宜的分析方法。但用于回归分析的变量也有一些限定。首先,处理变量、因变量和控制变量都应为连续变量,如果是定性变量,则需转化为多个虚拟变量后才能进入模型。第二,回归分析除了需要满足上面提到的方差分析的三个假定外,还要求处理变量和因变量之间存在线性关系。

在对调查-实验数据进行分析时还需要考虑其他一些问题,如数据的来源或研究的需求。如调查-实验数据是在现场采集,研究者不可能完全控制调查过程,所获数据不可避免地会同时面临两个问题:一个是“不遵从(noncompliance)”,即受访者没有完全遵照实验设计的预期来接受处理。另一个是“无应答(nonresponse),即有些受访者可能拒绝访问或者漏答问题,以至于没有获取到研究变量上的应答值。另外,如列举调查-实验,通过比较控制组和实验组受访者对于列举条目个数上应答的均值可以计算出敏感的行为或态度在受调查人群中的比例,然而却无法获知这种敏感行为或态度在不同特征人群中的分布情况。再如析因调查-实验一般采用组内和组间的混合研究设计,数据具有多层次的特征,研究者在选择分析手段时也应考虑这一点。

针对以上问题,已有研究者提出了新的分析思路或方法,如对于不遵从或无应答问题的处理(Horiuchi, Imai and Taniguchi, 2007; Imai, 2009; Imbens and Rubin, 1997),对于列举实验调查数据的个体分析(Imai, Park and Greene, 2015; Blair and Imai, 2012; Glynn, 2013; Imai, 2011),以及对析因调查-实验的多层次分析(Atzmueller and Steiner, 2010; Hox, Kreft and Hermkens, 1991)等。

2.2 调查-实验的设计

对上述问题有了充分的准备后,就要进入调查-实验的设计阶段。和其他实验研究一样,调查-实验的设计极为重要。设计合理不仅有助于得出可靠的结论,而且也可以简化数据分析工作。相反,如果设计不合理,任何复杂的统计分析方法也无法补救。

本节从三个方面来介绍调查-实验的设计:处理操纵设计、样本分配设计和样本抽选设计。处理操纵设计重点介绍启动效应实验、析因调查-实验和列举调查-实验的设计方法和注意事项。样本分配设计和抽选设计具体讲解如何实现随机分配及如何选取实验样本。这三方面的设计并非彼此割裂,而是要考虑彼此的适用性和实验效果,以及实施条件的限制。

2.2.1 处理操纵设计

调查-实验中对处理变量的操纵手段形式多样,总的来说可以分为直接处理和间接处理。直接处理对参与者来说很容易被察觉,比如在受访者回答研究问题前看一些图片、放一段视频,或者提供一些附加信息等。而间接处理对于参与者,甚至旁观者来说都没有那么显而易见,比如在受访者回答研究问题前,有的先回答一组相关的问题,有的却没有,受访者不容易发现这个处理的存在。

研究者可以根据研究需要设计最适合的处理操纵方式,比如同一个概念的不同测量方法,同一种现象的不同问法,同一个问题的不同选项设计等。下面主要介绍在社会科学主题研究中较为典型的三种处理操纵方法。

启动效应调查-实验

启动效应调查-实验的基本要点是在实验结果变量的问题前介入处理操纵,考察受访者对于结果变量问题的应答是否会受到处理变量的影响。启动效应调查-实验的处理操纵形式多样,根据作用方式可以分为两大类:潜移默化型和信息反馈型。

潜移默化型的设计思路是让实验单元回答一个或一组问题,实验单元对这个问题的思考会影响到其对于结果变量的应答。比如一个研究者想了解实验单元的情绪对于结果变量问题应答的影响,在提问前先请一组样本回忆人生中两件快乐的事情,请另一组样本回忆人生中两件悲伤的事情,以此来激发调查对象的情绪。还有一些基于固有印象(stereotype)的调查-实验,研究者会在实验组中先借助一组态度问题激发实验单元对某类人群(如黑人)的固有印象,然后再询问其对某个现象(如福利政策)的看法。这种处理操纵大多是间接的,不为实验单元所察觉,但对其关键问题的应答会有潜移默化的影响。

信息反馈型的设计也是先让实验单元回答一些问题,然后就实验单元的应答给予反馈,实验单元对这个反馈的反应会影响到其对于结果变量问题的应答。如实验组的访谈员在得知实验单元的家庭收入具体数目和自我感知的收入地位后,会告诉实验单元基于全国的收入分布,实验单元对自己家庭收入的估计地位是过高、过低还是差不多,目的是考察实验单元对于这个反馈信息的反应是否会影响到其对收入再分配的态度(Cruces, Perez-Truglia and Tetaz, 2013)。在这种类型的调查-实验中,反馈的信息也可以有意设计成错误的或随机产生的。如一项研究假设当男人的男子汉气概受到威胁时,这个男人会更敌视男同性恋者。调查-实验中首先请实验单元在网上完成一个关于“男子汉气概”的测试表，测试显示的得分并非根据测试表中真实的应答结果，而是随机产生的，实验单元会看到一个图表显示他的“男子汉气概”是在测试人群的平均线以上还是以下，然后隔几个问题后再询问实验单元对于同性恋的看法（Mutz, 2011）。需要注意的是，在采用虚假信息作为处理操纵手段时，研究者要在伦理方面证明对受访者不会造成伤害。

析因调查-实验

析因调查-实验以虚拟案例作为处理操纵手段。虚拟案例是精心设计的对人、物，或者所处情形的描述，是对影响因素各种特征的系统组合（Atzmueller and Steiner, 2010）。虚拟案例的形式多样，可以采用关键词或叙述文字，也可以采用动画、图片、音频或视频的方式。关键词的设计主要是为了方便纸版问卷调查，省去诸多版本问卷印刷的困难，但这种形式的虚拟案例比较机械，难以产生生动的案例情境。采用动画、图片、音频或视频的方式可以使受访者更好地置身在虚拟案例的情节中，增加了实验的真实性，但在设计中要注意一些实验外因素的搅扰。目前用得最多的还是文字描述风格的虚拟案例，下面将以此种形式为示例介绍析因调查-实验的设计。

设计虚拟案例的第一步是挑选要用到案例中的影响因子，也就是研究者认为会影响到结果变量的自变量，选取的依据一般是比较成熟的理论及其推论。因为需要预先确定因变量，如果设计中遗漏重要的因子，会造成分析时模型的错误设定，因此应尽可能地包括普遍认为有决定作用的因素。

下一步要确定因子（自变量）的测量方法。用于虚拟案例的因子多为定类变量，也可包括低级别的定序或定距变量。对于一些连续型变量，比如年龄，需要根据理论或模型的需要分组处理。

接下来要创建虚拟案例的总体。虚拟案例的总体就是这些因子和变量值级别的系统组合。例如一项研究中包含 k 个因子,每个因子的变量值级别为 $v_i(i=1,\cdots,k)$,那么虚拟案例总体所包含的案例数 m 为 $v_1 \times v_2 \times \cdots \times v_k$。虚拟案例中因子数或变量值的级别不宜过多,否则虚拟案例的总体数目就会增加,就要求有更多的样本量来保证有较好的统计功效。

然后要确定调查中需要采用的虚拟案例个数。在创建的所有虚拟案例中可能会存在一些逻辑上不合常理的组合,比如初中学历的大学教授。如果出现这样不现实的案例,需要首先将其去除。如果余下的案例较少,同时样本量足够大,则建议在调查-实验中使用所有可用的虚拟案例,这样可以保留所有主效应和交互效应的信息。然而如果案例较多,一般用两种方法来处理(Atzmueller and Steiner, 2010)。

一种方法是选取虚拟案例总体中的子样本(vignette subpopulation)来访问受访者。有两种选择机制:分数因子设计(fractional factorial design)和随机选择策略(random selection strategy)。分数因子设计根据因子的个数和变量值级别,选择虚拟案例总体的一半、三分之一、四分之一或八分之一等的案例请每一位受访者回答,也就是每一位受访者回答精心挑选的相同案例。这种设计会造成主效应和高阶交互效应的混淆,但低阶的交互效应可以较好地区分。随机选择策略是从虚拟案例空间中随机选取一个子样本用来访问,这种选择方法会造成复杂的随机混淆结构,主效应和低阶、高阶交互效应,甚至和其他主效应都会出现混淆。即使针对每一个受访者随机抽选不同的虚拟案例子样本进行访问,这个问题仍然不可避免。

还有一种方法是把虚拟案例总体拆分成数目相等的子集

(vignette sets),各组受访者在调查中接受不同的虚拟案例子集的问题。这种方法保证了所有虚拟案例总体中的问题都被问到。同样,拆分的方法可采用有目的的实验式拆分,和分数因子设计相似,尽量保证主效应和低阶交互效应的估计无混淆;也可采用随机的无放回的拆分方法,但这种方法无法控制主效应、交互效应,甚至和集效应(set effect)的混淆,因而在析因调查-实验中应用不多。

最后,当确定了用来访问的虚拟案例子总体或子集后,还要考虑虚拟案例的排列顺序对应答可能产生的影响,因此有必要在问卷设计时随机打乱虚拟案例的排列顺序来排除这一可能的效应。

以一项关于责任分布的研究为例(Nock, Kingston and Holian, 2008)。这项研究设计的虚拟案例中假定有人需要财务上的帮助,请受访者来回答受访者本人、对方的亲戚、教会或慈善组织以及政府该提供多少金额的帮助。

研究者花费一年的时间仔细研究以前关于个人责任的理论,最终决定选取六个因子来建构这个虚拟情境。

(1)需求类型。案例中虚拟的主人公处于以下四种情形之一:被解雇,需要职业培训;不能照顾自己,需要生活看护;需要看病,但是没有保险;被赶出住所,需要租房子。

(2)个人关系。假定需要帮助的人和受访者的关系包括从父母、子女、兄弟姐妹,到好友、同事、邻居和陌生人等14种。

(3)问题严重性。经济困难分为五级:困难很小、困难较小、困难不大、困难较大和困难很大。对于需要看护和治疗的情形,还补充了“可能会去世”和“非常可能会去世”。

(4)责任追究。假定需要帮助的人陷于这种状况有七种可能的责任,从可以完全避免到完全无法避免。

(5)解决问题的收益,包括精神上的感谢称赞和物质上的偿还。精神上的包括得不到任何感谢,到受到家人、朋友或社区邻居的赞扬五种可能;物质上的包括从得不到一点偿还到得到全部偿还四种可能。

(6)解决问题的代价。设计 100 元到 10000 元,每 100 元设定为一个级别。

根据这些因子及其因子取值的级别,建构虚拟案例的总体,共计 5488000 个案例。在预调查过程中,我们发现了一些因子变量值的组合不符合现实,如职业培训没有实现会导致死亡,或严重疾病可以在 1000 元以下解决问题,因而去除了这些不合理的案例。如把培训需要的金额上限定为 3500 元,而看护和医疗需要的金额下限定为 1500 元。

由于虚拟案例的总体过大,研究者采用随机选取策略,每个受访者用计算机随机选取 19 个案例,就每个案例回答 4 个问题。展现给受访者的虚拟案例示例如下:

> 想象你有一个亲密的朋友被诊断出有严重健康问题需要治疗,但是这个朋友没有医疗保险。如果没有得到帮助,你的朋友会在生活上遇到较大的困难。
>
> 如果你这个亲密的朋友在过去能更负责一些,这个问题勉强可以防止。如果你给予帮助,你的家人和朋友会称赞你的慷慨,但是收到偿还的可能不大。
>
> 解决这个问题需要花费 3500 元,为达到这个金额,你认为:
>
> a.你应该捐助多少?
>
> b.这个人的亲戚应该捐助多少?
>
> c.教会或其他慈善组织应该捐助多少?
>
> d.政府应该捐助多少?

列举调查-实验

列举调查-实验中处理的最基本操纵形式是设计一些不敏感问题的条目和一个研究者关心的敏感问题的条目，调查过程中分配给控制组中的实验单元回答不敏感问题的条目，而实验组中的实验单元回答的问题中除了和控制组同样的条目，还包括这个敏感问题的条目。

例如在 2008—2009 年美国全国选举研究（American National Election Studies，ANES）中随机分配的控制组回答下列问题：

> 下面有四件事情。请告诉我有多少件事情你不喜欢。我们不需要知道您具体不喜欢哪件事情，只需要知道有多少件。
>
> 1.听音乐
>
> 2.同性婚姻合法化
>
> 3.接到推销电话
>
> 4.做收垃圾的工人

实验组的受访人回答的题目和上面相同，只是多了一条：

> 5.黑人当总统

列举实验的设计看似简单，然而在实际操作时常会遇到的问题是：①该设计多少个条目？②该设计什么样的条目？③统计误差过大导致结果不显著怎么办？

首先，我们需要清楚列举实验设计的有效性是基于两个假设：

第一，实验单元对于控制条目的应答结果不会受到加入的敏感问题条目的影响。比如上例，假如实验单元在没有看到第 5 个条目时对前四件事情有三件不喜欢,在他看到所有五个条目后不会改变对这四件事情的态度,也就是说这四件事情中依然有三件不喜欢。这样才能保证实验组和控制组所回答条目数的差异仅是敏感问题条目的加入导致的。

第二,实验单元对于敏感问题的条目会给以真实的回答。也就是列举实验这种方式能够使实验单元感到个人隐私得到保护,从而愿意给出真实的应答。

其次,满足了这两个假设,列举实验才能有效地估算出调查样本对于敏感问题条目的选择比例,而不精心的设计则会导致失败的实验结果。比如,当控制条目对实验单元都适用时会产生"天花板"效应,而都不适用时会产生"地板效应",在这两种情形下,实验单元都会觉得自己对敏感条目的选择结果很容易被识别,于是不愿意给出真实的应答。

基于此,学者们对列举调查-实验的设计提出了以下建议(Imai, King and Stuart, 2008; Blair and Imai, 2012; Glynn, 2013):

第一,在条目个数的选择上要尽量避免过少,这样很容易造成天花板或地板效应;但同时也不宜过多,这样实验单元在记忆条目上会出现困难,从而造成漏报。

第二,在设计列举的控制条目时要避免那些大多数人都选取或都不选取的条目内容,比如选取一些在实验单元应答上彼此负相关的条目,可以防止天花板和地板效应。

第三,注意避免控制条目的应答不要受到敏感条目的影响,比如选择那些意义明确并且受访者通常有明确态度的条目,避免包括和敏感问题条目有依赖关系的控制条目。

Glynn (2013) 因此对 ANES 问卷中的列举条目做了一个小改

动，将"做收垃圾的工人"替换为"在公立学校同时教授智能设计论和进化论"，具体如下：

<u>控制条目组 A：</u>
1.听音乐
2.同性婚姻合法化
3.在公立学校同时教授智能设计论和进化论
4.接到推销电话

大多数人都不会喜欢"做收垃圾的工人"，这个条目的变异性差，而"在公立学校同时教授智能设计论和进化论"是一个具有争议性的话题，喜欢和不喜欢的都大有人在。而且这个新条目和"同性婚姻合法化"负相关，支持"智能设计论"的往往反对"同性婚姻合法化"，同时喜欢这两件事情的人会比较少。这样修订不仅可以避免天花板或地板效应，而且可以降低应答的偏差和方差。

然而这种标准的列举实验设计的弱点是在估计均值差(difference-in-means)时方差加大。如在一项关于种族态度的列举调查-实验中，在相同的样本规模下，采用直接提问的方式获取的均数差的方差为0.007，而通过标准列举实验方式获取的均数差的方差为0.050，后者约是前者的七倍(Blair and Imai, 2012)。估计方差的加大会造成统计检验不显著，从而拒绝真实的假设。列举实验的双列表设计(Double List Experiment)则可以在一定程度上弥补这个缺陷(Droitcour et al, 1991; Glynn, 2013)。

顾名思义，双列表调查-实验就是要采用两组列举的条目，比如除了上述的控制条目组 A 外，另外设计一组控制条目组 B：

控制条目组 B：

1.看电影

2.同性民事伴侣关系合法化

3.在公立学校同时教授创造论和进化论

4.做收垃圾的工人

控制条目组 B 和 A 的条目完全不同，但又十分接近。这样设计的目的是：①组内的各条目的应答保持负向关系，如条目 2 和条目 3 彼此有一定的互斥关系；②两个条目组的总体应答存在正向关系，如条目组 A 中的 2 和条目组 B 中的 2 正相关的可能性非常大。双列举实验在使用上仍是把受访者随机分为两组，其中一组先回答控制条目组 A 的问题，然后回答控制条目组 B 和敏感条目的问题；另一组则先回答控制条目组 B，然后回答控制条目组 A 和敏感条目的问题。这样就存在两个列举实验，每个组在一个实验中是控制组，同时也是另外一个实验的实验组。双列表实验设计会比标准设计明显减少估计误差（Droitcour et al，1991）。

然而在使用双列表实验设计时也有一些注意事项。首先，由于多了一个列举实验，会造成采访时间延长，增加调查成本；第二，为保证两个条目组的应答正相关，设计的条目内容比较接近，受访者应答时需区分条目间的微妙差异，会造成受访者认知上的困难；第三，在单列表实验中，研究者一般在控制组除了使用控制条目的问题外，还会直接询问受访者敏感问题来检验实验效果，而在双列表实验中，由于两组受访者的问题中都包括了敏感条目，就不宜再直接提问敏感问题了；第四，两组条目都要回答也会导致问题的顺序效应，对前面条目组的应答很有可能会影响到后面条目组的应答（Glynn，2013）。

2.2.2　样本分配设计

调查-实验的样本分配设计决定了该如何将实验单元分配到实验组和对照组，或者如何在实验单元中随机分配不同的实验处理。在调查-实验中较为常用的样本分配设计有简单随机化设计、随机化析因设计、区组随机化设计及分层随机化设计。[①]

简单随机化设计

简单随机化设计是最简单的实验设计，是复杂实验设计的基础。其设计程序被称为简单随机化分配（SRA），是将一个处理变量的 t 个水平随机分配给 N 个实验单元（也可以说是将 N 个实验单元随机分配给 t 个处理水平）的过程。在随机化分配过程中，一般要考虑两个因素：概率和规模。因而衍生出四种分配方法：等概率简单随机化分配（将每个实验单元以相同的概率分配给每个处理水平），不等概率简单随机化分配（将每个实验单元以不同的概率分配给每个处理水平），等规模简单随机化分配（每个处理水平上的实验单元数量相同），以及不等规模简单随机化分配（每个处理水平上的实验单元数量不同）。

具体操作步骤如下：

（1）获取实验单元名单，赋给每个实验单元一个顺序号。如果名单是电子版，也可以考虑先根据某一无系统特征的元素（如姓名的首字母）进行排序，然后再添加顺序号（参看表 2.1 的第 1 和第 2 列）。

（2）生成一组在 0 和 1 之间的随机数，个数与实验单元数量相同，按照随机数的原始顺序和实验单元顺序号匹配（参看表 2.1 的

① 更多样本分配设计请参考 Alferes（2012）。

第 3 列)。如在计算机上操作,可以对每一个实验单元生成 0 和 1 之间的随机数,但要注意,所有实验单元的随机数生成完毕后需固定,不允许再改变。

(3)将所有实验单元按照随机数从小到大排序(参看表 2.1 的第 3 列)。

(4)确定分配方案,并将实验单元分配给各处理水平。表 2.1 给出了四种分配方案的示例。首先,如果采用 $p=0.25$ 的等概率随机化分配方法,需根据随机数列表选取 0.25,0.50,0.75 作为分割点,将第一个处理水平(T_1)分配给随机数在 0 到 0.25(含)区间的实验单元,第二个处理水平(T_2)分配给随机数在 0.25 到 0.50(含)区间的实验单元,以此类推。如果采用不等概率的随机化分配,需要根据事先设定的概率来选取分割点,示例中选用了 0.30,0.30,0.20,0.20 四个概率,那么分割点就是 0.30,0.60,0.80,然后根据这些分割点来分配处理水平。等规模随机化分配要求接受不同处理水平的实验单元个数相同。如果实验单元总数恰好是处理水平个数的倍数,那么按实验单元对应的随机数从小到大的顺序来分配处理水平。如示例中共有 20 个实验单元,4 个处理水平,等规模分配的话就是分为 4 组,每组 5 个实验单元,那么就按顺序 5 个一组来分配处理水平。如果实验单元个数不是处理水平的倍数,就涉及该减少哪个或哪几个处理水平的实验单元数。推荐采用随机去除的方法,具体操作是将处理水平随机排序,然后去除排在最后的处理水平。举例说明,假如实验单元数是 19 个,处理水平数还是 4 个,这样不可能出现完全的等规模,只能是 3 个处理水平每个有 5 个实验单元,1 个处理水平有 4 个实验单元。那么该减少哪个处理水平的实验单元个数呢?随机去除的方法就是给每个处理水平一个随机数,然后按照这个随机数对 4 个处理水平排序,排在最后一个的处理水平分配 4 个实验单元，其他处理水平分配 5 个实验单元。这种随机去除的方法可以有效避免复杂样本分配设计中处理水平的样本不平衡问题。不等规模随机化分配就要按照研究者事先设定的样本个数来分配处理水平。如示例中研究者设定分配给第一个处理水平 7 个实验单元，分配给第二个处理水平 4 个实验单元。

表 2.1　简单随机化分配方法示例

			简单随机化分配			
			等概率	不等概率	等规模	不等规模
ID	实验单元	随机数	$p=.25$	$p=.30,.30,.20,.20$	$n=5$	$n=7,4,3,6$
2	××	0.001	T_1	T_1	T_1	T_1
4	××	0.058	T_1	T_1	T_1	T_1
19	××	0.059	T_1	T_1	T_1	T_1
16	××	0.142	T_1	T_1	T_1	T_1
8	××	0.256	T_2	T_1	T_1	T_1
13	××	0.268	T_2	T_1	T_2	T_1
1	××	0.301	T_2	T_2	T_2	T_1
9	××	0.493	T_2	T_2	T_2	T_2
11	××	0.518	T_3	T_2	T_2	T_2
3	××	0.550	T_3	T_2	T_2	T_2
5	××	0.554	T_3	T_2	T_3	T_2
12	××	0.598	T_3	T_2	T_3	T_3
7	××	0.615	T_3	T_3	T_3	T_3
18	××	0.691	T_3	T_3	T_3	T_3
10	××	0.768	T_4	T_3	T_3	T_4
15	××	0.798	T_4	T_3	T_4	T_4
6	××	0.906	T_4	T_4	T_4	T_4
20	××	0.955	T_4	T_4	T_4	T_4
14	××	0.974	T_4	T_4	T_4	T_4
17	××	0.994	T_4	T_4	T_4	T_4

在调查-实验的操作过程中还有可能遇到两种情形：一种情形是实验单元名单在调查开始时不是完备的，而是在调查过程中单个连续补充，或是以组的形式加入；另一种情形是在调查前已获取完整的实验单元名单，但会因时间或其他外部条件的限制而中断调查。

对于第一种情形可以采用简单连续随机化分配方法。首先还是要先给实验单元分配样本代码。可以按照招募的先后顺序编码，如果遇到以组的形式加入时，在组内选择一个变量排序后，再按顺序赋予代码。然后确定处理水平对应的概率或实验单元个数。如采用等概率的分配方法，就根据处理水平个数分配随机数区间。假如处理变量有三个处理水平，那么设定第一个处理水平对应的随机数区间为[0,0.3333]，第二个处理水平对应的随机数区间是(0.3333,0.6666]，第三个就是(0.6666,1)。第三步是给每一个已得的实验单元分配随机数，这个随机数落在哪个区间，这个实验单元就被分配给对应的实验水平。例如，新招募了一个实验单元获取随机数 0.5663，这个随机数在(0.3333,0.6666]区间内，那么这个新招募的实验单元就被分配给第二个处理水平。

对于第二种情形，如果在完成全部样本的访问前调查被强行终止，就可能会破坏样本随机化分配。为应对这种情形，可以将全部样本分为等规模的几个部分(一般 2~4 个部分为佳)，然后在每个部分内部采用简单随机化分配方法。假如一项调查-实验要求在规定日期前结束，而在规定日期前完成全部访问的可能性不大，这时最保险的方法是将执行期分为 2~4 个时间段，每个时间段分配相同的样本个数，并采用简单随机化分配的方法分配处理水平。

随机化析因设计

随机化析因设计应对的是调查-实验中有两个或两个以上处理变量。应用这种设计时首先需要确定处理变量的个数及其因子水平，然后根据处理变量间的交叉或嵌套关系组合处理水平，最后将处理水平的组合随机分配给每个实验单元。因而随机化析因设计主要有两种形式：一个是基于处理变量间交叉关系的完全随机化析因设计（Completely Randomized Factorial Design）；另一个是基于处理变量间嵌套关系的完全随机化等级设计（Completely Randomized Hierarchical Design）。

例如，一个调查-实验中包含三个处理变量：处理变量 A 有 2 个因子水平，处理变量 B 有 4 个因子水平，处理变量 C 有 2 个因子水平。在完全随机化析因设计下，每个处理变量的每个因子水平都与其他处理变量的任一因子水平组合，这样就形成 16 个实验处理（表 2.2 所示）。假定处理变量 B 嵌套在处理变量 A 中，那么就形成完全随机化等级设计。如表 2.3 所示，处理变量 B 的因子水平 B_1 和 B_2 嵌套在处理变量水平 A_1 中，而因子水平 B_3 和 B_4 嵌套在 A_2 中，这样就只形成 8 个实验处理。有的调查-实验由于处理变量或其因子水平过多，会生成数量巨大的实验处理，这时研究者可以采用完全随机化分数析因设计，按照一定的分数值随机或有意选取部分实验处理。表 2.4 就是一个分数值为二分之一的示例。但这样做在数据分析时会在一定程度上混淆单个处理变量的主效应和处理变量间的交互效应。

表 2.2　完全随机化析因设计示例

	B_1		B_2		B_3		B_4	
	C_1	C_2	C_1	C_2	C_1	C_2	C_1	C_2
A_1	$A_1B_1C_1$	$A_1B_1C_2$	$A_1B_2C_1$	$A_1B_2C_2$	$A_1B_3C_1$	$A_1B_3C_2$	$A_1B_4C_1$	$A_1B_4C_2$
A_2	$A_2B_1C_1$	$A_2B_1C_2$	$A_2B_2C_1$	$A_2B_2C_2$	$A_2B_3C_1$	$A_2B_3C_2$	$A_2B_4C_1$	$A_2B_4C_2$

表 2.3　完全随机化等级设计示例

	B_1		B_2		B_3		B_4	
	C_1	C_2	C_1	C_2	C_1	C_2	C_1	C_2
A_1	$A_1B_1C_1$	$A_1B_1C_2$	$A_1B_2C_1$	$A_1B_2C_2$				
A_2					$A_2B_3C_1$	$A_2B_3C_2$	$A_2B_4C_1$	$A_2B_4C_2$

表 2.4　完全随机化分数析因设计示例

	B_1		B_2		B_3		B_4	
	C_1	C_2	C_1	C_2	C_1	C_2	C_1	C_2
A_1	$A_1B_1C_1$	$A_1B_1C_2$					$A_1B_3C_1$	$A_1B_3C_2$
A_2			$A_2B_2C_1$	$A_2B_2C_2$			$A_2B_4C_1$	$A_2B_4C_2$

实际上，随机化析因设计是简单随机化设计的延伸。二者不同之处在于后者的实验处理是处理变量的一个因子水平，而前者的实验处理是多个处理变量的因子组合。而二者采用的实验处理分配方法是完全一致的，等概率、不等概率、等规模、不等规模的分配方法均适用。

随机化析因设计的优点有二：一是可以用相对较小的样本获取更多的信息，如与对两个处理变量分别进行简单随机化设计实验相比，随机化析因设计将节约样本量的 1/2；二是可以研究多个处理变量各自的主效应和彼此间的交互效应。析因设计的缺点是当处理变量个数增加时，实验处理的组数会呈几何倍数增加，因此在处理变量及其因子水平的选择上应尽量精练，避免生成过多的实验组。

区组随机化设计

区组随机化设计是在简单随机化设计的基础上利用已知信息加以限制，以提升实验组内的同质性，提高数据分析的统计效能。当只有一个处理变量时，区组随机化设计有两种形式：简单区组随机化设计和广义区组随机化设计。前者要求每组实验单元的个数等于处理变量水平数，后者要求每组实验单元的个数是处理变量水平数的倍数。调查-实验由于样本数量较大，这种广义区组随机化设计更为适用。

进行广义区组随机化设计可采用下述步骤：

(1)选择与实验结果变量密切相关的特征变量作为区组变量。这个分组变量不能是研究中关注的影响因子，也不能和处理变量之间存在交互效应。另外区组个数不宜过多，因为在对随机区组设计的实验结果进行统计分析时，区组个数会提高分析的自由度(degree of freedom)，从而降低统计检验的强度。

(2)根据区组变量将调查样本进行分组，每组的实验单元数目须为处理变量水平数的倍数。

(3)在每个区组内采用简单随机化分配的方法将实验处理分配给每个实验单元。

例如在一项调查-实验中处理变量 T 有 T_1、T_2、T_3和 T_4四个处理水平，调查样本数为 1200 人，调查样本的性别和年龄已知。区组随机化设计中采用性别和年龄两个变量作为区组变量，计划设计 6 个区组，每个区组 200 人。见表 2.5，操作时首先给每个样本一个唯一且固定的编码，然后按照性别分为男女两个大组，每组各 600 人。接着在每一性别组内，按照年龄从小到大的顺序每 200 人分为一组，这样所有样本共形成 6 个区组。最后，在每一个区组内按照等规模随机分配的方法将四个处理水平分配给实验单元（如表 2.5 的第 1 和第 4 区组所示）。

表 2.5　区组随机化设计示例

区组	序号	编码	姓名	性别	年龄	随机数	处理
1	1	21	××	男	33	0.197	T_1
1	…	…	…	…	…	…	…
1	50	125	××	男	37	0.331	T_1
1	1	460	××	男	27	0.351	T_2
1	…	…	…	…	…	…	…
1	50	130	××	男	19	0.497	T_2
1	1	52	××	男	23	0.592	T_3
1	…	…	…	…	…	…	…
1	50		××	男	28	0.739	T_3
1	1		××	男	23	0.741	T_4
1	…	…	…	…	…	…	…
1	50	324	××	男	39	0.912	T_4
2	1	1011	××	男	41	0.318	T_1
2	…	…	…	…	…	…	…
2	50	878	××	男	57	0.992	T_4

续表

区组	序号	编码	姓名	性别	年龄	随机数	处理
3	1	289	××	男	58	0.196	T_1
3	…	…	…	…	…	…	…
3	50	576	××	男	75	0.904	T_4
4	1	1121	××	女	25	0.197	T_1
4	…	…	…	…	…	…	…
4	50	125	××	女	31	0.331	T_1
4	1	460	××	女	35	0.351	T_2
4	…	…	…	…	…	…	…
4	50	130	××	女	21	0.497	T_2
4	1	52	××	女	22	0.592	T_3
4	…	…	…	…	…	…	…
4	50	979	××	女	35	0.739	T_3
4	1	374	××	女	27	0.741	T_4
4	…	…	…	…	…	…	…
4	50	824	××	女	18	0.912	T_4
5	1	527	××	女	39	0.211	T_1
5	…	…	…	…	…	…	…
5	50	1094	××	女	52	0.977	T_4
6	1	1110	××	女	53	0.074	T_1
6	…	…	…	…	…	…	…
6	50	416	××	女	75	0.752	T_4

区组随机化设计也适用于在调查-实验前没有获得完备的实验单元名单，需要在调查过程中不断补充样本，且没有时间限定的情形。这时需要注意，一旦某区组内实验单元数目已满则应停止该区组实验单元的招募。对于有时间限定、调查可能被强制中断的情形则不能采用随机化区组设计。

区组随机化设计的优势在于能够有效地降低实验组和对照组之间的随机或系统差别，通过降低组内方差的办法来提高统计强度，以便有效确认显著的处理效应。但是这种设计需要预先获取调查对象的一些背景信息，并且需在选择区组变量上十分谨慎，一方面区组不宜过多，另一方面该变量不能和处理变量存在交互效应。另外每个区组的实验单元数量也有限制，需要是处理变量水平数的倍数。

分层随机化设计

在概率样本的调查-实验中，区组随机化设计的一些条件可能无法满足。如表 2.5 的示例中按照性别和年龄将样本划分成 6 个区组，但各区组内样本数量可能不等，而且可能不是处理水平数目的倍数，这时可以考虑采用分层随机化设计。

分层随机化设计的操作和区组随机化设计十分相似，首先是要选取一个或少数几个背景变量将样本划分为内部同质性较高的层，然后在每一个层内采用简单随机化分配的方法在实验单元间分配处理水平。如果某个层内的样本数量不是处理水平数的倍数，这时可以采用前面介绍的随机去除的方法来获取等规模随机分配。

在上例中以性别(男/女)和年龄组(老/中/青)为分层变量将 1200 个样本分为 6 层，概率抽取的样本中分到各层的样本数极有可能是不相同的。如表 2.6 所示，假定第 1 个区组中的样本数为 189 人，处理变量有 4 个因子水平，这时每个因子水平分配 47 个实验单元后还余下 1 个实验单元。对 4 个因子水平进行随机排序，获得 T_2, T_3, T_4, T_1 的顺序，这样采用随机去除的方法，将第 2 个因子水平（T_2）分配给这个实验单元。在第 2,4,5 区组也遇到不能平均分配的情形，都可以采用这种方法处理。

表 2.6　分层随机化设计示例

区组	性别	年龄组	总样本数	T_1 样本数	T_2 样本数	T_3 样本数	T_4 样本数
1	男	青年	189	47	48	47	47
2	男	中年	206	51	52	52	51
3	男	老年	192	48	48	48	48
4	女	青年	195	49	49	48	49
5	女	中年	210	53	53	52	52
6	女	老年	208	52	52	52	52

分层随机化设计由于各层的样本数不同，和区组随机化设计相比在统计分析上略占劣势，但由于分配时多了一些背景因素的控制，其统计强度要优于简单随机化设计。

设计调查-实验时该选取哪种样本分配的方法通常还要考虑到处理操纵的设计。如完全随机设计、区组随机化设计和分层随机化设计在启动效应实验和列举调查-实验应用较多，而随机化析因设计是析因调查-实验的主要方法。同时，调查-实验中也可以多个样本分配方法结合使用，如析因调查-实验中一个实验单元往往要对多个虚拟案例进行判断，每个虚拟案例包含一个处理变量水平的组合，所以在随机化析因设计的基础上结合了主体内设计的方式。

在一项关于信息和投票率的调查-实验研究中（Horiuchi, Imai and Taniguchi, 2007），研究者认为性别和投票计划[①]可以有效预测日本选民的投票率。他们通过样本筛选调查获取了调查样本的背景信息，包括性别和投票计划两个变量，然后在大选前对符合资格的选民进行第二次调查。该调查共设计了 2 个实验组和 1 个控制组。第一个实验组的选民要访问日本自民党或民主党其中一个党派的官方网站查看有关养老金改革的政策提议；第二个实验组的选民要查看两个党派官方网站上的政策提议，一部分人先访问民主党，后访问自民党，另一部分人则顺序相反；控制组的选民只参与了筛选调查，没有参加这次选举前调查。

在这次调查中研究者们采用了分层随机化设计[②]，根据性别和投票计划将调查的选民分为 6 层，然后在每层内采用不等规模完全随机化设计将选民分配到实验组和对照组。如表 2.7 所示，总调查样本是 2000 人，6 层人数不等，每层内第一个实验组的选民人数占 50%，第二个实验组的人数占 30%，控制组的人数占 20%。在每个实验组内又随机将调查样本分为数量相等的两个组，接受不同的实验处理。

① 这个变量是基于问卷中的问题“在即将来临的大选中你会去投票吗?”答案分为计划去投票、没有计划投票和不确定三类。

② 作者们认为这是一个区组随机化设计，然而由于区组规模不等，笔者认为严格地讲该设计应属于分层随机化。

表 2.7 日本选举实验的分层随机化设计

	层						
	Ⅰ	Ⅱ	Ⅲ	Ⅳ	Ⅴ	Ⅵ	
	计划投票		没有计划投票		不确定		
	男	女	男	女	男	女	总数
实验组 1							
民主党官网	194	151	24	33	36	62	500
自民党官网	194	151	24	33	36	62	500
实验组 2							
民主党/自民党官网	117	91	15	20	20	37	300
自民党/民主党官网	117	91	15	20	20	37	300
控制组							
没有访问	156	121	19	26	29	49	400
层样本规模	778	605	97	132	141	247	2000

2.2.3 样本抽选设计

社会科学的实验研究多采用大学的学生作为实验单元，如1990—2006 年在美国顶级政治学刊物上发表的实验文章中有25%的实验采用学生样本。这样做有几个优势：首先大学的学生一般在时间上弹性大，离科研机构的实验室距离近，所以用起来比较方便；第二是学生要求的报酬相对较低，可节约实验成本；第三是学生对科研实验比较感兴趣，能够积极参与。然而采用大学生作为样本也有诸多局限：如学生样本的代表性较差，不能将实验结果有效推论到广泛的研究总体；学生样本同质性强，会影响到统计的显著性检验，实验结果可能不适用于内部差异较大的群体，等等。

调查-实验借助社会调查的样本选取方法,主要有概率抽样和非概率抽样两种。这些方法在社会调查的方法论教科书中有详细讲解,本书仅对此概要介绍。

概率抽样,又称随机抽样,是以概率理论和随机原则为依据来选取调查样本,具体的抽样方法包括简单随机抽样(Simple Random Sampling)、系统抽样(Systematic Sampling)、分层抽样(Stratified Sampling)、整群抽样(Cluster Sampling)和混合抽样(Mixed Sampling)等。

简单随机抽样的方法是给抽样框中的每一个单元赋予一个独特不重复的号码,然后按照预定的样本量随机选取同样数目的号码。用于简单随机抽样的技术主要有抽奖的方式,随机数表的方式以及计算机生成随机数的方式。抽奖的方式就是每次随机选取一个数字,直到满足样本量的要求。随机数表的方式是在随机数表上随机确定一个起点,然后横向或纵向选取和样本量相同数目的随机数,根据随机数来确定入选的样本号码。这两种方式主要适用于样本量较小,并且采用纸版问卷的调查。而对于采用计算机辅助模式的调查,用计算机生成随机数从而确定入选样本的方式更为简便。简单随机抽样适用于目标总体小,抽样框易得,并且没有其他辅助抽样的信息的调查-实验。这是调查-实验最基本的抽样方法,其他方法被看作是对它的修正,以便得到更实用、经济或更精确的设计。

在实施抽样时,由于系统抽样较为简单实用,常常用来代替简单随机抽样。系统抽样的方法是首先确定样本框中所有单元的个数和计划选取的样本个数,用前者除以后者得到的数保留整数部分作为间距个数,然后将抽样框中的单元随机排序,或者按照某一个相关因素排序,以起到隐含分层的作用。选取样本时先随机确定一个起点,然后每隔一个间距,选取一个单元作为调查样本。如果起点小于间距，被称为线性系统抽样；如果起点是 1 到样本总数 N 之间的任一个数值，则被称为环形系统抽样；如果多个随机起点，抽选多个样本，然后组合为一个样本，则称为重复系统抽样。系统抽样的缺点是如果抽样间距恰巧和某一周期重合会增大变异性，并且选择的第一个样本决定了其他样本的选择，违背了样本间的独立性原则，方差估计也会比简单随机抽样复杂。

分层抽样也是抽样调查常用的抽样方法。这种方法首先将目标总体分成若干个彼此互斥，且内部同质性高的分割，称为层，然后在每个层内采用简单随机抽样或系统抽样的方法选取调查对象。所有层中选取的调查对象汇合在一起构成该调查的整体样本。分层的目的是降低样本估计量的方差，因而分层变量的选取尤为重要，一般是与研究目的相关，特别是与调查中的关键变量相关。在抽样调查中多采用人口规模、人口密度，经济发展水平等附加变量作为分层依据。另外，如果总体各部分实际分布差别大，或者可用的抽样框差别大，或者适宜的访问方法差别很大，那么不同层中可以采用不同的抽样方法和步骤。分层抽样有三个注意事项：一是总体中的每一个单元一定属于并且只属于某一个层，并且所有层的总和构成总体；二是尽可能使层内单元的指标值相近，层间单元的差异尽可能大；三是同时使用多个分层变量时要小心变量间可能会抵消彼此效应；最后就是要考虑实施的简便易行。

当目标总体的样本框很难获取，或者目标总体在地理上分布较为分散，造成访问成本过高时，可以采用整群抽样的方法。这个方法首先要基于自然或已存在的地理或物理上的聚集体确定群的划分，如一个街区、一所学校、一个车间等，然后采用简单随机或系统抽样的方法选择群，最后将每个选中的群内的所有单元汇总在一起构成调查样本。这样，在整群抽样中按照随机原则选取的是调查对象的聚集体，而非直接是调查对象本身。这种方法对群内异质性较强，而群和群之间差异较小的调查总体最为适宜，常用的分群标志如行政或地域的划分，或研究变量的特点等。整群抽样中群的大小直接关系到抽样效率的高低，然而在实际操作中有的是可以控制群规模的，有的则无法控制群规模。对于前者，分群时应注意群规模不宜过大。其他分群的注意事项和上面所述分层的注意事项基本相同。

简单随机抽样、系统抽样、分层抽样和整群抽样是获取概率样本的基本抽样方法，其优缺点总结在表 2.8 里。

表 2.8　概率抽样方法及优缺点

	优点	缺点
简单随机抽样	• 操作简单，容易理解 • 统计分析方法简单 • 不需要其他辅助抽样的信息	• 总体很大时难以获得抽样框 • 个体或者抽样单位分散不易实施，执行成本高 • 抽样单位的规模如果差异悬殊，则误差会比分层抽样、系统抽样等获得的样本误差大 • 个体如果异质性非常强，则也比上述其他抽样方法的误差大
系统抽样	• 操作简单，容易理解 • 样本框无须排序（地址样本框） • 如果样本框是随机排序，系统抽样可以得到类似随机抽样的样本 • 如果样本框根据某个变量排序，则产生隐含分层，这时系统抽样会比随机抽样更为有效 • 样本在总体中分布较为分散	• 如果抽样间距恰巧和某一周期重合会增大变异性 • 选择的第一个样本决定了其他样本的选择，违背了样本间的独立性原则 • 方差估计比简单随机抽样复杂

续表

	优点	缺点
分层抽样	• 允许层上推论，并且跨层比较 • 在代表性上更好 • 执行成本可能降低 • 允许层内使用不同的抽样方法 • 允许对每一个层进行分析并单独报告结果	• 需要事先获取分层变量的信息 • 方法相对复杂 • 每层至少要有 2 个样本 • 数据分析方法较复杂 • 如果是不等比例分配，需要使用权重来调整
整群抽样	• 如果是地理上的自然群，整群抽样可以降低执行成本，缩短执行周期 • 不需要得到目标总结完整的抽样框 • 允许在群内再抽样 • 可以估计群特征	• 在同等样本规模下，整群抽样获取的样本代表性比简单随机抽样的样本要差 • 样本方差也比简单随机抽样大 • 统计分析方法较复杂 • 产生较大的抽样误差

大多数抽样调查并不是采用单一的抽样方法，而是几种抽样方法的组合，即混合抽样。如在全国概率个人样本的选取上，一般先按照东部、中部、西部或按照城市、乡村分层，在层内按照概率和人口规模成比例（PPS）[①]的方式选取县级行政单位，然后随机选取一定数目的村级行政单位，在最后一级行政单位下采用系统等距抽样的方法选取调查的家户，在家户里再用简单随机抽样的方法选取最终的调查对象。

虽然调查-实验在概率样本上能具有较好的总体效度，然而对于某些研究项目，由于受到研究经费、时间、人员、设备的不足，以

① 即每个单元被抽中的概率都和这个单元的规模大小成比例。

及抽样框不可得等因素的限制,这种情况下非概率抽样更为适用。非概率抽样方法下单元中的元素入选概率不知,而且存在某些单元没有机会入选的情形。其优点是节省费用和时间、方便快捷;缺点也很明显,就是代表性差,研究结果不能有效地推断总体。非概率抽样的方法多样,应用到调查-实验中较为推荐的是目的抽样(Purposive Sampling)和配额抽样(Quota Sampling)方法。

目的抽样中研究者要根据研究目的或需求设定样本纳入或排除的标准,只有符合这个标准的单元才被邀请或允许成为调查对象。这种样本选取方法适用于特定人群中的调查-实验,总体的抽样框不存在或不可得,需要根据这个标准来筛选。这种方法可以在一定程度上减少选择偏差,对于混淆变量有一定控制。如在某些析因调查-实验中,其虚拟案例可能存在一定的适用对象,而不是普遍人群,这时可以考虑采用目的抽样的方法。

配额抽样是研究者将目标人群按照某些特征分为几个互斥的组别,然后调查员或数据采集者从每个组内找出一定数量的样本作为调查对象。配额抽样在具体实施时研究者告知调查员数据采集标准及配额,然后调查员根据这个标准寻找调查对象,并且完成和配额一致的访问量。用于做配额控制的变量多为人口或态度特征,如性别、年龄、民族、职业,支持或是反对。配额抽样可以保证样本中包含不同子总体的人群,并且介入一定程度的分层,有助于比较亚群体的特征,特别是人数较少的组群。同时按照总体比例进行配额的抽样有一定的代表性。但是这种抽样方法现场执行的控制比较困难,而且当组内采用方便抽样方法时会降低样本代表性。

抽样设计的另一个重点就是样本量的确定。概率抽样设计首先要根据统计公式确定样本量。方法是先确定主要研究变量，如有多个研究变量，在分别计算样本量后选用最大的样本量。然后决定估计统计公式：如果变量是定类的，选用比例的方法；如果变量是连续的，选用均值的方法。在计算公式中还要考虑可容忍的误差幅度，一般来说，研究越重要，误差幅度越小。根据公式计算出样本量后，还要根据实际调查过程中可能发现的不符合资格比例、无应答比例、损耗或死亡比例进行调整，此外，当样本规模大于总体 5% 时，通常要使用有限总体修正系数（Finite Population Corrector Factor, FPC）进行调整，当采用简单随机抽样以外的抽样设计时，还要考虑设计效应（Design Effect, DEFF）对于样本量的需求。感兴趣的读者可参看相关参考书，此处不再赘言。

对于非概率方法选取调查-实验样本，这里只能从经验出发给出所需样本的建议。对于探索研究或调查-实验的预调查，可以选取 20 到 150 个参与者；对于单一主题的社区或全国性研究，建议选取 400 到 2500 个调查样本；对于多个主题的全国性研究，则建议选取 10000 到 15000 个样本。

2.3 调查-实验的执行

一项高质量的调查-实验不仅要设计严谨，执行过程也至关重要，比如通过预调查来检测设计的有效性，通过过程监控来保证实验环境的有效控制和实验处理的有效操纵等。另外在实际执行过程中还有一些问题需要引起研究者的注意。

2.3.1　预调查

预调查是社会抽样调查的一个必要步骤，在这一环节，要对数据的采集工具（问卷）和采集模式进行测试，也可以说是正式调查之前的彩排。对于调查-实验来说，预调查尤为重要，其作用不仅是测试或演练，甚至一些实验处理的设计必须经过预调查的检测后才能确定。

列举调查-实验的控制条目如果出现天花板效应、地板效应或其他设计效应，会直接影响到处理的效果。研究者们一般会在预调查中对条目设计进行检测。如为了解调查对象对于控制条目的应答情况，研究者们可以在预调查时直接提问控制条目，这时需要注意的是和列举实验尽可能保持一致，最好将所有控制条目同时列出，而非逐个提问。还有，为评估列举设计对敏感问题应答的影响，研究者也会在预调查的问卷中包括对敏感条目直接提问的方式，同时需要注意的是：直接提问的敏感问题应该放在列举的条目问题之后，以免不能准确评估列举实验设计的效果。另外，在双列举实验中，还有必要通过预调查来检测调查对象的认知困难，以及问题顺序对于应答的影响。

对于析因调查-实验，预调查也至关重要。虚拟案例该包括多少变量、多少维度，一个调查对象该回答多少个虚拟案例问题，这些问题除了有理论和设计的考虑外，还需要考虑到调查对象的承受能力，如认知上的困难和精力上的疲累等，这些也需要通过对预调查数据的分析来确定。

在预调查中，对于处理操纵情况的检测也是一个重点（Mutz，2011）。实验处理的操纵效果可以体现在两个方面：一方面是操纵对处理变量的影响,即有效导致了调查对象对于处理变量应答的变异;另一方面是处理变量对于因变量的影响,即因为不同的处理导致实验结果发生变化。第二种效果和理论是否成立有关,而第一种效果则体现了是否对调查对象实现了有效的操纵。操纵的检测主要有两方面内容。一是调查对象是否真正接受了操纵后的处理。比如在启动效应实验中,调查对象是否真的按照指示去查看了外部网站的信息,或者思考了一些快乐的事情。再如在析因调查-实验中,调查对象是否注意到虚拟案例中的人物是男是女,或是否结婚等。检测的另一个内容是对操纵外因素的控制。假定实验处理是一条信息,控制组的问卷题目中没有包含这条信息,而实验组的问卷题目中含有这条信息,那么在控制组的调查对象是否有可能在接受调查前就已经了解到了这条信息？如果是,这个调查-实验就已经受到污染了。

在实践中,对于操纵的检测问题可以直接放在处理问题的后面,但更多情形是放在因变量问题的后面,以避免受访者对于处理操纵的过度注意。然而,要想提高操纵的效果,Mutz(2011)建议操纵的方式要尽量简短,特别是在电话访问模式的调查-实验中,即使访问员完整地读出了操纵的问题,也不能保证受访者能够完全理解并记住信息。如果操纵手段是一段长文本的信息,如报纸上的一个新闻报道,则可以分成几段请受访者阅读,在每段后设计一两个问题用来刺激受访者的注意力。还有就是可以采用音频视频的操纵手段来吸引受访者的注意力。这些方法都需要通过预调查来检测其有效性。

2.3.2 过程监控

调查-实验的执行场所是调查实地,而且调查对象人数众多、分布分散、异质性高，和实验室研究相比，研究者对调查过程的掌控更为困难，这时需要注意对调查-实验实施过程数据的采集。

在社会调查方法学中，调查过程的数据又称为并行数据（Couper，2005；任莉颖、严洁，2014）。这些数据主要包括访员分派的记录、访员和调查对象联系的记录、调查对象合作情况的记录、使用计算机辅助访问系统时记录的痕迹数据和访问录音数据，以及访员采访过程中的观察记录等。如果调查-实验采用了计算机辅助访问模式，那么可以采集到丰富的并行数据，为调查-实验过程的监控提供必要的信息。

第一，在调查-实验执行过程中需要监测的是访员的分配。采用面访或电话访问的调查-实验，一个访员往往要采访多个调查对象，而访员采访的技巧、个人的特征都有可能造成访员效应，导致测量误差。对于调查-实验，要特别小心处理效应和访员效应的混淆。比如为调查方便，由几个访员负责一个版本问卷的采访，而另外一些访员负责另一个版本问卷的采访，这种情况要尽量避免。理想的方式是将不同实验处理的问卷，或者将实验组和对照组中调查对象随机分派给访员，以降低访员效应对调查-实验的影响。

第二，在调查过程中，研究者也需要及时掌握调查的进展情况。对于完全随机分组和随机化区组设计，当各组应答人数相同或相近时，分析方法较为简单。如果应答人数差异较大，则有必要采用较为复杂的分析方法。因此，在调查-实验执行过程中要对调查对象的应答情况进行及时分析，监测实验各组应答的人数。如果发现某些区组访到率较低，则需采取措施，加大这些区组的访问力度，降低因无应答而造成的分析偏差。

第三,研究者还可以根据计算机记录的访问痕迹数据和访问录音数据来分析监测实验处理是否得到调查对象的关注。如在键盘录入的痕迹数据中可以提取出每道题的访问时长,如果调查对象处理问题访问时长过短,则意味着处理没有得到充分的关注。在网络调查-实验中,调查对象的视线轨迹也可以被记录下来,通过对视线的跟踪可以了解到调查对象对于处理问题的关注。此外,在得到调查对象同意的情况下,一些需要访谈的调查-实验可以全部或部分录制采访过程的对话,通过对这些录音的核查,也可以发现访员是否完整准确地提问以及处理问题。

此外,在采用访员面访的调查-实验中,也可以借助访员观察来了解实验处理的操纵情况,或者发现其他可能影响调查-实验结果的因素。访员观察数据和访问痕迹数据结合分析可以帮助研究者剔除调查-实验中"不遵从"的样本,降低分析时的组内方差,提高统计功效。

2.3.3 其他事项

调查-实验的质量会受到诸多因素的威胁。一般来说,调查-实验需要最大限度地排除自变量以外其他因素的影响,然而执行过程中常有一些情形会污染到实验条件。

比如,为了使研究者可以用少量的经费来开展自己感兴趣的研究项目,常见的做法是采用一个调查搭载多个实验。然而这种实验方式要很小心不同实验处理手段的交互影响,或称之为外溢效应(spillover effects)(Gaines, Kuklinski and Quirk, 2006; Transue, Lee and Aldrich,2009)。想象一个调查中嵌套了多个实验,如果每个实验的受访者都是随机独立的分组,这种外溢效应可以得到较好的控制。但如果没有实现独立分组,或者实验过多,即使独立分组也可能无法避免实验之间存在系统的交互影响,而且这种影响的后果可能不是简单的加减关系,而是彼此之间会存在抑制或膨胀效应。

另一个对实验条件的可能污染来自现实世界。调查-实验的研究主题一般都是真实存在的社会政治现象,如果现实中不存在这种现象,那么也就没有研究价值了。而且处理手段也是现实中可行的,甚至就是从现实中提取的。同时调查-实验要在现实条件下执行,这就意味着受访者在接受调查前可能已经在个人的正常生活中体验过这种处理手段。虽然研究者可以通过随机分组,使控制组和对照组中包含相同比例的已有过处理体验的人,但实验效果会被大大地削弱,而且如果实验结果与受到的处理次数高度相关,则还会带来研究结果的偏差(Gaines, Kuklinski and Quirk, 2006)。

对于调查-实验处理变量的操纵也有一些注意事项(Gaines, Kuklinski and Quirk, 2006;Barabas and Jerit, 2010)。如大多数调查-实验是单次的跨地区截面调查,处理只能执行一次。而在现实世界中,研究者关心的影响因素一般不是这种一次性、稍纵即逝的,而是反复性、多次出现的。为了在一个调查-实验中能最大限度地表现出处理变量的作用,实验组往往会使用过度的操纵手段。如故意把处理性问题(自变量)设计得很醒目,以使受访者不至于忽略;或者在处理性问题后紧接着问结果性的问题(因变量)。研究者们假定通过这样一次性"大剂量"的处理可以得到和现实中多次"小剂量"的处理同样的效果。显然这一假定成立与否还有待论证。

2.4　调查-实验的分析

调查-实验在设计和实施中控制了混淆因素对结果变量的影响，在分析时就可以采用较为简单的方法。一般来说，实验研究所广泛应用的分析方法都适用于调查-实验的分析，现仅列举调查-实验和析因调查-实验，在实际中则需要根据具体设计和研究需求选用复杂一些的分析手段。

2.4.1　常规分析方法

在实验研究中普遍应用的分析方法有方差分析、因子水平均值分析、回归分析和协方差分析，下面将简要介绍这些分析方法的原理和模型。

方差分析

方差分析（Analysis of Variance，ANOVA）又称 F 检验，主要用来检测两个及两个以上样本均数差别的显著性检验，可以用于完全随机化设计、随机化析因设计、区组随机化设计和分层随机化设计的实验数据分析。

对于完全随机化设计，调查-实验中只有一个处理变量时，应采用单因素方差分析，其分析模型有两种表达形式：

单元格均值模型：$Y_{ij}=\mu_i+\varepsilon_{ij}$

处理效应模型：$Y_{ij}=\mu_{.}+\tau_i+\varepsilon_{ij}$

假定该处理变量的因子水平数为 r，每个因子水平对应一个实验组，那么上述模型中 Y_{ij}表示第 i 组的第 j 个观察值，μ_i 表示第 i 组的均值，$\mu_{.}$ 表示总体均值，τ_i 表示处理变量在 i 水平下对因变量的效应，ε_{ij}为一个服从正态分布的随机变量，代表随机误差。

在单元格均值模型下，方差分析检验的假设为各组的均值是否完全相等，即

$$H_0:\mu_1 = \mu_2 = \cdots = \mu_r$$

$$H_1:\text{不是所有的}\ \mu_i\ \text{都相等}$$

而在处理效应模型中，方差分析检验的是处理变量在各组中的效应是否有变化，零假设和对应的研究假设为

$$H_0:\tau_1 = \tau_2 = \cdots = \tau_r$$

$$H_1:\text{不是所有的}\ \tau_i\ \text{都相等}$$

方差分析的基本原理是认为调查-实验所获取的因变量数据存在差异，主要体现在每个实验组内部的差异，以及不同实验组之间的差异。实验组内部的差异属于随机误差，用 SSE 来表示，而实验组之间的差异是因不同处理所造成的，记作 SSTR，方差分析的 F 检验就是要基于这两个差异的均值进行比较，即

$$F^* = \frac{\text{SSTR}/(r-1)}{\text{SSE}/(n_T - r)}$$

其中 r 是处理变量的因子水平个数，n_T 是样本总量。当 F 统计值服从自由度为$(r-1)$和(n_T-r)的 F 分布时，零假设成立，即所有的均值或处理效应相同；如果不服从这个 F 分布，则研究假设成立，即至少有一个均值或处理效应不同。

区组随机化设计和分层随机化设计除了要考虑处理变量，还要考虑区组/层变量，这时应采用无交互作用的双因素方差分析，原理和单因素方差分析相同，只是增加对区组/层变量效应的分析。

具体来说，这两种设计方差分析的模型为

$$Y_{ijk}=\mu_{..}+\rho_i+\tau_j+\varepsilon_{ijk}$$

其中，$i=1,\cdots,n_b$，表示区组/层的序号，$j=1,\cdots,r$ 表示处理变量的因子水平序号，$k=1,\cdots,d$ 表示每个区组/层内每个实验组内的观测序号。这样，Y_{ijk}表示第 i 个区组/层内的接受 j 水平处理的第 k 个观察值，$\mu_{..}$表示总体均值，ρ_i 表示因变量在 i 区组/层内的变异，τ_j 表示处理变量在 j 水平下对因变量的效应，ε_{ijk}为一个服从正态分布的随机变量，代表随机误差。注意此模型中限定 $\sum\rho_i=0$ 和 $\sum\tau_j=0$。

这时调查-实验因变量数据的变异会有三个来源：不同区组/层间的差异（记作 SSBL），不同实验组间的差异（记作 SSTR），以及随机误差（记作 SSBL.TR）。由于实验处理的效应是研究所关心的，因此只需检验下列假设：

$$H_0:\text{所有}\tau_j=0$$

$$H_1:\text{不是所有的}\tau_j\text{都相等}$$

F 统计值为

$$F^*=\frac{\mathrm{SSTR}/(r-1)}{\mathrm{SSBL.TR}/(n_b-1)(r-1)}$$

当 F 统计值服从自由度为 $(r-1)$ 和 $(n_b-1)(r-1)$ 的 F 分布时，零假设成立，即所有的处理效应相同；如果不服从这个 F 分布，则研究假设成立，即至少有一个处理效应不同。

对于随机化析因设计，处理变量有多个，并且处理变量间可能存在交互关系，这时需选用双因素或多因素的方差分析，计算原理与区组/分层随机设计的方差分析相似，只是要补充交互效应的分析，但计算过程要复杂得多。以双因素的方差分析为例，其模型为

$$Y_{ijk} = \mu_{..} + \alpha_i + \beta_j + (\alpha\beta)_{ij} + \varepsilon_{ijk}$$

F 检验也要针对 α 或 β 的主效应及其交互效应。

每种统计分析方法都基于一些假定，方差分析也是如此，具体要满足三个条件：

(1)各组的观测样本彼此独立抽选

(2)各组观测样本均选自正态分布的总体

(3)各组样本观测到的研究变量的方差相等

第一个条件可以通过研究设计来确认。例如同时抽选两个样本(如丈夫和妻子)，然后分为两组，就显然违背了第一个条件。第二、三条则可以通过统计分析来检验。

因子水平均值分析

研究者一般不仅要关心实验组和对照组均值是否有差别，而且还要关心差别的大小和方向，而上述的方差分析显然不能满足这个需求，这时需要对实验数据进行因子水平均值分析(Analysis of Factor Level Means)。

因子水平均值分析是针对实验处理不同因子水平所产生效应的大小、差异，以及关系的显著性检验，一般来说适用于以下几种情形的分析：

(1)处理变量的某一因子水平上的均值

(2)处理变量两个因子水平上均值的差异

(3)处理变量多个因子水平均值的对比

(4)处理变量多个因子水平均值的线性组合

对于某一因子水平的均值 μ_i，其估计值 $\hat{\mu}_i$ 为 $\overline{Y}_{i.}$，在 $1-\alpha$ 水平

上的置信区间为

$$\overline{Y}_{i.} \pm t(1-\alpha/2;n_T-r)s\{\overline{Y}_{i.}\}$$

其中 $i=1,\cdots,r$,表示因子水平的序号。

在调查-实验中应用最多的第二种情形又称均值差(Difference of Means)。对于两个因子水平上均值的差异 D,其估计值 $\hat{D}$ 为 $(\overline{Y}_{i.}-\overline{Y}'_{i.})$,在 $1-\alpha$ 水平上的置信区间为

$$\hat{D} \pm t(1-\alpha/2;n_T-r)s\{\hat{D}\}$$

当 $\hat{D}$ 的置信区间包括 0,表明这两个因子水平上的均值差异在 $1-\alpha$ 置信水平上不显著;如果置信区间不包括 0,则可以根据估计值 $\hat{D}$ 判断处理效应的强弱。

此外,这种方法还可以用来分析多个因子水平均值的对比。所谓对比,就是指两个或者更多因子水平均值之间的组合比较。如果用 L 来表示这个比较,可以表示其为一个有限制的线性组合:

$L=\sum_{i=1}^{r}c_i\mu_i$,其中 $\sum_{i=1}^{r}c_i=0$

如 $L=\mu_1-\mu_2$,$L=\frac{\mu_1+\mu_2}{2}-\frac{\mu_3+\mu_4}{2}$,

或者 $L=\mu_1-\frac{\mu_1+\mu_2+\mu_3+\mu_4}{4}$等

只要 L 表达式的系数相加为 0,即为对比分析,可以计算出 L 的置信区间并推论。如果系数相加不为 0,即为多个因子水平均值的无限制的线性组合,也可以用这种方法分析。

对于多因子水平处理变量效应的分析,常常需要同时对多个因子水平均值的差异或关系进行显著性检验。如果研究仅关注因子水平均值两两之间的比较,Tukey 多重比较法得到的置信区间

会更短；如果对比的个数少于或等于因子水平的个数，Bonferroni 多重比较法会比 Scheffe 多重比较法具有较高的效率。

回归分析

因为调查-实验的随机分组设计可以排除或降低不可知、不可测量，或没有被加入到模型中的因素对实验结果的影响，在调查-实验数据上应用回归分析（Regression Analysis）会比在观察数据上应用得到更可靠的分析结果。

回归分析的基本原理是自变量观测值之间的线性或非线性的组合计算结果与因变量的观测值存在不同程度的拟合，而在调查-实验中研究者最为关注的是，在控制其他混淆变量的影响的前提下，处理变量对于因变量的作用如何。

回归分析适用于两个或两个以上处理变量的调查-实验。例如，对于两个处理变量，并且无交互作用的回归分析，其模型形式为：

$$Y_{ij} = \beta_0 + \beta_1 X_{i1} + \beta_2 X_{i2} + \varepsilon_{ij}$$

如果处理变量间有交互作用，回归分析的模型为：

$$Y_{ij} = \beta_0 + \beta_1 X_{i1} + \beta_2 X_{i2} + \beta_3 X_{i1} X_{i2} + \varepsilon_{ij}$$

回归模型就是要估计 β 参数，并且对其进行统计检验，来确定处理变量对于因变量是否有作用及作用大小。

调查-实验中的处理变量多为定类或定距的变量，每一个实验处理的效应可能不同，这时不能将变量直接放到回归模型中，而是需要将其转化为二分变量或虚拟变量（dummy variable）使用。如对于一个有 5 个因子水平的处理变量，需要转化为 5 个二分变量，而在建模时，选择一个二分变量作为控制变量，将其他 4 个变量放入模型中。这样估计出来的回归效应就是实验组和控制组均值的比较结果。

除了可以分析多个处理变量的主效应及交互效应外，回归分析还可以通过模型控制在实验设计中没有包括或者没能有效控制的混淆变量，或者是和处理变量存在交互作用的变量的影响，对于设计上的缺陷或实施中的问题这可以起到一定的补救作用。

协方差分析

协方差分析（Analysis of Covariance, ANCOVA）结合了方差分析和回归分析，可以应用于单因素的完全随机化设计，多因素和随机化区组/分层设计和随机化析因设计。用于协方差分析的协变量（covariate）必须是连续的定量变量，主要是用来降低方差分析中的实验组内部的变异。

对于只有一个处理变量的调查-实验，协方差分析的模型为

$$Y_{ij} = \mu. + \tau_i + \gamma(X_{ij} - \overline{X}_{..}) + \varepsilon_{ij}$$

注意这个协方差的模型比方差分析的模型多出一个部分 $\gamma(X_{ij} - \overline{X}_{..})$，其中 X_{ij} 是协变量在第 i 组第 j 个观测值，$\overline{X}_{..}$ 是该协变量的观测总均值，γ 是回归系数。与一般回归模型稍有不同的是，协方差分析模型中的协变量一般转换为和总均值的差异，这样可以保证 $\sum(X_{ij} - \overline{X}_{..}) = 0$。同样，也要求 $\sum \tau_j = 0$，以便更好地估算处理效应。

对于随机化区组/分层设计和随机化析因设计下获取的调查-实验数据，协方差分析的模型分别为

$$Y_{ij} = \mu_{..} + \rho_i + \tau_j + \gamma(X_{ij} - \overline{X}_{..}) + \varepsilon_{ij}$$

$$Y_{ijk} = \mu_{..} + \alpha_i + \beta_j + (\alpha\beta)_{ij} + \gamma(X_{ij} - \overline{X}_{..}) + \varepsilon_{ijk}$$

同样，也是在方差分析的模型中补充了协变量的控制效应。

用于方差分析和因子水平均值分析的检验方法和置信区间的

计算方法也同样适用于协方差分析。

2.4.2　高级分析方法

对于常见的研究设计，如完全随机化设计、随机化析因设计、区组随机化设计和分层随机化设计，以上介绍的数据分析方法可以有很好的应用。然而对于一些需要特别处理手段的设计，研究者们根据研究需要或数据特征提出了一些复杂的数据分析方法，如应用到析因调查-实验上的多水平分析，以及应用到列举调查-实验上的多元回归分析。

析因调查-实验

在样本量足够大，并且虚拟案例个数不多的情况下，析因调查-实验可能采用主体间设计，这种情况下，上述的方差分析、因子水平均值分析、协方差分析、回归分析都可以使用。然而，大多数析因调查-实验采用主体间和主体内的混合设计，这样调查-实验数据结构就呈现出两个水平：虚拟案例水平和应答者水平。因此，在数据分析时要同时考虑两个水平对实验结果的影响，此时多水平模型分析更为适宜（Hox, Kreft and Hermkens, 1991）。

基于析因调查-实验数据建构多水平模型时一般需要考虑三个效应：应答者特征变量对于因变量的效应；虚拟案例中的处理变量对于因变量的效应；以及应答者特征变量对于处理变量和因变量的效应。

在进行多水平模型分析时，把虚拟案例看作个体层面，即水平 1 上的元素，而应答者看作组层面，即水平 2 上的元素。具体的建模过程大致包括以下几个步骤：

(1)首先，在对析因调查数据分析时需要判断多水平模型是否适用，这时需要借助组内相关系数(Intraclass Correlation Coefficient, ICC)。ICC是组间方差和总方差的比值，计算公式为

$$\mathrm{ICC}=\frac{\sigma_b^2}{\sigma_b^2+\sigma_w^2}$$

其中，σ_b^2 是组间方差，σ_w^2 是组内方差，二者之和构成总方差。ICC的取值范围为0至1，如果接近0，意味着一般的单水平回归分析即可，没有必要使用多水平模型；如果ICC大于0，则意味着存在水平1上的因素对水平2模型的影响，从而需要使用多水平模型。

为计算ICC，研究者先要从建构二水平的空模型开始，即不包含任何影响因子的模型。

在水平1上的空模型为：$Y_{ij}=\beta_{0j}+r_{ij}$，

在水平2上的空模型为：$\beta_{0j}=\gamma_{00}+\mu_{0j}$，

组合在一起为：$Y_{ij}=\gamma_{00}+\mu_{0j}+r_{ij}$。

其中 i 为虚拟案例的序号，j 为应答者序号，Y_{ij}就是第 j 个应答者对第 i 个案例的回答结果。

空模型不仅可以用来计算ICC，还可以提供因变量的总均值及在各组中的均值，了解其间差异，因此建构多水平模型的第一步就是要运行空模型的分析。

(2)接下来就是考察水平2上的因素对于因变量的影响，也就是上述的第一个效应。假设 W 是应答者的一个特征变量，那么水平2应答者层面的回归模型为

$$\beta_{0j}=\gamma_{00}+\gamma_{01}(W_j-\overline{W})+\mu_{0j}$$

加入水平1上的空模型后形式为：

$$Y_{ij} = \gamma_{00} + \gamma_{01}(W_j - \overline{W}) + \mu_{0j} + r_{ij}$$

这个模型中 W 的斜率 γ_{01} 是固定的，也就是说在水平 2 上各组的回归线斜率相同，截距不同。

(3)模型中进一步要加入水平 1 上的处理变量，以考察虚拟案例中处理变量对于因变量的影响。假设虚拟案例中只包括一个处理变量 X，那么水平 1 虚拟案例层面的回归模型为

$$Y_{ij} = \beta_{0j} + \beta_{1j}(X_{ij} - \overline{X}_j) + r_{ij}$$

其中，X_{ij} 是第 j 个应答者回答的第 i 个案例中的处理变量，$\overline{X}_j$ 是第 j 个应答者回答的虚拟案例中该处理变量的均值。

与水平 2 上的回归模型组合后的形式是：

$$Y_{ij} = \gamma_{00} + \beta_{1j}(X_{ij} - \overline{X}_j) + \gamma_{01}(W_j - \overline{W}) + \mu_{0j} + r_{ij}$$

对于水平 1 上的处理变量的斜率有两种情况：

如果斜率是固定的，即 $\beta_{1j} = \gamma_{10}$，模型表现为

$$Y_{ij} = \gamma_{00} + \gamma_{10}(X_{ij} - \overline{X}_j) + \gamma_{01}(W_j - \overline{W}) + \mu_{0j} + r_{ij}$$

如果斜率是随机的，即 $\beta_{1j} = \gamma_{10} + \mu_{1j}$，模型表现为

$$Y_{ij} = \gamma_{00} + \gamma_{10}(X_{ij} - \overline{X}_j) + \mu_{1j}(X_{ij} - \overline{X}_j) + \gamma_{01}(W_j - \overline{W}) + \mu_{0j} + r_{ij}$$

至于斜率是固定还是随机，一方面要研究者基于理论或前人研究的经验，另一方面也可以通过统计检验来判断。

(4)最后还要考虑一种情形，即应答者特征变量不仅影响到因变量，对虚拟案例中的处理变量也有影响，这时水平 1 模型中的参数 β_{1j} 也受到水平 2 变量的影响，即

$$\beta_{1j} = \gamma_{10} + \gamma_{11}(W_j - \overline{W}) + \mu_{1j}$$

这时模型就加入了一个水平 1 处理变量和水平 2 特征变量的交

互项：

$$Y_{ij} = \gamma_{00} + \gamma_{10}(X_{ij} - \overline{X}_j) + \mu_{1j}(X_{ij} - \overline{X}_j) + \gamma_{01}(W_j - \overline{W}) + \gamma_{11}(X_{ij} - \overline{X}_j)(W_j - \overline{W}) + \mu_{0j} + r_{ij}$$

多水平模型分析也需要满足一系列的假定条件，包括水平1模型的残差要求是正态分布，均值为0，方差为常数；水平2模型的残差须是多元正态分布，也是均值为0；并且水平1和水平2模型的残差彼此独立。

在多水平回归模型的选择上主要基于-2LL数值，即-2倍的对数似然比（log likelihood ratio）。-2LL数值越小，表明模型对于数据的拟合程度越好。

列举调查-实验

列举调查-实验多采用完全随机化设计、区组随机化设计或分层随机化设计，因此适用单因素方差分析和因子水平均值分析方法。一般情形就是采用均数差的方法，分别计算出控制组和实验组应答的条目数均值然后相减得到差数，作为对敏感问题给以肯定回答的比例估计值，并计算出均数差的方差用以检验该估计值是否统计上显著。

具体地说，假如一个列举实验有N个调查对象，在完全随机化设计下，人们将这些调查对象分为控制组（$T_i = 0$）和实验组（$T_i = 1$），人数分别为N_1和N_0。用Y_i来代表第i个受访者对于列举实验条目问题的应答结果，那么均数差的估计值$\hat{\tau}$为：

$$\hat{\tau} = \frac{1}{N_1}\sum_{i=1}^{N} T_i Y_i - \frac{1}{N_0}\sum_{i=1}^{N}(1 - T_i)Y_i$$

这个公式清楚地显示出均数差方法的估计值基于三个要素：①受访者的应答结果；②受访者属于控制组还是实验组；③控制组和实

验组的样本规模。这样仅能估计出选择敏感问题条目的比例，却无从知道选择敏感条目的人具有哪些特征，而后者却是研究者们极想探究的。

为了解决这一难题，Imai(2011)深入探讨，提出了两种方法的多元回归模型。第一个是用两阶段非线性最小二乘法(Nonlinear Least Squares, NLS)来估计。模型的因变量是 Y_i，依然代表第 i 个受访者对于列举实验条目问题的应答结果，自变量是 X_i，是影响受访者应答结果的因素。模型由两个非线性回归模型相加构成，一个是 $f(x,\gamma)$，是基于自变量的控制条目应答的条件期望；另一个是 $g(x,\delta)$，是基于自变量的敏感条目应答的条件期望，用数学公式表示为：

$$Y_i = f(x_, \gamma) + T_i g(x_i, \delta) + \varepsilon_i$$

估计(δ,γ)时分为两个阶段：首先从控制组(即 $T_i = 0$)计算 NLS 估计值 $\hat{\gamma}_{NLS}$，然后设定 γ 等于第一步估计出来的 $\hat{\gamma}_{NLS}$，从实验组(即 $T_i = 1$)计算 NLS 估计值 δ_{NLS}。

这个模型有两个特殊的情形。一个是当模型中没有考虑任何的自变量因素，即 $f(x,\gamma) = \gamma$，$g(x,\delta) = \delta$ 时，可以得出和均数差方法相同的估计值 $\hat{\tau}$；另一个是当 $f(x,\gamma)$ 和 $g(x,\delta)$ 均为线性模型时，这个模型转化为有交互项的线性模型。

另一种方法是基于控制组受访者的应答 $Y_i(0)$ 和实验组受访者是否选择敏感问题条目 $Z_{i,j+1}(1)$ 的联合分布，用最大似然法(Maximum Likelihood, ML)来估计。

$$g(x,\delta) = Pr(Z_{i,J+1}(1) = 1 \mid X_i = x)$$

$$h_z(y,x,\psi_z) = Pr(Y_i(0) = y \mid Z_{i,J+1}(1) = z, X_i = x)$$

其中，y 是对控制组条目问题的应答结果，控制条目一共有 J 个，那

么 $y=0,\cdots,J$。敏感问题的条目则标注为 $J+1$。z 是表示是否选择,取值为 0 和 1。

在计算过程中,鉴于似然方差过于复杂,Imai(2011)还提出了用最大期望算法(Expectation Maximization, EM)来简化运算过程。

比较这两种估计方法,ML 估计值有更好的统计功效,而 NLS 估计值则在稳健性上略有优势。

2.4.3 分析的误区

调查-实验数据相对于实验室数据来说具有调查对象多、变量信息丰富的特点,而对于社会调查数据来说,则具有一些设计上的优势,这些优势可以简化数据分析。然而,Mutz(2011)发现研究者们在对调查-实验数据进行分析时常常存在着一些误区或困惑。

首先,为了证明调查-实验分组随机化,研究者们倾向于比较实验组和控制组在一些特征上的差异,并且把差异不显著作为成功分组的标志。Mutz 认为这种检验是一种误导,这种做法证明了研究者对于随机分配的误解。随机分配并不保证某个随机化操作可以使实验各组在各个方面都完全相同,而是说多次独立的随机化分配下实验各组很可能在各个方面完全相同。这是统计意义上的相同,而非每次随机分配都可以实现这一点。并且,随着样本量的加大,这种实验各组间出现差异的可能性就会降低。因此,只要在调查-实验中按照随机化的规范严格操作,随机化分配就是成功的,这个成功是基于定义,无须对数据进行校验。

其次,为了显示模型界定的完备,研究者们倾向于在模型中包含大量的协变量。Mutz 认为这种做法是对随机化分配的另一个误解。调查-实验中随机化分配的目的就在于控制实验处理以外其他因素对实验结果的影响,因此对协变量的控制已经内嵌在实验设计中。同时,研究者在分析模型中添加协变量的目的在于降低组内方差,提高统计功效。然而,当协变量对于实验结果没有重要影响时,不但不能降低组内方差,还会减少自由度,从而降低统计功效。此外,在模型中加入大量的协变量也会使分析结果的报告变得复杂,不利于读者理解。如果研究者认为一些协变量会影响实验结果,最好在实验设计时就考虑采用区组或分层随机化的方式给予控制。

第三,让研究者常常感到困扰的是对调查-实验数据的分析是否该使用权重。Mutz 介绍了两种加权的方式。一种是使全部样本反映出总体参数;另一种是使每一个实验条件下的样本反映出总体参数。前者在社会调查中比较常见,后者更适用于调查-实验,但目前对此的研究较少。Mutz 认为,如果研究的目的是估计总体平均处理效应,或者实验处理与权重中包含的调查对象特征变量存在交互关系,这时分析时使用权重较为合宜。但使用权重会降低统计功效,如果实验处理效应较小,加权分析结果则可能无法证明这个效应的存在。因此研究者有必要在代表性和统计功效之间权衡,然后决定是否在分析中使用权重。Mutz 建议研究者需要了解构建权重的具体变量有哪些。如果这些变量对于处理效应没有影响,那么权重对于这些研究就没有意义;如果这些变量对于处理效应有重要影响,那么最好事先基于这些变量采用区组或分层随机化设计,否则就只能根据需要选择使用上述的两种权重。

概括地说,基于调查-实验的设计,数据分析不需要复杂的模型和过多的协变量,相反,简单的分析方法正是调查-实验设计优越的体现。

2.5 小结

本章介绍了调查-实验的前期准备工作——调查-实验的设计、执行和分析的主要方法和注意事项。

调查-实验从精心的准备工作开始。这一阶段要对调查-实验的各个环节作出决定。比如根据研究的内容和目的确定调查-实验的方法是否适用，根据要验证的理论确定处理变量和结果变量及其测量方法，根据技术和信息的可得来确定随机化分配的方法，以及根据财力、物力和人力等的限制来确定样本的来源和选取方法，以及调查执行的方式。最后还要根据调查-实验的设计选取适宜的分析方法。研究者基于这些准备工作形成调查-实验的操作方案，指导下一步的具体实施工作。

调查-实验的研究设计包括三方面内容：处理的操纵设计、样本的分配设计和样本的抽选设计。处理操纵设计是关于实验处理的测量形式和介入方式。本章重点介绍了启动效应实验、析因调查-实验和列举调查-实验。启动调查-实验的操纵手段多种多样，可以是问题词句或影像的暗示，问卷以外的信息等；析因调查-实验设计时要注意影响因子及其因子水平的选择，虚拟案例的选择，以及虚拟案例的排列顺序等；列举调查-实验在设计时则要注意避免天花板或地板效应，以及条目设计等。样本分配设计也有多种形式，常用的有完全随机化设计、随机化析因设计、区组随机化设计，以及分层随机化设计。在设计时要最大可能利用已有的信息，并且确保受访者的随机分配。调查-实验样本的选取方法主要有概率抽样和非概率抽样两种。本章简要介绍了概率抽样中的简单随机抽样、系统抽样、分层抽样、整群抽样和混合抽样,以及非概率抽样中的目的抽样和配额抽样方法。

调查-实验的执行也至关重要。首先在正式调查之前有必要进行预调查,不仅要对数据的采集工具(问卷)和采集模式进行测试,重要的是要对实验处理的操纵设计进行检测以确保达到效果。另外,调查-实验的样本规模大、异质性高,并且实验地点分散、情况多样。在正式调查过程中,研究者需要及时了解调查过程中实验处理的操纵情况,实验环境的控制情况,以及实验样本的流失情况等,因此有必要通过对并行数据的收集、加工与分析来监控执行过程。此外,执行过程中一些特殊情形也可能会影响到调查-实验的质量。

调查-实验数据的分析方法相对简单。对于大多数常规调查-实验、简单的方差分析、因子水平均值分析、协方差分析,以及回归分析就可以实现对数据的有效分析。对于析因调查-实验数据,建议使用多水平模型分析。对于列举调查-实验数据,采用多元回归分析会得出更丰富的研究结论。本章对这些分析方法做了简要介绍,并提醒研究者注意分析中有关随机化检验、协变量和权重的使用等方面的注意事项。

/ 第 3 章 /

调查-实验法应用案例评析

本章选取了四个典型的调查-实验法应用案例，希望借助对这几个案例的评析，使读者对调查-实验的研究和发表有更深入的认识。

调查-实验在国内社会科学研究还处于起步阶段，现阶段中文发表的调查-实验学术文章寥寥无几。仅有的几篇文章在实验设计和分析上相对简单，不能满足案例评析的需要，因此只能从国外顶级学术刊物中发表的英文文章中选取评析案例。

案例选取有三个标准：第一是选自不同的应用领域，这四个案例分别属于调查方法学、经济学、社会学和政治学；第二是选用多样的调查-实验技术，这四个案例涵盖了常规调查-实验、启动效应调查-实验、析因调查-实验和列举调查-实验；还有就是与中国研究相关，这四个案例中的一个是直接研究中国问题的，其余三个也对中国的社会科学研究具有参考意义，具体见表3.1。

表3.1　本章调查-实验案例概要

序号	主要作者	学科领域	调查-实验类型	研究主题	发表年
1	Tourangeau and Smith	调查方法	常规调查-实验	敏感问题的应答与抽样调查技术	1996
2	Cruces	公共经济	启动效应实验	收入分配的主观感受与对再分配政策的偏好	2013
3	Jasso and Opp	社会学	析因调查-实验	社会行动规范的测量	1997
4	Meng	政治学	列举调查-实验	中国地方官员对民意的回应性	2014

评析的重点在于分析案例为什么采用这种调查-实验技术，是如何对调查-实验进行设计的，设计中存在哪些问题，如何进行数据处理和分析，分析时用了哪种统计方法，如何解读调查-实验研究结果，等等。

3.1　调查方法学案例

在社会抽样调查中，受访者会受到社会期许的影响，对一些敏感性的问题或是规避或是不实报告。而社会抽样调查研究者的一个重要任务就是要获取高质量的调查数据，他们为此尝试了多种方式，并且要对各种方式的效果进行比较分析，Tourangeau 和 Smith（1996）的研究就是其中之一。

在这项研究中，Tourangeau 和 Smith 采用了析因设计的常规调查-实验方法，围绕男性和女性受访者报告性伴侣个数的问题，检验了三种计算机辅助调查模式、问题格式，以及问题情境对于报告水平的影响。这三个因子共产生 18 种组合方式。实验中把受访对象随机分为 18 组，每组给以一种实验处理，然后比较不同处理下的实验结果。

作者在实验实施和数据分析上的每一个步骤都做了精心处理，例如排除了不同实验条件下的外溢效应，处理了因变量非正态分布的问题，以及考察了离群值的影响等。在文章撰写上十分规范，分为研究背景、文献综述、研究设计、研究方法、分析结果，以及讨论总结几大部分。尤其是在研究方法方面详细介绍了样本的抽样选取，调查问卷的多版本设计，以及实验随机分组设计每一个步骤的操作方法。同时在数据分析和解读上严谨充分，结构清晰，对于调查-实验初学者可以起到很好的示范作用，因此选择此篇文章作为第一个案例来评析。

例文

Abstract

This study compared three methods of collecting survey data about sexual behaviors and other sensitive topics: computer-assisted personal interviewing (CAPI), computer-assisted self-administered interviewing (CASI), and audio computer-assisted self-administered interviewing (ACASI). Interviews were conducted with an area probability sample of more than 300 adults in Cook County, Illinois. The experiment also compared open and closed questions about the number of sex partners and varied the context in which the sex partner items were embedded. The three mode groups did not differ in response rates, but the mode of data collection did affect the level of reporting of sensitive behaviors: both forms of self-administration tended to reduce the disparity between men and women in the number of sex partners reported. Self-administration, especially via ACASI, also increased the proportion of respondents

解析

摘要中介绍了本项调查-实验研究的内容有三：(1)比较三种调查模式对采集性行为和其他敏感问题的影响；(2)比较开放式和封闭式问题设计对回答性伙伴个数的影响；(3)比较问题情境设置对回答性伙伴个数的影响。因此这个调查-实验要对三个处理变量进行操纵。

admitting that they had used illicit drugs. In addition, when the closed answer options emphasized the low end of the distribution, fewer sex partners were reported than when the options emphasized the high end of the distribution; responses to the open-ended versions of the sex partner items generally fell between responses to the two closed versions.

Over the past 2 decades, two trends have transformed survey data collection in the United States. The first trend has been the introduction and widespread adoption of computerized tools for surveys; these tools have automated many survey tasks, including data collection...

At the same time that computerization has altered the methods of collecting survey data, a second trend has altered the content of surveys. Surveys are collecting increasingly sensitive information, information about illegal or embarrassing activities, such as drug use and sexual behavior...

文章开始介绍了研究的背景，指出了近 20 年来美国抽样调查数据采集的两个趋势：一个是计算机技术的应用；另一个是对敏感信息采集需求的增长。

采集敏感信息数据时遇到的严峻问题就是信息的准确性，对此存在着两个主要的威胁：一个是受访者拒绝回答；另一个是受访者回答不实。

通过这样的介绍，读者可以明白本项研究的意义。

Although the need for information about these topics is clear, it is not clear whether the data collected about them in surveys are accurate. One potential threat to accurate results is nonresponse. Members of the sample may refuse to take part in the survey at all, or they may decline to answer specific questions. Either way, the very persons with the most sensitive information to report may be the least likely to report it...

A second potential threat to accuracy is reporting error. The mere fact that a respondent answers a question provides no assurance that the answer is accurate...

Mode effects and sensitive questions. The literature on sensitive questions demonstrates that the method of collecting the data can affect the answers that are obtained. Table 1 summarizes the findings from some of the key methodological studies. Several of these studies have demonstrated that self-administration of sensitive questions increases levels of reporting relative to administration of

接下来，是文献综述部分。作者总结了一些主要的方法论文章，这些文献证明数据采集模式会影响到敏感问题的回答。首先，受访者自答会比访员访谈得到更高的报告水平；其次，计算机辅助模式下的自答和传统纸笔模式下的自答在结果上没有显著差别。进而总结为，根据

the same questions by an interviewer. …

…

Early comparisons of computer-assisted self-administration (via CASI) with paper-and-pencil interviews suggest that computer administration of survey items produces gains similar to those from conventional self-administration. …

The basic finding from the study was that computerization per se had little effect on the level of reporting; consistent with the results of prior studies, however, self-administration-whether computer assisted or not-had a clear impact on reporting, especially the reporting of sexual behavior…

…

Because CASI requires respondents to read the questions, it is subject to some of the same limitations as other methods of self administration. The requirement that respondents read the questions and follow the directions may make it difficult to use CASI among populations with poor reading skills. Because it

目前的文献发现对于敏感信息的采集，受访者自答或访员访谈有明显不同，而是否使用计算机辅助模式则影响不大。

在计算机辅助模式下的访员自答访问也分为两种形式：一种是访员提问，受访者录入答案，即 CASI；另一种是计算机语音提问，受访者录入答案，即 ACASI。后者比前者能更好地保护受访者的隐私。但是，

features auditory presentation of the questions, ACASI may circumvent this restriction. ACASI may thus preserve the privacy of self-administration without imposing the same demands on respondent literacy. To date, methodological research on ACASI is limited.

…

Variables underlying mode differences. The revolution in computerized data collection has multiplied the methods available for face-to-face interviewing; at least six methods can be used to collect data: (1) paper-and-pencil personal interviews (PAPI); (2) paper-and-pencil self-administered questionnaires (SAQ); (3) Walkman-administered questionnaires (audio-SAQ); (4) computer-assisted personal interviews (CAPI); (5) computer-assisted self-administered interviews (CASI); and (6) audio computer-assisted self-administered interviews(ACASI)…

A second difference among these six methods of in-person data collection

目前对于 ACASI 的研究较少，这意味着本项研究的成果将对扩展 ACASI 调查技术的知识文献有所贡献。

作者在三个维度上来划分访问模式：一是根据访问技术的不同分成 6 种方式；二是根据答题方式的不同分为受访者自答和访员访谈；三是根据提问方式分为读给受访者听和访员自己读。

这三个维度上不同选择的组合形成了多种访问模式。

involves whether the questions are self-administered or administered by an interviewer…

A final difference among the methods involves whether the questions are read to the respondent or by the respondent…

Study design. This study compared the three methods of computer-assisted data collection-CAPI, CASI, and ACASI-currently available for face-to-face interviewing. Computer-assisted personal interviewing (CAPI) differs from the other two modes in that the questions are administered by an interviewer rather than directly by the computer. Computer-assisted self-administered interviewing (CASI) differs from the other two in its reliance on visual presentation of the items. The three modes were compared in a cross-sectional sample of respondents from Cook County. The key outcome variables were nonresponse rates and levels of reporting, particularly reporting of illicit drug use and sexual behavior. Our hypotheses were that, relative to CAPI

作者接下来介绍本项研究的设计，包括三个方面：研究问题、研究变量和研究假设。

第一个研究问题：

计算机辅助访问的三种模式（CAPI，CASI，ACASI）比较。

因变量：无应答率；吸毒和性行为的报告水平。研究假设：

（1）和 CAPI 相比，CASI 和 ACASI 模式下期望获得较高的吸毒人数比例和较低的男女性伴侣人数差异。

（2）期望自答的访问模式会对男性和女性报告自己性伴侣个数上有相反的效果。

（3）期望不同模式下访问的应答率没有差别。

data collection, CASI and ACASI data collection would increase the proportion of respondents admitting illicit drug use and decrease the disparity between the average number of sex partners reported by men and women. More generally, we predicted that, by offering greater privacy to the respondents, the two self-administered modes would reduce the effects of social desirability on the answers. Because a large number of partners is often seen as undesirable for women and a small number of partners is often seen as undesirable for men, we expected self-administration to have opposite effects on the number of sex partners reported by men and women. We did not anticipate a difference in overall response rates by mode.

Because of our interest in the reporting of sex partners, the design included two other variables besides data collection mode that were designed to affect responses to the sex partner questions; these variables were the format and context of the sex

第二个研究问题：

问题设计的格式对受访者应答的影响。

因变量：受访者性伴侣的个数。

研究假设：

(1)封闭式提问方式

partner questions. ... It is possible that the use of closed items may increase the discrepancy between the number of sex partners reported by men and women by suggesting that inexact answers are legitimate; it is also possible, on the other hand, that the use of broad categories (especially at the upper end) will make it easier for women to report large numbers of partners. To test the effect of the answer options presented in the closed questions, we used two versions of each closed item-one with categories mainly at the low end of the range and a second version with categories concentrated at the high end of the range. In addition to these two closed forms, we also included an open form of each of the sex partner questions.

会加大男女报告性伴侣个数的差异。

(2) 封闭式提问方式下选项范围的划分也会影响到受访者的应答结果。

This study also examined the effects of prior items on the reporting of sex partners. Just before the sex partner questions, respondents answered one of two sets of questions about their sexual attitudes. One set of items was designed to encourage respondents to report large numbers of

第三个研究问题：

问题设计的顺序对受访者应答的影响。

因变量：受访者性伴侣的个数。研究假设：

(1) 在研究问题前设计一组对性行为持容

sex partners; these questions consisted of statements expressing "permissive" views about sexual activity. The other set of questions was designed to discourage reporting large numbers of partners; these statements in this set expressed more "restrictive" views about sex. ... We thought that, because reports about sexual behavior may be affected by attitudes toward sex, the permissive items would encourage female respondents to admit how many partners they had and that the restrictive items would encourage male respondents to admit how few they had.

许态度的观点问题会鼓励女性受访者多报性伴侣个数。

（2）在研究问题前设计一组对性行为持约束态度的观点问题会鼓励男性受访者少报性伴侣个数。

Method

Sample selection. We selected an area probability sample of dwellings in Cook County, Illinois. At the first stage of selection, we selected a systematic sample of 32 area segments, with the first-stage selection probabilities proportional to the number of housing units on the segment (according to 1990 census data). Each segment consisted of a single block or several adjoining blocks. Prior to selection, all blocks in the

作者在"方法"部分介绍了研究的样本选取、问卷设计、实验设计和数据采集情况。

作者首先简练但系统地介绍了整个抽样和应答情况，使读者可以对调查-实验中的概率抽样有初步的认识。

本研究目标总体是居住在美国伊利诺伊州

county had been sorted by census tract and, within census tract, by block number. A systematic sample of segments was selected that gave proportionate representation to all areas of the county. Seventeen of the 32 sample segments were located in the city of Chicago. The remainder were drawn from the balance of Cook County.

库克郡的 18 到 45 岁的居民。第一阶段采用概率抽样方法抽选了 32 个区域样本。

At the second stage of selection, we designated a sample of 1,122 housing units (HUs) for a short screening interview to determine whether anyone living there was in the 18-45-year age range. The screening sample constituted an equal probability sample of the housing units in Cook County. Fifty-three of the sample HUs were unoccupied; screeners were completed at 975 of the 1, 069 occupied HUs, for a completion rate of 91.2 percent.

第二阶段的抽样是对样本资格的认定,对第一阶段抽中的 32 个区域样本中的 1122 个住宅单元进行过滤调查,结果是 53 个住宅无人居住,在有人居住的住宅中完成了 975 份过滤问卷,完成率为 91.2%。

Eligible persons were identified at 643 of the HUs that completed the screener. When more than a single HU resident was eligible for the study, we randomly designated one of them to be the respondent. Residents

如果一个住宅里有一个以上符合调查资格的居民,则从中随机选取一人进行访问。最终选取 643 个受访者,365 人成功完成访问,应答

selected for the main interview were told that the survey concerned health and was supported by funding from the National Science Foundation. Of the 643 potential respondents selected in this way, 365 completed the main interview, for a final completion rate of 56.8 percent. Unfortunately, the study used a new version of AutoQuest to administer the items, and a design flaw in this version of the program prevented some 79 of these initial interviews from being downloaded from the laptops. Subsequently, the error was corrected, and 53 of the original cases were reinterviewed under the same experimental conditions they had been assigned to originally. (Twenty-five ACASI interviews, 12 CAPI interviews, and 16 CASI interviews were redone.) The results presented here are, except where noted, based on 339 completed cases (including the 53 reinterviewed cases). The results are not appreciably altered if the reinterviews are excluded from the analysis.

率为 56.8%。作者还说明了因为技术原因，79 条调查数据丢失，但其中 53 个受访人成功做了二次访问，于是最终数据库中的案例个数为 339 个。

Questionnaire. The questionnaire included items concerning a range of sensitive topics. It was divided into five major sections. The first section included standard demographic questions (asking about the respondent's sex, date of birth, marital status, and educational attainment). The next section asked about a number of health conditions, among them several sexually transmitted diseases. The third section consisted of items on marriage and cohabitation, pregnancy, and sex partners; the sex partner items asked about the number of opposite-sex sex partners during the past year, the past 5 years, and over the respondent's lifetime. In each version of the questionnaire, the sex partner items followed a set of three or four questions on sexual attitudes; these attitude items were designed to encourage or discourage full reporting of sex partners. The fourth section of the questionnaire contained two items on AIDS risk and a series of items on condom use. The fifth section of the questionnaire included several items

作者在这部分介绍了问卷的结构。

其中第三部分是关于婚姻、同居、怀孕，以及性伴侣的情况。本项调查-实验主要关注的敏感问题，即性伴侣个数的问题就放在这个部分。这个问题询问的是异性伴侣个数，设计的时间点有三个：去年，过去5年，以及一生。研究者还设计了两组对两性关系态度的问题。每个版本的问卷中在性伴侣个数这道问题的前面放置其中一组态度问题。

作者指出问卷中的问题主要来源于目前已有的一些知名调查。这样做的好处有二：一是知名调查中的问题一般经过多轮测试，具有较好的信度和效度；而采用相同的问题，可以方便调查结果的横向比较。人们在设计调查-实验问卷时也可以借鉴这种做法。

on illicit drug use. The interview concluded with a few questions assessing attitudes toward abortion and the legalization of marijuana.

The questions were mostly drawn from existing sources. The bulk of the items in the questionnaire were taken from an earlier study-the Women's Health Study-conducted as a pretest for Cycle V of the National Survey of Family Growth (NSFG; see Jobe et al. [in press]). Most of the items in that study were taken from earlier cycles of the NSFG. The sex partner items in the questionnaire were quite similar to those used in a series of supplements to the General Social Surveys (GSS); the only difference is that the GSS items asked about partners since age 18 rather than over the lifetime. The items on illicit drug use were modeled on those used in the National Household Survey of Drug Abuse (see, e. g., Turner, Lessler and Gfroerer, 1992).

Experimental design. Prior to screening, each HU was randomly assigned to an experimental condition; the data collection mode variable was crossed with the context and format of the sex partner items, producing a total of 12 conditions. Random assignment was done within segments to assure that the experimental conditions were not confounded with geographic areas.

作者在本部分介绍了本项研究的实验设计。这个调查-实验中共有 3 个处理变量形成 12 个处理条件，在进行资格过滤前，就在每个区域分割内将每一户随机分配给这些实验组。然而，在接下来的详细介绍中，读者会发现作者实际上设计了 3 个实验变量上的 18 种情形，而非 12 个。作者在这里应该是个笔误。

The main experimental variable was the mode of data collection: respondents were assigned to data collection by computer-assisted personal interview (CAPI), computer-assisted self-administered interview (CASI), or audio computer-assisted self-administered interview (ACASI)...

第一个处理变量是三种数据采集模式。

The sex partner items were the subject of two additional experimental variables. The first was whether the sex partner questions used an open or closed format and what response op-

第二个处理变量是性伴侣问题的格式设计。作者选取了三种形式：第一种是开放式提

tions were offered in the closed format. Three versions of the sex partner questions were used. The open version simply asked for the number of partners; for example, the 1-year question administered to women respondents asked: "During the last 12 months, that is, since August/September 1993, how many men (if any) have you had intercourse with? Please count every partner, even those you only had sex with once." A number was entered as the answer. The closed versions of this question presented the same question followed by a set of response options. The response options presented to one group of respondents were 0, 1, 2, 3, 4, and 5 or more; the options presented to the other group were 0, 1-4, 5-9, 10-49, 50-99, and 100 or more. A follow-up item asked respondents in the closed format groups the exact number of partners (when that could not be inferred from the response category they had selected). Respondents received the same version of the sex partner item for all three recall

问，请受访者直接报告性伴侣的个数；第二种是封闭式提问，设计了0,1,2,3,4和5个及以上共六个选项；第三种也是封闭式提问，但选项设计为0,1—4,5—9,10—49,50—59,100及以上。在两种封闭式提问的问题后会紧接着请受访者报告具体数字。

periods (1 year, 5 years, and lifetime); moreover, the same set of response options was used for all three items. We will refer to the three groups of respondents as the open, closed-low, and closed-high respondents.

最后一个处理变量是提问的情境。分为两种,一种是在性伴侣问题前安放一组对性行为持容许态度的观点问题;另一种是在性伴侣问题前安放一组对性行为持约束态度的观点问题。

这样,第一个和第二个处理变量各包括 3 种情形,第三个处理变量包括 2 种情形,所以应该一共是 18 种实验条件,而非作者前文中报告的 12 种。

The final experimental variable consisted of the items that preceded the three sex partner questions. Each of these context items consisted of a statement with which respondents were to indicate their agreement, using a 5-point scale. We created two sets of attitude statements for each sex, one that expressed relatively "permissive" views about sexual activity and a second set that expressed more "restrictive" views...

数据采集部分作者详细介绍了访问时间、访员情况和设备使用情况。对于二次访问的样本,作者也特意做了说明。

Data collection. The initial 365 interviews were completed in August and September of 1994. The 53 reinterviews were completed in February of 1995. A total of 22 interviewers conducted the interviews that make up the final data set. All but one of them were women. Because of the need to manipulate the sound files, the ACASI condition required faster machines than the CAPI or CASI conditions. As a result, we rented a limited number of Compaq Conturas and ASTs (386 laptops) for the ACASI interviews and assigned these machines to eight of the interviewers; these eight interviewers completed only ACASI interviews. The remaining field staff received slower Compaq LTEs (286 laptops) and were assigned to conduct both CAPI and CASI interviews.

至此，关于本项研究的方法介绍完毕。调查-实验的关键在于设计和执行，因此在报告研究结果之前非常有必要对此详细介绍。

Available interviewers from both groups were used to conduct the reinterviews. Nine interviewers ultimately completed cases in all three modes of data collection, 10 completed only CASI/CAPI interviews, and three completed only ACASI cases.

Results

The analysis examines three main issues: the impact of the different modes of data collection on participation in the study (i.e., on unit nonresponse); the

作者采用了 SUDAAN 软件来执行分析。SUDAAN 软件主要

effects of mode, question context, and format of the questions on responses to the sexual behavior items; and the effect of mode on responses to the questions on illicit drug use. Because the sample was clustered by area segment, we analyzed the data using SUDAAN, which uses Taylor Series approximation to estimate standard errors and compute significance tests (Shah et al. 1993). However, because of the experimental design we used (in which the experimental factors were crossed with area segments), the SUDAAN standard errors were consistently smaller than those computed under the assumption of simple random sampling. Similarly, in every case, the significance levels were more extreme when we used SUDAAN to take the clustering into account than when we ignored the clustering. As a result, we report the inferential statistics from the analyses that assume a simple random sample. In every case where the results differed, this is the conservative approach. In general, these differences involved higher-order interaction terms with no clear interpretation.

用于对复杂抽样设计的调查数据及复测或整群相关实验数据的分析。因为这些数据间彼此不独立,因此分析在估计标准误时采用泰勒多项式逼近(Taylor Series Approximation)方法。此软件多用在医学和生物统计分析上。在 STATA 和 SAS 软件中,如果分析时使用权重,分析结果也是采用泰勒多项式逼近方法估计标准误。

作者虽然使用 SUDAAN 软件,但分析时没有设为复杂抽样设计,而是假定简单随机抽样设计,这样在检验实验结果的差异时可以得到较为保守的结论。

Unit nonresponse. We examined nonresponse in the initial wave of interviewing. The overall response rate for this wave was 56.8 percent (365 completed interviews out of 643 eligible cases). The response rates did not differ significantly by mode of data collection. Of the 211 cases assigned to ACASI data collection, 55.5 percent (117) completed the interview; of the 220 assigned to CAPI, 57.7 percent (127) completed the interview; and of the 212 assigned to CASI, 57.1 percent (121) completed the interview. There were also no significant differences in refusal rates by mode, although the refusal rate was somewhat lower among the CASI (22.7 percent) than among the ACASI (42.4 percent) and CAPI (34.9 percent) cases...

The response rates did not differ significantly by mode of data collection. Because differences in the composition of the three groups could explain any apparent differences in the levels of reporting, we compared. the groups on marital status, educational attainment, age and sex. These

本文采用了方差分析的方法来比较不同实验组的差别。

首先是单元无应答的情况。作者先分析了三种调查模式的应答率和拒访率，均未发现统计上的显著区别。

作者又进一步分析了不同调查模式的应答者在婚姻、教育、年龄和性别上的分布。除了教育外，没有发现应答者在其他人口变量上的显著差异。作者在这一步的分析一方面是对第一个研究假设的验证，同时也是为了排除这个实验对后两种实验的影响（即外溢效应）。因为应答者的性别、年龄、婚姻等背景变量很有可能会影响到性伴侣个数的应答，而此处检验不显著，避免了对后面分析结果的混淆。作者在这点上很审慎。

analyses are based on the 339 cases for whom questionnaire data ultimately were obtained. Little information about the nonrespondents is available beyond the segment from which they were selected and the experimental condition to which they were assigned.

There were no significant differences in the three mode groups in marital status, age or sex; there was, however, a significant difference in educational attainment (XI = 20.16; $p=0.01$). Table 2 shows the composition of the three mode groups by the background characteristics...

Reporting of sex partners. Respondents were asked to report the number of their sex partners over three time periods (past year, past 5 years, and lifetime)...

The distribution of the reported number of sex partners for each time period was quite skewed. To reduce this skewness, we transformed the sex partner data by adding .5 to the reported number and taking the natural logarithm of the result. A fur-

接下来作者分析受访者报告的去年,过去 5 年,以及一生的性伴侣个数。

作者发现这些报告的性伴侣个数不是正态分布。因为作者要运用方差分析的方法来比较各实验组结果的差异,而方差分析方法适用的前提是分析变量的数据呈正态分布。为了提高分析的有效性,降低数据

ther problem with the sex partner data was the presence of outliers. Two cases reported 50 partners in the prior year, one reported more than 100 partners during the previous 5 years, and two reported more than 100 partners in total. We dropped these outliers from the analyses reported here; their removal had little impact on the conclusions drawn. We then carried out analyses of variance on the transformed reports for each time period. The factors included sex, mode of data collection, format of the question, and context of the items.

分布的偏态，作者对数据做了转换：原始数据值加0.5，然后结果取自然对数。

此外作者还检查了离群值，去掉了几个过高的报告数字。然后运行方差分析，分析的因素有性别、数据采集模式、问题格式和问题语境。

For all three time periods, there were significant main effects for the sex of the respondent. As has been found in prior studies, the male respondents reported more partners than their female counterparts...

There were significant main effects for all three of the experimental variables. For all three time periods, ACASI elicited the highest mean number of reported sex partners. ... For the 1-year and 5-year periods, the closed item with the high-response

作者报告了分析结果。

首先，和以往研究发现一致，男性应答者平均比女性应答者报告了更多的性伴侣个数；

第二，接受ACASI调查模式的应答者比其他调查模式下的应答者报告的性伴侣个数更多。

第三，在问题格式上，使用高位选项封闭式问卷的应答者平均报

categories elicited the highest level of reporting and the closed item with the low-response categories, the lowest; in both cases, the open item produced intermediate levels of reporting. ... Finally, the restrictive context elicited higher numbers of sex partners than the permissive context for all three time periods; however, this "backfire" effect was significant only for the 5-year data-$F(1,256) = 4.03$ ($p < .05$)-and the effect of context was qualified by higher-order interactions. A potential complication here is that the permissive and restrictive items may have differed in their effectiveness. Overall, the permissive items elicited lower levels of support than the restrictive items did; ...Some of the respondents apparently found the permissive items a little too permissive.

告的性伴侣个数最多，低位选项封闭式的最少，开放式的居于中间。

最后，性伴侣问题前放置对性行为持容许观点的问题会得到受访者更高的报告数字，但只是在"过去 5 年内"时间期限内统计显著。作者推测应答者对"容许"和"约束"的感受程度可能不同，因而存在高阶的交互效应。

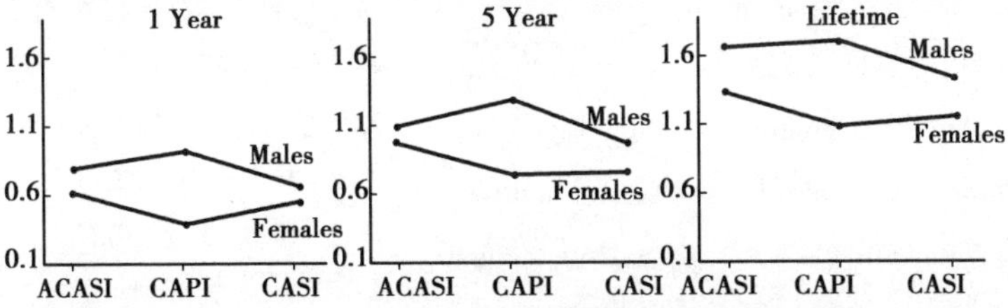

Figure1. Mean reported sex partners by mode and sex (transformed data)

The data in table 3 show the usual discrepancy between men and women in the reported number of sex partners. We expected this discrepancy to be reduced when the questions were self-administered. Moreover, we expected the impact of self-administration to differ by sex-with males reporting fewer partners and women more partners under the two self-administered modes than under the interviewer administered mode. The results in figure 1, which plots the means of the transformed sex partner reports by sex and mode of data collection, are consistent with these hypotheses. For all three time periods, the disparity between the number of sex partners reported by men and women was largest under CAPI; in addition, CAPI yielded the highest level of reporting for the men and the lowest level for the women. However, none of the mode-by-sex interactions was significant. The two-way interactions apparent in figure 1 were qualified by higher order effects involving the context variable. Figure 2 graphs the means for each combination of data collection mode, respondent sex, and item context. The three-way

如前所述，以往的抽样调查结果发现男性应答者倾向于多报告性伴侣个数，而女性应答者则倾向于少报告。这个调查-实验的一个目的就是考察不同的实验处理是否可以降低男女在这一问题上的报告差异，因此作者在以下的分析中引入交互效应，并且用折线图来展示分析结果（注意折线图中的纵轴是性伴侣报告个数转换后的均值）。

首先，图 1 很直观地展现出在 ACASI 和 CASI 两种自答的调查模式下，男女应答者报告数字的差距最小，而在面访 CAPI 模式下差距最大。然而这个分析结果在统计上是不显著的。

作者进一步分析了三个变量——数据采集模式、受访者性别和问题情境——之间的交互关系，发现在约束性观点的问题语境下，男性和女性受访者报告性伴

interactions were significant for both the 1-year and lifetime reports: $F(2,257)=5.10$ ($p<0.01$) for the 1-year data and $F(2,256)=3.71$ ($p<0.05$) for the lifetime data. The patterns apparent in figure 1 were far more pronounced among respondents who received the restrictive context items than among those who received the permissive items. Within the restrictive context groups, the mode of data collection had a large impact on the reported number of sex partners, and the gap between men and women is widest under CAPI data collection; within the permissive context groups, the mode of data collection had relatively little impact on the number of partners reported, and the disparity between the reports by men and women remained apparent under all three modes of data collection. Figure 2 also reveals that the overall trend toward backfire effects apparent in table 3 was, in fact, mainly produced by the women respondents, especially those in the CASI condition

Besides the three-way interaction plotted in figure 2, we found one other consistent interaction effect, involving the mode of data collection and item format...

侣个数的差异和调查模式有关,在 CAPI 模式下差异最大。而在容许性观点的问题语境下,调查模式没有表现出影响作用。这个结果在一年和一生性伴侣个数的报告上是统计显著的。作者还发现数据采集模式和问题格式间也存在稳定的交互关系,在 CAPI 模式下,问题格式的影响最小,并且结果统计上显著。

Rounding of sex partners. Prior research indicates that many respondents answer the sex partner questions using round numbers, suggesting that their answers are, at best, approximations (Tourangeau et al, 1995). In this study, a total of 66 respondents reported eight or more lifetime sex partners, 37 of them reporting a total that was a round value-that is, an exact multiple of five. We analyzed the proportion of the respondents reporting at least eight lifetime partners who used round values to report their answers. ... Neither the sex of the respondent nor the mode of data collection significantly affected the proportion of respondents reporting a round number of lifetime sex partners.

作者又提出了另外一个问题：受访者在报告性伴侣个数上会倾向于取整数。分析发现，这种取整数的倾向会受到问题情境和格式的影响，但与受访者性别和调查模式无关。

Other sexual behavior. In addition to the sex partner items, respondents were asked about some specific sexual behaviors, including how frequently they had had oral and anal sex over the past 5 years...

除了性伴侣个数外，作者还分析了数据采集模式对受访者报告其他性行为和非法药品使用行为的影响。

Reporting of illicit drug use. The mode of data collection also had some effect on the proportion of respondents who admitted using illicit drugs…

Discussion

The study provides further evidence that computer-assisted self-administration increases respondents' willingness to make potentially embarrassing admissions in surveys. Across a range of items involving sexual behavior and drug use, ACASI and CASI generally elicited higher levels of reporting than CAPI did…

The only consistent exception to the rule that questions administered directly by computer increased reporting relative to questions administered by interviewers involved the number of sex partners reported by men; men tended to report either fewer or no more sex partners under CASI and ACASI than under CAPI…

The findings on the reported number of sex partners are consistent with the view that responses to questions about sexual behavior are strongly affected by self-presentation concerns…

…

作者在文章的最后一个部分总结了前述的研究发现，点出此项研究的局限，并且在最后部分提出了一个分析调查模式效应的研究框架。

One possible limitation on the findings presented here involves the relatively young, well-educated, and urban sample (see table 2 for statistics on the composition of the sample). It is certainly possible that CASI and ACASI will be less readily accepted by older respondents or other groups who have limited prior experience with laptop computers (Couper and Rowe, 1995).

…

作者也指出了本项研究的局限：样本在构成上偏向受过良好教育的城市青年。计算机辅助自答模式对于老年或没有使用笔记本电脑的人群可能会较难接受。

Tourangeau 和 Smith（1996）的研究是针对长期以来社会调查中存在的一个问题，即受访者对于某些敏感问题会给出不真实的应答，这个问题的后果就是调查数据的失真。他们选择了性伴侣个数这个敏感话题，发现在以往的数据中，男性和女性在性伴侣数目报告上存在和常识不符的严重差异。他们想考察先进的计算机辅助访问手段能否降低受访者的应答疑虑，以及不同的问卷设计是否也是造成这个不正常差异的原因。

这项研究的对象是调查技术，目的是发现这些技术对于敏感问题应答的影响，属于因果关系的研究，这种情形下调查-实验方法是最佳选择。同时在一项研究中要考察多个调查技术的效果，适宜采用多个处理变量的随机化析因设计，将受访者分为多组，每组接受的实验处理为这些调查技术的一个组合。

然而本调查-实验中只有 339 个成功访问的案例，也就是说，如果应答者在 18 个组内平均分配的话，每个组只有不到 19 个人，对调查-实验数据的分析必然会受到小样本的影响。同时调查对象来自美国北部一个包含大城市的郡县，虽是概率随机抽样获取，但和全国样本相比在一些背景特征上会有明显差异。这些局限会影响到本项研究数据分析的统计功效和结果推论。如果该调查-实验能够在全国性大样本的调查中实施，并且能够根据调查对象的性别采用随机区组设计，将会提高本项研究的质量和价值。

当前国内也开始重视提高调查数据的质量，开展调查方法学的研究。中国的社会调查有独特的社会环境，在实施上会遇到不同于西方国家的调查困难。如何在中国的社会调查中减少受访者的拒访情形，促进受访者的真实应答，防范访员的不规范访问行为，以及控制预算降低成本等，都可以采用调查-实验的方法来探讨。如严洁等（2012）对于访员臆答和干预效果的研究采用了准实验设计，如果能采用调查-实验法，研究结果将更为严谨有效。

3.2　经济学案例

在现实生活中，人们对事实的感知会影响到他们对一些事件的看法。Cruces 等（2013）的研究是要考察人们对家庭收入地位感知的改变是否会带来其对收入再分配政策态度的改变。他们采用了启动效应实验的方法，并在阿根廷的一项地区性概率抽样调查中实施。调查问卷设计为两个版本，一个版本包括常规的两道关于家庭收入地位的判断和对国家收入再分配政策的态度问题；另一个版本的问卷则在两道问题间插入实验处理，即告知受访者基于研究统计数据受访者对于家庭收入地位的判断是过高、过低还是差不多。受访者被随机分为两组，控制组使用第一个版本的问卷，实验组使用第二个版本的问卷。研究结果发现，当受访者获知自己家庭真实的收入地位后，那些高估家庭收入地位的人会倾向于支持更高水平的再分配政策。

这篇文章结构非常清晰。首先介绍了此项研究的学术价值及研究的概况；然后从理论上论述对收入分配的主观感知、感知偏误，以及对收入再分配政策的偏好。第三部分详细介绍了数据来源和实验设置，接下来的两部分是对数据的分析，证实了感知偏误的存在及对收入再分配政策态度的影响。下面的评析将侧重在调查-实验的设计与分析上。

Abstract

…This study examines how individuals form these perceptions and explores their potential impact on preferences for redistribution. A tailored household survey provides original evidence on systematic biases in individuals' evaluations of their own relative position in the income distribution. … The impact of these biased perceptions on attitudes toward redistributive policies is studied by means of an experimental design that was incorporated into the survey, which provided consistent information on the ownranking within the income distribu-

作者在摘要里简练地概括了研究背景、研究主题和研究发现。

该研究采用调查-实验法来考察个人的看法如何影响到其对再分配政策的态度。

研究发现，当了解自己家庭真实的收入地位后，那些高估收入地位的人会倾向于支持更高水平的再分配政策。

tion to a randomly selected group of respondents. The evidence suggests that those who had overestimated their relative position and thought that they were relatively richer than they were tend to demand higher levels of redistribution when informed of their true ranking.

1. Introduction

…

The empirical results presented in this paper are based on the Survey on Distributional Perceptions and Redistribution, a study of 1100 representative households in Greater Buenos Aires in Argentina. The survey was designed and implemented in 2009 for the specific purpose of testing the posited mechanisms for the formation of distributional perceptions. Data were collected on each respondent's household income and on his or her assessment of its ranking (to the closest decile) in the overall income distribution.

The first finding is that systematic biases are present in perceptions of own income rank: a significant portion of poorer individuals

从文章开篇的介绍部分可以了解到调查-实验的概况。

首先该调查-实验的样本来自 2009 年阿根廷一个地区的概率抽样。样本量为 1100 个家户。

这个抽样调查发现了人们对自己收入水平的主观感知与客观收入水平之间存在偏差。

调查-实验的目的是想探讨对收入分配情况的误解与对收入再分配政策态度之间的因果关系。

place themselves in higher positions than they actually occupy, while a significant proportion of richer individuals underestimate their rank...

Finally, the study explores how these misperceptions about the income distribution may affect attitudes toward redistribution. ... This study presents the results from a unique randomized experiment that was implemented within the survey: for a randomly assigned treatment group, the interviewer highlighted any discrepancy between the subjective assessment of the respondent's ranking and that respondent's actual position, effectively correcting any bias that was present. ... in this survey experiment, biased subjects were provided with feedback and were actually confronted with accurate information.

The results from the experiment indicate that confronting agents' biased perceptions with accurate information had a significant effect on their stated preferences for redistribution. Those who underestimated their income ranking did not change their

作者在此部分简要介绍了调查-实验的设计及其方法上的贡献。可以看出，此项调查-实验是以真实准确的信息提供作为处理手段，并且是根据调查对象客观的家庭收入来决定处理的具体内容，因而属于一种“量体裁衣”式的启动效应实验。

实验结果发现，当受访者被告知自己真实的收入地位后，那些低估自己收入水平的人不会改变其对再分配政策的态度，而那些高估的人则会比控制组的受访者要求更多的再分配。

attitudes toward redistribution when provided with accurate information about their income ranking. However, those who overestimated their relative position (i. e., who thought that they were relatively richer than they are) and who were provided with accurate information demanded more redistribution than those in the control group…

2. Subjective income distributions, potential biases and preferences for redistribution

…

3. Data source and experimental setup: Survey on Distributional Perceptions and Redistribution

3.1. Survey on Distributional Perceptions and Redistribution

The discussion in the previous section covered the formation of subjective income distributions, the possibility of systematic biases, and their implications for attitudes toward redistribution. The empirical research described in this paper is based on the Survey on Distributional Perceptions and Redistribution, a study of

文章此部分是理论上的阐释和探讨。

文章第 3 部分详细介绍了此项研究的数据来源和调查-实验的设置。

首先介绍了调查项目的名称、实施地点和时间、样本代表性及规模执行方式，以及问卷的主要内容。这是一篇规范的基于调查数据分析的学术文章所必须具备的内容。

1100 representative households representative in Greater Buenos Aires, Argentina. The survey was carried out in March 2009 and consisted of face-to-face interviews with a random sample of that population. It was specifically designed to test the mechanisms discussed in the previous section and, to that end, collected data on a set of individual and household characteristics and on respondents' labor-market and other socioeconomic outcomes, as well as their answers to a series of questions about their political views and attitudes. It also gathered information on the respondents' actual household income and on their perceptions of their own income rank within the distribution for the whole country.

There are several ways of recovering subjective probability distributions for a continuous variable such as income, which include eliciting quantiles, moments or points of the distribution ... The Survey on Distributional Perceptions and Redistribution relied on an original instrument

为获取受访者对于家庭收入的主观地位感知，这个调查采用了一个原创的测量方式。具体的问题为："在阿根廷有1亿个家户。在这1亿个家户中，你认为有多

(the income-rank evaluation question), which elicited a specific value for the cumulative subjective distribution: its evaluation at the point where each respondent thought his or her household stood. [4] The question was worded as follows: "There are 10 million households in Argentina. Of those 10 million, how many do you think have an income lower than yours?" [5] The survey also collected data on the households' total monthly income by intervals. While distributional indicators often rely on per capita or adjusted income, a pilot conducted in December 2007 indicated that individuals compare incomes in terms of total monthly household levels. The intervals were chosen by the research team to correspond to the boundaries of deciles of the total national household income distribution at the time of the survey in order to facilitate the comparison of objective and perceived positions in the distribution using the experimental design. [6]

少家庭的收入低于你们家?"这样的设计一方面受访者容易理解,另一方面经过简单转换就可以获取一个 0 到 100 的连续变量,其变量值可对应概率分布的分位值。

在获取家庭客观收入数据时,该调查询问了受访者家庭月收入的区间值。之所以询问家庭月收入而非人均收入,以及收入区间该如何设计,本文都给出了解释。

3.2. The survey experiment setup

Besides the income-rank question, the second and most innovative aspect of the survey was the implementation of an experimental design that was incorporated into the questionnaire. …

… the experimental setup for this survey involved randomly allocating two different types of questionnaires to interviewees, although the questions posed to the respondents were the same. The original feature of this setup has to do with the nature of the treatment, with the interviewer providing feedback to respondents in the treatment group in the form of accurate information concerning the income distribution. Specifically, after collecting information on household characteristics, income levels and positional perceptions, the interviewer informed respondents in the treatment group whether their estimates of relative income coincided with those of the research team. The interviewer read the following statement (with X and Y being determined by previous answers): "Based on your income

调查-实验是本研究的另一个创新之处。

该调查-实验采用随机化分配的方式将样本分为控制组和实验组。

实验的处理变量是受访者获知自己的主观地位判断是过高、合宜，还是过低。对处理变量的操纵方式采用了访员根据受访者的应答结果而给出反馈，具体表达为："根据您的收入水平，我们大学最新的研究结果显示全国有X百万的家户收入水平低于您家，然而您刚才说低于您家收入水平的有Y百万户。"然后，访员会根据X和Y的比较读出下面三句话之一：(1)"实际上收入低于您家的家户比您想的要多"；(2)"收入低于您家的家户数目和您想的差不多"；(3)"实际上收入低于您家的家户比您想的要少"。

调查-实验的结果变

level, the latest studies conducted by the University indicate that there are X million households with an income lower than yours, while you stated that there were Y." The interviewer then read out one of the three following statements, depending on the accuracy of the X/Y comparison: (1) "In fact, there are more households with a lower income than yours than you thought", (2) "You were right about how many households have a lower income than yours", or (3) "In fact, there are fewer households with a lower income than yours than you thought." The presence of a bias in their perceptions was thus explicitly pointed out to respondents in the treatment group. After the treatment, the questionnaire was used to collect information on attitudes about specific redistributive policies of interest in Argentina within the political context existing at the time of the survey. The questionnaire for the control group did not contain the "feedback" section, but was exactly

量是受访者对阿根廷当时再分配政策的态度。

用于控制组的问卷除了不包括"反馈"的部分,其他地方和实验组的问题相同。

the same in all other respects …

…

4. Evidence on perceptions of income distributions

4.1. Subjective income distributions

This section presents an analysis of the distribution of objective and perceived income rankings derived from the Survey on Distributional Perceptions and Redistribution. Fig. 2a gives the income distribution of the Greater Buenos Aires survey sample as a function of deciles of the national distribution at the time of the survey… Fig. 2b, in turn, presents the respondents' perceptions of their households' positions in the distribution, which were elicited by posing the income-rank evaluation question described in the previous section. …

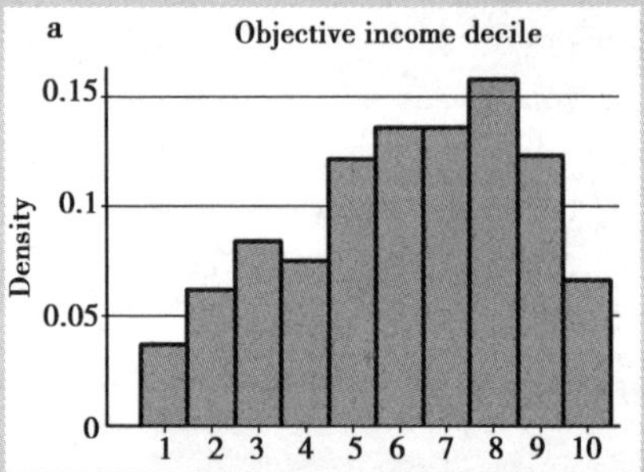

对于数据的分析，作者首先在图 2 中展示了应答者的客观收入分布和主观感知的收入分布情况。这种展现方式可以让读者直观地看出二者存在着明显的差异。

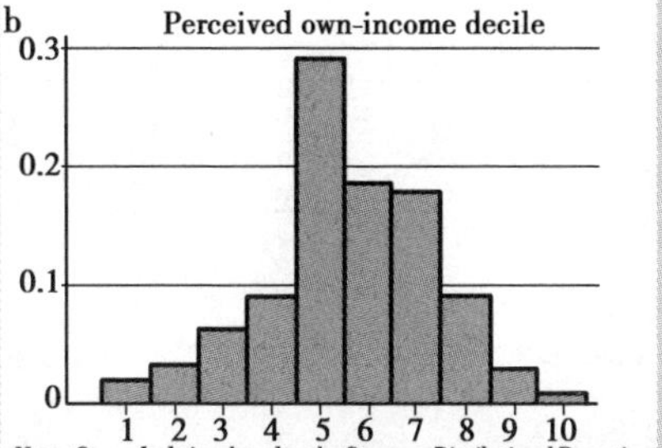

Notes: Own calculations based on the *Survey on Distributional Perceptions and Redistribution*. See Table A1 for definitions. N=1,060.

Fig 2. Distribution of objective and perceived own-income decile

The difference between the two panels in Fig.2 indicates the presence of a bias in distributional perceptions. … Table 1 presents summary statistics for this variable by objective income quintile. …

作者又采用了另外一种方式来展现主观感知上的偏差,即具体计算了客观收入十分位数和自我评估收入的十分位数的差,负值代表低估了自己的收入水平,正值则代表高估。分析结果总结在表 1 里。这种展现方式可以让读者对偏差的程度有进一步的认知。

Table 1 also illustrates the relationship between the distributions of objective and perceived relative income levels depicted in Fig.2. …

并且,作者对表 1 进行了深入解读,总结出对家庭收入水平的主观感知偏差的规律,即收入居中的人感知偏差最小,然后随着收入的增加或减少,偏差呈负向或正向逐渐增加。

Table 1
Objective income decile, perceived own-income decile and bias by quintile of objective income.

Quintiles of population income	Average objective decile	Average perceived own decile	Mean bias	Proportion with positive bias	Average positive bias	Proportion with negative bias	Average negative bias
Lowest	1.62	4.60	2.98	0.85	3.02	0.04	−0.04
Second	3.47	4.96	1.49	0.71	1.71	0.16	−0.21
Third	5.53	5.38	−0.14	0.30	0.60	0.40	−0.74
Fourth	7.54	5.89	−1.64	0.07	0.09	0.81	−1.73
Highest	9.35	6.48	−2.88	0.00	0.00	0.97	−2.88
Total ($N = 1060$)	6.12	5.60	−0.53	0.30	0.75	0.55	−1.28

Notes: the bias is defined as the perception of income decile minus objective income decile (see Table A1 for detailed definitions).
Source: Own calculations based on the Survey on Distributional Perceptions and Redistribution.

4.2. Reference groups and biased perceptions of income distribution

…

4.3. Alternative explanations

…

4.2 和 4.3 部分是对感知偏差原因的探讨，和调查-实验无关，此处不做评析。

5. Biased perceptions and preferences for redistribution: experimental results

5.1. Identification strategy

As described in Section 3, the survey included a field questionnaire-experiment: the interviewer provided a randomly assigned group of respondents with unbiased estimates of their positions in the income distribution, pointing out the degree and direction of the bias in each respondent's self-assessment (if any). This section discusses the causal effect of this information treatment on preferences for redistribution.[13]

…

作者在对调查-实验数据具体分析前先从理论层面讨论了该实验的因果效应。感兴趣的读者可以阅读原文。

Given these potential assymetries, the most natural choice is to estimate the effect of the informational treatment for three groups: those with a positive bias, those with a negative bias, and those without any bias. For respondents with no bias, the treatment simply confirms their perception of their own rank in the distribution ... The treatment ought to prompt those who overestimated their own rank to demand more help for the poor, insofar as it makes them more likely to consider themselves as potential beneficiaries of this type of policy. Finally, for those who underestimated their rank, the treatment can be expected to make them less likely to believe that they will benefit from the program, so self-interest should induce them to demand less redistribution (although the non-monotonicity of d(·) may prevent this from happening).

基于多种考虑，作者将受访者分为主观感受偏差为正、为负，及没有偏差三组人群，分别分析实验处理的效应，并且就不同的实验处理提出不同的研究假设。

5.2. Experimental results

...

The dependent variables in Table 3 are the different measures of

调查-实验的结果变量是受访者对收入再分配政策的态度，作者采用

preferences for redistribution (mean support, standardized mean, help with money and help with food) and a fifth dependent variable, which equals 1 if the respondent reports having made a donation in the past 12 months (this is used as a falsification test, as discussed below). The results are presented for each of the treatment subgroups: those with a negative bias, those with a zero bias, and those with a positive bias. The first two rows in each panel display the means for each dependent variable by treatment status. The following row shows the difference between the two and the standard error of this difference, with stars denoting the significance of the mean difference test. Finally, the last row in each panel presents the results from the regression version of the test, i.e., the coefficient of the treatment indicator in an OLS regression that includes the same control variables from columns 5 and 6 of Table 2 (standard errors are also clustered at the neighborhood level).

了 5 种方式来测量因变量：第一个是三个关于再分配政策问题的合成变量的均值，第二个是该合成变量的标准化均值，第三和第四个是其中两个关于再分配政策的问题，而第五个是一个用来证伪的问题①。

实验组除了上面提到主观感受偏差为正、为负和没有偏差三组人群以外，分析时还将正向偏差在 1 个十分位以上的人群提取出来专门分析。

表 3 报告了数据分析结果，即针对每一个因变量，计算了每个实验组和控制组的均值及标准误，二者之间的均值差及标准误，以及协方差分析获取的回归系数及标准误。

分析结果显示，对于主观感受出现负偏差的受访者，均值差很小且不显著；没有偏差的受访者，虽然均值差较大，但统计上仍然不显著；

① 这个问题的主要目的是证明因变量和自变量之间不是虚假相关，后文会进一步说明。

The results shown in the second column of Table 3 indicate that some of the point estimates of the differences between treatment and controls for those with a zero bias are non-negligible...

The first column of Table 3 presents the treatment effect for individuals with negative biases. The differences between the treatment and control groups are relatively small for all the dependent variables considered (positive for help with money and negative for help with food, and very close to zero for the two aggregate variables), with the exception of the donations variable, which exhibits slightly higher differences. None of the point estimates, however, are statistically significant at conventional levels.

Finally, the results for individuals with positive biases (those who overestimate their rank), shown in the third column, point to a series of relatively large and statistically significant differences between treatments and control groups...

...

只有出现正偏差的受访者,才有显著的差异,并且对于正偏差在 1 个十分位以上的受访者处理效应尤为强烈。

Table 3

Biased perceptions of income distribution and preferences for redistribution: experimental results.

	Negative bias: Treatment = telling respondents that position is higher	No bias: Treatment = confirming respondent's positional perception	Positive bias: Treatment = telling respondent that position is lower	Positive bias: More than one decil
	(1)	(2)	(3)	(4)
Mean of three government-support-to-the-poor questions (money, food, jobs)				
Treatment group [obs.]	0.459 [296]	0.532 [84]	0.538 [150]	0.559 [99]
Control group [obs.]	0.463 [286]	0.495 [72]	0.509 [152]	0.500 [112]
Difference [s.e.]	−0.003 [0.018]	0.036 [0.041]	0.029 [0.029]	0.059 [0.034]**
Conditional diff. [s.e.]	−0.003 [0.015]	0.015 [0.066]	0.071 [0.026]***	0.096 [0.042]**
Standardized mean (Kling et al, 2007), support questions (money, food, jobs)				
Treatment group [obs.]	−0.067 [296]	0.126 [84]	0.109 [150]	0.192 [99]
Control group [obs.]	−0.063 [286]	0.026 [72]	0.048 [152]	0.009 [112]
Difference [s.e.]	−0.004 [0.049]	0.101 [0.108]	0.060 [0.084]	0.182 [0.094]**
Conditional diff. [s.e.]	−0.004 [0.045]	0.035 [0.183]	0.179 [0.082]**	0.259 [0.116]**
Government should help the poor with money				
Treatment group [obs.]	0.111 [296]	0.226 [84]	0.212 [151]	0.242 [99]
Control group [obs.]	0.108 [287]	0.153 [72]	0.176 [153]	0.150 [113]
Difference [s.e.]	0.003 [0.026]	0.073 [0.063]	0.035 [0.045]	0.092 [0.054]**
Conditional diff. [s.e.]	0.010 [0.021]	0.063 [0.119]	0.084 [0.046]*	0.132 [0.067]*
Government should help the poor with food				
Treatment group [obs.]	0.284 [296]	0.381 [84]	0.424 [151]	0.444 [99]
Control group [obs.]	0.303 [287]	0.347 [72]	0.373 [153]	0.381 [113]
Difference [s.e.]	−0.019 [0.038]	0.034 [0.078]	0.051 [0.056]	0.064 [0.068]
Conditional diff. [s.e.]	−0.024 [0.034]	−0.010 [0.105]	0.118 [0.046]**	0.124 [0.071]*
Falsification test: Made donations in the last twelve months				
Treatment group [obs.]	0.866 [292]	0.788 [85]	0.719 [153]	0.687 [99]
Control group [obs.]	0.831 [284]	0.845 [71]	0.742 [155]	0.722 [115]
Difference [s.e.]	0.035 [0.030]	−0.057 [0.063]	−0.023 [0.051]	−0.035 [0.063]
Conditional diff. [s.e.]	0.044 [0.030]	−0.024 [0.082]	0.029 [0.054]	0.031 [0.064]

Notes: * represents statistical significance at the 10% level; ** at the 5% level; and * at the 1% level. These levels correspond to the test for the unconditional difference – the p-value for $\mu_T<\mu_C$ for cases of negative bias (column 1), $\mu_T=\mu_C$ for those with no bias (column 2) and for $\mu_T>\mu_C$ for those with positive bias (columns 3–4). The conditional difference is computed from a regression of the outcome of interest against a treatment indicator, neighborhood fixed effects and a series of individual controls. The conditional difference is the estimate of the coefficient of the treatment indicator, and the significance levels underlying the stars are derived from standard errors clustered at the neighborhood level. The individual controls in the regressions include the sex of the respondent, whether the respondent is the household head, his or her age, indicators for his or her education level (from primary incomplete and lower up to postgraduate degree), whether the respondent has a spouse, indicators for the spouse's education level (if present), whether the respondent is a public employee, whether the respondent is unionized, and whether the household has any extra source of income besides labor earnings. The bias is defined as the perception of own income decile minus objective income decile. See Table A1 for further variable definitions.

Source: Own calculations based on the Survey on Distributional Perceptions and Redistribution.

Finally, the bottom panel in Table 3 presents a falsification test designed to capture the presence of any spurious effects of the treatment on respondents. These are estimates of the effect of the informational treatment on the variable defined by the post-treatment question: "Have you made any donations to an individual or charity during the past 12 months?" This donation variable was included in the survey because of its close relationship to a willingness to provide assistance to the poor. If the treatment has an effect through a change in the perceptions of own-income rank,

本研究的另一个亮点是在分析时对处理变量的操纵进行检测，也就是表 3 中对于用来证伪的因变量的分析。作者在此解释了用意：为了验证实验处理的启动效应改变了受访者对自己收入水平的感受，而非引发出受访者关怀或慈善的情感，从而导致他们对收入再分配政策上的不同态度。对于启动效应实验，这种方法有助于检查实验处理作用的机制。

it should have an impact on stated preferences, but should not affect the reporting of past actions. If, on the contrary, the provision of information induces more caring or generous statements from the respondent through a shaming effect, then the treatment should also have a (spurious) impact on statements about what the respondent did in the past. The results shown in the last rows of Table 3 indicate that, despite some sizeable differences between treatments and controls for some of the groups, none of these differences (conditional or unconditional) are statistically significant at the standard levels.

…

6. Conclusion

…

The findings in this paper indicate how perceptions may affect stated preferences for redistribution. Further research could focus on the impact of biases and information on actual behavior, such as voting patterns. Moreover, it would be interesting to explore how mispercep-

在文章的最后一部分再次总结了本项研究的发现和学术价值，并对将来的相关研究提出建议。

tions affect individuals' reactions to redistributive policies (e.g., as expressed through charitable contributions and tax evasion) and to learn whether the provision of information on broader issues that go beyond such matters as rules and regulations (e.g., Chetty and Saez, 2009) may have implications for public finance models. Finally, the results of the analyses conducted in connection with this study could be attributable either to limited information or to limited cognitive ability — further research will be needed in order to pinpoint the source of the observed biases in distributional perceptions.

Cruces 等(2013)的研究是将启动效应调查-实验应用到社会科学主题研究中,需要重点关注的是调查-实验的效度,即本书第1章中介绍的建构效度、因果效度、总体效度和外部效度。

本研究中的调查-实验部分要检验的理论假设是个人对于收入分配的感知会影响到他们对于再分配政策的反应。很明显,前者是因,后者是果。该调查-实验对这两个概念有较好的测量,对于收入分配的感知操作化为受访者认为的全国低于本人家庭收入的户数,而对再分配政策的反应则是询问受访者是否认为政府应该帮助穷人，以及该以哪种方式（现金、食物或者工作）帮助。在实验设置上遵照因先果后的原则，并且通过随机分组的方式排除了受访者个人特征对于实验结果的影响。而且为了验证实验处理的启动效应是受访者对于自己收入地位感知的改变，而非被引发出个人的关怀或慈善的情感，还采取了辅助因变量的证伪测试。可以认为此调查-实验具有较好的建构效度和因果效度。另外，在调查对象上该调查-实验使用的是阿根廷某一地区的代表性家户样本，对于这一地区的家户而言具有较好的总体效度。至于外部效度则需要通过在其他地区，甚至在其他国家实施同样的调查-实验来提高。

启动效应调查-实验也可以应用在对中国问题的研究上。如中国也存在收入不平等的现象，但有学者认为这种不平等在中国民众的日常生活中并不突出，并且在中国文化传统中为民众所接受，所以至少近期不太可能造成社会不稳定（谢宇，2010）。如果让民众真正认识到自己在全国的收入水平，是否会改变民众对于收入不平等的接受程度？甚至是否会引起民众对政府的不满？这些疑问可以利用启动效应调查-实验来探究。

3.3　社会学案例

现实中个人作出的决定或者判断往往会受到一些社会规范的制约。例如，大量理论和研究证明规范是人们参与集体行动的决定因素，然而该如何测量规范一直是个难题。Jasso 和 Opp（1997）的研究就是要对政治行动规范的特征进行测量，而他们使用的测量工具就是析因调查-实验中的虚拟案例。

在这个调查-实验中，作者选取了六个影响因素构成虚拟案例的维度，它们分别是对政治或经济的不满、抗议的形式是否合法、感受的个人影响、感受的个人风险、预期参与的人数，以及当事者的性别，这样共构成 468 个有意义的虚拟案例总体，然后从中选取 47 个案例样本及其复本随机发放给受访者，每个受访者被随机分配到的案例数为 10 个。对于每个案例中描述的情形，受访者要判断当事人在多大程度上应该参与不参与，用来打分的尺度为“-5”到“5”，其中“0”代表没有义务。对于政治行动规范的测量就是根据受访者打分所表现出来的规律。

文章内容上作者们首先从理论上提出了规范的四个方面：极性、条件性、强度和一致性。然后详细地介绍了析因调查-实验的设计以及对规范的测量方法。最后在德国莱比锡市的一个抽样调查中应用了这种方法，通过对调查-实验数据的分析展示了规范的四个方面的测量结果。

虽然多层次模型被认为是析因调查-实验最适宜的分析方法，然而在已发表的社会科学研究文章中应用此方法的却很少，这篇文章在对规范的一致性的特征分析时采用了多层次模型分析方法，因此可以更全面地示范析因调查-实验的设计与分析。

例文

Abstract

The purpose of this paper is twofold: first, to contribute to the methodology for measuring norms; and second, to measure the norms of political action among a sample of respondents in Leipzig, in the former East Germany, in 1993. We highlight four aspects of norms: (1) polarity, whether a norm is prescriptive, proscriptive, or bipolar; (2) conditionality, whether a norm holds under all circumstances; (3) intensity, the degree to which individuals subscribe to the norm; and (4) consensus, the extent to which members of a society share a norm. We show how the factorial survey pioneered by Rossi (1951, 1979) enables development of procedures for measuring these four aspects of norms, and we carry out for the first time a factorial survey analysis of the norms of political action. …

Social norms are important elements for explaining behavior, and understanding their emergence and operation is a central task for social

解析

摘要中说明了此篇文章的贡献，一是在于对“规范”概念的测量，二是对具体区域的研究。作者从理论上概括规范的四个方面：极性、条件性、强度和一致性，并展示如何利用析因调查-实验的方法来测量这几个特征。在摘要的最后报告了调查-实验的发现。

文章开头强调了对社会规范测量的重要性。

science (Blake and Davis 1963; Gibbs 1965, 1968; Williams 1968a; Cancian 1975; Hechter 1983; Akerlof 1984; Ostrom 1986; Cole, Mailath, and Postlewaite 1992; Posner 1997). In the extensive literature on norms, two questions are largely neglected: One concerns how specific norms emerge; the other concerns how norms can be appropriately measured. ... Building on the factorial survey pioneered by Rossi (1951, 1979), we develop a method for measuring norms, and we use this method to study norms governing political action.

A norm is visible in two types of individual behavior. The first involves the individual reflexively and consists of the felt obligation to behave according to the norm, together with the ensuing configuration of sentiments, decisions, and behaviors. The second involves the individual as a sanctioning agent and consists of the held view that others are obligated to behave according to the norm, together with the ensuing configuration

强调本项研究侧重于个人对他人行为规范的判断。

of sentiments, decisions, and behaviors. In this paper we examine the latter type, investigating individuals' judgments about how others ought to behave. Other-focused behavior is crucial, for if sanctioning ceases, the norm dies.

We highlight four aspects of norms. The first three are properties of a norm to which an individual subscribes: (1) polarity, that is, whether a norm is prescriptive, proscriptive, or bipolar; (2) conditionality, that is, whether a norm holds under all circumstances; and (3) intensity, the degree to which the individual subscribes to a norm. (4) The fourth aspect is consensus, the extent to which members of a society share a norm. We show how Rossi's factorial survey method enables development of procedures for measuring these four aspects of norms, and we carry out for the first time a factorial survey analysis of the norms of political action. Our data were collected in 1993 from a sample of residents of Leipzig, in the former East Germany.

提出了规范的四个方面：极性、条件性、强度和一致性。

NORMS AND POLITICAL ACTION: THEORETICAL AND EMPIRICAL BACKGROUND

…

研究综述部分，主要论述了规范的四个方面的含义和对其测量的困难，指出规范是政治行动参与的决定因素。

METHOD: FACTORIAL SURVEY ANALYSIS AND THE NORMS OF POLITICAL ACTION

Our objective is to measure norms of political action, focusing on four aspects of norms-polarity, conditionality, intensity, and consensus. To reach our objective, we use Rossi's factorial survey method (Rossi 1951, 1979; Rossi et al. 1974; Rossi and Anderson 1982; Rossi and Berk 1985). In brief, we present to respondents hypothetical protest situations that combine the factors identified as potentially norm-relevant, and we ask the respondents to judge whether the protagonist in each situation has an obligation to participate in the protest, or has an obligation not to participate in the protest, or has no obligation of any kind. For each respondent, we measure the norm that the respondent

简要介绍研究中所应用的析因调查-实验的设计和对规范不同方面的测量。

析因调查-实验有三个重要环节：选取调查样本，随机选取虚拟案例并随机分配给受访者，基于案例情形打分的任务。本部分对此逐一介绍。

subscribes to and is applying to the fictitious protagonists. The polarity and conditionality of this norm can be unambiguously characterized; and we attempt to measure the intensity of each respondent's norm. Finally, to measure cons-ensus, we compare the norms measured for all the respondents.

The design of the data collection in a factorial survey (also called "vignette analysis") has three main ingredients: a sample of respondents, a population of hypothetical situations (the vignettes) from which random samples are drawn and randomly assigned to respondents, and a rating task.

The Vignette Samples

Vignette characteristics. The first step in constructing the vignettes was to select those characteristics of a protest situation potentially relevant to the norm governing participation in the protest. We were guided by the literature on collective action and, more proxi-mately, by the results of an empirical study carried out in 1990 by Opp and his colleagues (Opp

首先介绍虚拟案例的设计和选用。

设计虚拟案例最核心的工作是筛选影响因素或自变量。本项研究中作者选取影响因素的依据是集体行动方面的文献和已有经验研究的发现。

1994; Opp and Gern 1993; Opp et al. 1995), who interviewed a representative sample of 1,300 citizens of Leipzig, in the former German Democratic Republic (GDR). ...

What were these conditions affecting the felt obligation to protest? The major condition seemed to be an increasing and relatively high degree of discontent. High discontent appeared to be a universal and necessary condition for protest to become a duty.

"Protest" encompasses various kinds of political action, ranging from participation in peaceful demon-strations to assassination of political figures. A factor relevant to the felt moral obligation to participate is therefore the kind of protest itself. In Western societies, participation in illegal protest actions seems to be regarded as immoral (Wolfsfeld et al. 1994). This also holds for violent forms of protest (e.g., seizing construction sites) because they are a subset of illegal actions. The Leipzig study indicates that under Communist rule violence was regarded as morally

基于此，作者梳理出认为驱使人们参与抗议的条件：第一个是“不满”程度的强弱，第二个是“抗议的形式”是否合法。第三和第四个条件是“感受的个人影响”和“预期的个人风险”。还有一个条件就是“预期参加的人数”。

very questionable.

Perceived personal influence seemed to be an important factor affecting the felt obligation to protest, as was the expected personal risk from participating in protests against the regime.

If a GDR citizen thought that nobody else would protest and that she or he alone would bear the costs of doing something to effect reforms, this citizen was considerably less likely to regard participation as obligatory. Thus, the higher the expected number of participants in a protest, the more the citizens felt an obligation to participate.

The conditions that were norm-relevant in East Germany in 1989 seem to be norm-relevant more generally. Thus, we built those conditions into the vignettes we used to study protest norms in 1993, when the moving from a Communist society to a Western democracy. In a factorial survey, the choice of vignette characteristics is based on the conjecture that the characteristic may be relevant

在选择虚拟案例包含的影响因素时，作者提出两点注意事项：第一，这些案例特征的选择是基于对受访者想法的猜测，但是受访者可能会忽略这些特征。第二，这些特征的选取不必基于单一的理论推理，而可能是综合多个理论，这些理论甚至可以是结论相反的。

in the eyes of some respondents; respondents, of course, are free to ignore characteristics.

Inclusion of characteristics may, but need not, be supported by formal theoretical reasonings; moreover, included characteristics may reflect several theoretical frameworks and may even reflect the competing predictions of rival theories. For example, several theories may each contribute distinct vignette characteristics. Alternatively, a particular vignette characteristic may be contributed by several theories, and the theories need not have uniform predictions concerning the operation of the characteristic. To illustrate, inclusion of the "expected number of participants" factor is consistent with both Olson's (1965) and Gould's (1993) reasonings; the two accounts predict opposite effects, both of which may be operating, though possibly at different strength. Similarly, "expected personal risk" is consistent with both biological and rationalchoice frameworks, the latter including as a special

这也是我们在设计虚拟案例时需要注意的事项。

case formulations in which externalities play a major part.

Levels/values of vignette characteristics. In the factorial survey method, the vignette characteristics become regressors in a regression equation that is estimated separately for each respondent. Thus, the need to conserve degrees of freedom dictates that, while the number of categories of a quantitative variable can be large, the number of categories of a qualitative variable should be kept small. Accordingly, we designed the categories of the qualitative characteristics so that their number was small, yet captured potentially normatively relevant situations. Table 1 presents the vignette characteristics. …

确定了虚拟案例中的影响变量，接下来就是要确定这些变量的测量水平。因为这些变量要作为自变量进入回归模型，为了保留较多的自由度，案例特征的类别要尽可能精炼。

Table 1 Characteristics of the Protest Vignettes: Leipzig Study, 1993

Discontent (Economic/Political)
(1) There will be an increase in rents of about 30 percent.
(2) There is a new law stating that persons can be arrestled and held for two weeks without being given any reasons for this.

首先，对于“不满”变量，作者只设计了两个类别，一个是经济不满；另一个是政治不满。并且不满的程度都比较高。

Continue

Kind of Protest (*Legal/Illegal*)

(1) To protest against this. A could participate in a legal demonstration in the city.

(2) To protest against this. A could participate in a traffic blockade in the city. This is illegal.

Perceived Personal Influence (*Low/High*)

(1) A believes that his/her protest would make a difference.

(2) A believes that his/her protest would hardly make a difference.

(3) This characteristic is not mentioned in a vignette.

Expected Personal Risk (*Police Action/No Problem*)

(1) A violent police action is expected where many participants might be injured.

(2) No problems are expected.

(3) This characteristic is not mentioned in a vignette.

Expected Number of Participants

(1) About 20 participants are expected.

(2) About 100 participants are expected.

(3) About 1,000 participants are expected.

(4) About 10,000 participants are expected.

(5) About 100,000 participants are expected.

(6) It is unknown how many people will participate.

(7) This characteristic is not mentioned in a vignette.

Gender[ii]

(1) Mr.Muller

(2) Mrs.Meier

[ii]Gender is indicated by the name of the person described in the vignctte.

“抗议的形式”作者也选取了两种，一种是合法的非暴力的抗议；另一种是非法的有一定暴力程度的抗议（封锁交通）。

“感受的个人影响”分为有和几乎没有两类，同时还有第三类就是没有提及此因素。

“感受的个人风险”分为警察的暴力干预和没有两类，再加上没有提及此项。

“参加人数的预期”分为 20，100，1000，10000和 100000 五档，补充两类分别是不知道和未提及该项。

最后是参与者的性别，以称呼（先生或夫人）来区分。

Population of vignettes. We next constructed the population of all possible vignettes (i.e., all possible combinations of the values of the characteristics). The number of possible vignettes (Cartesian product) is: $2\times2\times3\times3\times7\times2=504$.

Not all the possible vignettes were meaningful. We excluded one combination of values of "kind of protest" and "expected number of participants"-namely, a traffic blockade at which 100,000 participants are expected. Few illegal actions in Western countries involve such a large number of participants. Excluding this combination eliminated 36 vignettes, leaving an effective modified population of 468 meaningful vignettes. One vignette is presented below as an illustration; vignette characteristics are italicized:

There is a new law stating that persons can be arrested and held for two weeks without being given any reasons for this. To protest against this, Mrs. Meier could participate in

根据虚拟案例每个特征变量的类型一共可以建构 504 个案例，去除掉不合常理的组合，最终余下 468 个案例。

案例的陈述方式如正文斜体字部分所示。

a traffic blockade in the city. This is illegal. Mrs. Meier believes that her protest would hardly make a difference. A violent police action is expected where many participants might be injured. About 100 participants are expected.

Drawing vignette samples. Two final decisions involved how many vign-ettes to present to each respondent and how many ratings to obtain for each distinctly different vignette.

With respect to the number of vignettes to present to each respondent, there is a tradeoff. On the one hand, it is desirable to obtain as many ratings as possible from each respondent; this makes it possible to increase the number of factors in the vignettes and to investigate interaction effects, and it increases the precision of the obtained estimates. On the other hand, the number of ratings requested must not be so large that the respondent refuses to carry out the rating task or that fatigue interferes with

虚拟案例设计还需研究者做出两个决定：一个是该分配给每个受访者多少个虚拟案例；另一个是每个案例该得到多少个受访者的打分。

这是两个非常现实的问题。第一个问题既要从研究者角度考虑尽可能获得较多的案例变量信息，也要考虑到受访者所能承受的限度。于是作者采纳当地调查机构的建议，将每个受访者回答的案例定在了10个。

对于第二个问题作者的处理方法是从案例总体中抽选了47个样本，然后将这些案例的副本随机分配给受访者。

the quality of the ratings. Because this research was the first factorial survey in a formerly socialist country, we followed the advice of local professional survey institutes and asked each respondent to rate 10 vignettes, a small number relative to the usual number of vignettes rated by each respondent (e. g., 60 in Jasso and Rossi [1977] and 40 in Jasso [1988]). For future research, increasing the number of vignettes per respondent is a high priority.

With respect to the number of ratings of each distinctly different vignette, a hallmark of Rossi's method is that, in order to maximize the richness of the study, a large fraction of the generated vignettes is presented to respondents. Indeed, in some studies, each respondent receives a unique sample of vignettes drawn from the vignette population. In our case, we drew 47 samples from the vignette population and presented replicates of each of the 47 samples to randomly selected subsets of respondents.

作者没有详细介绍如何从案例总体中选取样本,每个样本使用多少副本,以及如何随机选取受访者的子集。

The Rating Task

The vignettes were presented to each respondent at the end of a personal interview (carried out using a standardized questionnaire). It was first explained that the respondent's task was to judge to what extent a person is obligated to protest or to not protest in certain situations, or, alternatively, is not obligated either way. A vignette was then presented as an example. The respondent was asked to rate the illustrative vignette on a scale consisting of 11 values, ranging from −5 to +5, including the value 0. Positive numbers represent an obligation to protest, negative numbers represent an obligation to not protest, and 0 represents the absence of any obligation at all; the absolute value of the number indicates the strength of the judged obligation. The meaning of the extreme points and of the value 0 was explained in a figure presented to the respondent (see Figure 1) and in the questionnaire, which provides detailed comments on the figure. A rating of −5 corresponds to the judgment that the vignette protagonist "should by no

析因调查-实验中虚拟案例提供了研究中自变量的信息，一般在每个案例的后面要紧接着一个问题，以获取因变量的信息。在这项研究中，在展示给受访者虚拟案例前就先说明了受访者的任务是基于案例的信息来判断主人公多大程度上有义务参与抗议活动，并在每个案例后采用下图所示的量表来确定程度的级别。

这个量表包含了−5到5共11个级别，其中0代表没有义务，左边的负值越小表示主人公越不应该参与，右边的正值越大代表主人公越应该参与。这样设计使"0"代表中间位置，即应该或不应该参与的分界点。

means participate" in the protest, and a rating of +5 corresponds to the judgment that the vignette protagonist "should by all means participate" in the protest. The respondent was then asked to rate the 10 vignettes in the randomly drawn sample of vignettes, using the same 11-point scale.

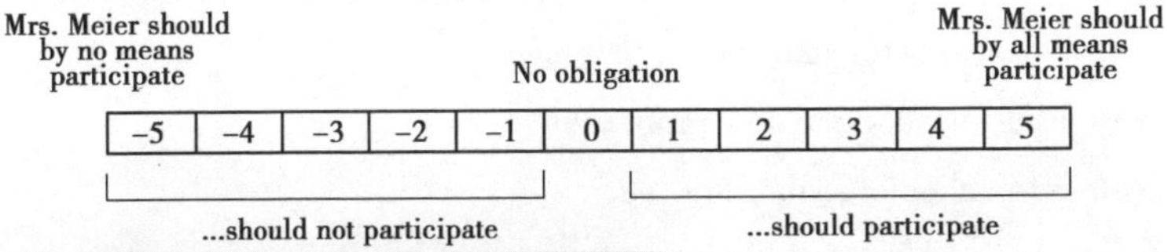

The Respondent Sample

The respondent sample consists of the second wave of a panel drawn from the population of Leipzig. The first wave was a random sample of 1, 300 citizens drawn in 1990 (Opp and Gem 1993, Opp 1994, Opp et al. 1995). In the summer of 1993, a total of 513 respondents from the first wave were located and reinterviewed. Such a relatively low response rate in panel studies is not uncommon in East Germany, which has experienced substantial out-migration since the fall of communism.

析因调查-实验设计的下一步就是要选取调查样本。

这项研究的调查样本来自1990年在莱比锡城市抽取的一个随机样本,共1300名居民。

然而在1993年对其跟踪调查时只访问到513人,不足40%。访到率如此之低会威胁到调查样本的代表性。

对此作者也做了探究,发现追访流失的样本确实在一些观测到的特征上有小但是显著的

To examine the extent to which the second wave was a representative sample of the first wave, we compared the subset of the first wave who were interviewed in the second wave with the subset who were not interviewed. As one would expect, the subset interviewed in the second wave includes a higher proportion of persons who are married or living with a partner and smaller proportions with low schooling and low occupational education. Although these differences are statist-ically signi-ficant, they are relatively small. There are no statistically significant relationships between participation in the panel and gender, religious affiliation (yes/no), or income. Although participants and nonparticipants in the panel might differ in unobserved characteristics, they do not differ appreciably on measured characteristics.

不同，但在一些重要的特征，如性别、宗教信仰和收入变量上没有显著差异。

Measuring Polarity, Conditionality, Intensity, and Consensus

A norm's polarity and conditionality, as well as the absence of a norm, are inferred from the pattern of

作者将在下面介绍如何基于对虚拟案例的打分来建构对社会规范四个方面的测量指标。

ratings. In factorial surveys, the case where a respondent assigns the same rating to all vignettes plays an important part. The precise meaning of the actions of these "zero-variance" respondents depends on the substantive context. In the current research, a zero-variance rating pattern can signify either a nonexistent norm or an unconditional norm.

Nonexistent norm. If a respondent assigns a rating of 0 to all 10 vignettes, we interpret this as indicating that the respondent does not subscribe to any protest norm whatsoever.

首先，如果受访者对 10 个虚拟案例的打分都是 0，那就说明对这位受访者而言不存在有关抗议的规范。

Polarity. If all 10 of a given respondent's ratings are negative, we assume that the respondent unambiguously subscribes to a proscriptive norm; the norm is termed "strongly proscriptive." If all 10 ratings are positive, we assume that the respondent unambiguously subscribes to a prescriptive norm; the norm is termed "strongly prescriptive." If a respondent's ratings are nonnegative, that

对极性的测量作者构建了五个指标：强禁令性、弱禁令性、强指令性、弱指令性，以及两级化。

is, include both 0 and positive numbers, the norm is called "weakly prescriptive"; if the ratings are nonpositive, that is, include both 0 and negative numbers, the norm is called "weakly proscriptive." The terms "prescriptive" and "proscriptive," used without an adjective, encompass both strong and weak forms of the norm. If the respondent's ratings span both negative and positive numbers, then we assume that the respondent subscribes to a bipolar norm.

Conditionality. If a respondent assigns the same nonzero rating to all 10 vignettes, then the respondent's norm is interpreted as an unconditional norm. In all other cases, the norm is regarded as a conditional norm.

当受访者对10个虚拟案例的打分相同，但不为零时，认定为不受制约的规范；否则属于条件性规范。

Intensity. Measuring intensity is more problematic. We propose two procedures, one applicable to respondents with unconditional norms and the other to respondents with prescriptive or proscriptive norms, but none for respondents with bipolarnorms. Among respondents who subscribe to unconditional norms, we measure intensity

作者仅对无条件性规范、指令或禁令性规范测量了其强度，对于两极化表现的规范，表示还有待研究。

同时作者也提出这种强度的测量方法存在问题，就是可能反映的是受访者的应答风格，如

by the rating used; for example, among respondents subscribing to an uncon-ditional prescriptive norm, a rating of +5 indicates a greater intensity than a rating of +1. Among respondents with prescriptive or proscriptive norms, we use the equation intercept as a measure of intensity. Unfortunately, the ratings and intercepts may also reflect the respondent's response style; what we call intensity may merely be differential expressiveness. As for respondents who subscribe to bipolar protest norms, there is no obviously good way to measure intensity; one possibility is to take the average of the absolute values of the ratings (in two versions, with and without 0 ratings). Formulating better measures of intensity remains a task for future research.

习惯性给高分或低分，而不纯粹是规范的强度。

Consensus. Examination of the ratings immediately yields information on the polarity and conditionality of the protest norms, thus signaling the degree of normative agreement. Among non-zero-variance respondents, consensus is more formally investigated

在一致性上，作者对于 10 个案例有不同打分的受访者首先用模型估计了虚拟案例中每个条件的影响作用，然后又做了同质性的统计检验。

by, first, estimating, for each respondent separ-ately, an equation describing the effects of the conditions on the judged protest obligation; and second, carrying out statistical homogeneity tests.

RESULTS

Of the 513 respondents in the Leipzig 1990 representative sample interviewed in 1993, almost 95 percent (486 respondents) rated all 10 vignettes presented to them. Slightly over 2 percent (11 respondents) did not rate any of the vignettes; and slightly over 3 percent (16 respondents) rated fewer than 10 vignettes. The analyses reported here use the subsample who rated all 10 vignettes (N = 486). 6 To establish whether each respondent subscribes to a norm and, if so, to measure and characterize the norm, we examine the respondent-specific pattern of ratings and, for non-zero-variance respondents, estimate a respondent-specific regression.

作者说明分析结果是基于对10个虚拟案例都进行打分的486个受访者的应答。

Nonexistent Protest Norm

Of the 486 respondents, 46 assigned a rating of 0 to all the vignettes (Table 2). Thus, almost 10 percent of the sample consists of individuals who do not subscribe to any protest norm at all. Exactly one-half of these nonorm respondents were men and one-half were women.

首先，数据显示在486名应答者中，46个人在所有案例上的打分都是0，这些人被认为"不存在抗议规范"。

Polarity of the Protest Norm

Of the 486 respondents, 100 (20.6 percent) subscribe to a prescriptive protest norm, and 38 (7.8 percent) subscribe to a proscriptive protest norm (Table 2). Thus, prescriptive norms are almost three times as common as proscriptive norms. Bipolarity, how-ever, characterizes a large majority of the sample-302 of the 486 respondents, or slightly more than 62 percent. Restricting attention to the 440 respondents who subscribe to a protest norm, 22.7 percent of the norms are prescriptive, 8.6 percent are proscriptive, and 68.6 percent are bipolar.

在486个应答者中，认为具有"指令性"抗议规范的占20.6%，具有"禁令性"抗议规范的占7.8%，大多数人的抗议规范具有"两极性"特征。

同时指令性和禁令性抗议规范的强弱也各有分布。

Among the 100 prescriptive norms, 22 are strongly prescriptive and

78 are weakly prescriptive. Among the 38 proscriptive norms, 22 are strongly proscriptive and 16 are weakly proscriptive. Thus, there is a marked tendency for prescriptive norms to be weak and proscriptive norms to be strong. This is an interesting and potentially important result. Whether, across behavioral domains, weakness is a characteristic of prescriptive norms and strength a characteristic of proscriptive norms is a question for future research.

Conditionality of the Protest Norm

Because 62 percent of the total sample subscribe to bipolar norms, we know already that the majority of respondents subscribe to conditional norms. Additionally, 97 of the 100 prescriptive norms are conditional, as are 25 of the 38 proscriptive norms. Thus, 424 of the 440 measured norms are conditional-over 96 percent (Table 2).

440 个存有抗议规范的应答者中，大约96%的人认为规范具有条件性。

Only 16 of the 486 respondents assigned the same nonzero rating to all 10 vignettes. Of these, 3 provided blanket approval for protest participation, and 13 opposed protest participation in all the vignette situations. Although the numbers are small, these results suggest two things: first, unconditionality is a rare condition. Second, unconditionality is a characteristic of proscriptive norms rather than of prescriptive norms.

Intensity

Of the 13 respondents subscribing to unconditional proscriptive norms, 9 chose a rating of −5, 2 chose a rating of −3, and 1 each chose ratings of −4 and −1. Of the 3 respondents subscribing to unconditional prescriptive norms, 2 chose a rating of +5 and 1 a rating of +4. Sample sizes are too small to draw any inferences; however, among respon-dents holding proscriptive norms, there is a clear propensity for the extreme categories.

对于无条件性的规范，由于样本量太少(只有 13 个)，对强度的测量结果没有什么意义。但对于条件性的规范，作者则发现了禁令性规范的强度要略高于指令性规范。

As for the conditional norms, examination of intensity utilizes the intercepts in the equations estimated for the respondents subscribing to prescriptive and proscriptive conditional norms. Restricting attention to the "strong" forms of the norms, the mean of the equation intercepts for the 19 respondents with strong prescriptive conditional norms is 2. 8, while the mean for the 9 respondents with strong proscriptive conditional norms is −5. 3. Among the respondents with weak forms of the norms, the mean intercept for the 78 respondents with weak prescriptive norms is.98, while that for the 16 respondents with weak proscriptive norms is −3.8.

Thus, the evidence from both unconditional and conditional norms suggests that intensity is greatest among respondents subscribing to proscriptive norms.

Consensus

The rating patterns indicate disagreement among respondents. For almost 10 percent of the sample, the protest situation does not evoke a norm. Moreover, the remaining 90 percent display three kinds of norms-prescriptive among more than 20 percent of the sample, proscriptive

对于规范的一致性的测量，首先作者认为应答者的打分表现出来的模式已经说明了受访者之间存在差异。

among almost 8 percent of the sample, bipolar among 62 percent. Furthermore, while over 87 percent of the sample subscribe to conditional norms (constituting over 96 percent of the measured norms), a tiny minority maintains an absolutist stance and adheres to an unconditional norm.

To more formally investigate consensus, we carry out the multivariate estimation and testing that has become standard for factorial surveys. In this analysis, we eliminate the 62 zero-variance respondents (the 46 with no norm and the 16 with unconditional norms), as their data cannot be analyzed using the usual factorial survey procedures. For example, the attempt to estimate respondent-specific equations yields a vector of parameter estimates equal to 0, and R^2 is not defined (total variation in the dependent variable is 0). More importantly, in order to carry out conservative homogeneity tests, it is important to remove the zero-variance respondents from the sample, as their

作者又应用了析因调查-实验正规的分析方法对此进行探究。出于分析的需求,他们排除了 62 个在 10 个案例上应答方差为 0 的受访者。

presence would militate against homogeneity even if the remainder of the sample had similar views.

Of course, the 424 non-zero-variance respondents need not agree with each other on the relevant conditions or the weights to place on them. To examine interrespondent disagreement, we estimate a separate equation for each respondent and then compare the equations across respondents, carrying out the complement of homogeneity tests. For example, the equations of all respondents may be so similar that a single equation can be used to represent all their judgments. Alternatively, respondents may have such different views that each respondent has to be described by a personal equation.

对于余下的424个受访者，作者首先对每个受访者分别估计模型等式，然后实施同质性检验来判断等式是否近似。这是判定是否有必要采用多水平模型分析的一个方法。

Formal multivariate analysis begins with estimation of three models and testing of three homogeneity hypotheses. Model 1 assumes that all respondents can be characterized by a single regression equation, that is, that all respondents have the same tendency to approve or disapprove

模型1是一般线性回归模型，即假设对虚拟案例的打分没有因受访者不同而受到影响。

protest participation and that all place the same weight on the conditioning factors. The single equation specified by Model 1 for all respondents is given by:

$$R_{iv} = \beta_0 + \sum \beta_k X_{kiv} + \varepsilon_{iv}, \quad (1)$$

where R denotes the rating, the X_k represent the regressors (that is, the vignette characteristics), β_0 denotes the intercept, the β_k denote the slope coefficients (that is, the weights associated with the vignette characteristics), ε denotes the error, i indexes the respondent, and v indexes the vignette. Model 1 assumes that the errors are distributed independently and with constant variance across respondents and vignettes, an assumption to be discussed, and relaxed, later.

Model 2 allows each respondent to have a unique intercept for the 10 vignettes he or she rated, but retains the restriction that a single slope vector characterizes all respondents:

$$R_{iv} = \beta_{0i} + \sum \beta_k X_{kiv} + \varepsilon_{iv}. \quad (2)$$

That is, although the overall

模型 2 是斜率固定、截距不同的多水平回归模型，假定受访者对虚拟案例的打分存在不同的倾向，但案例中所包含的影响因素的作用没有因受访者不同而存在变异。

tendency to approve or disapprove protest participation may differ across respondents, the conditioning effects of situational factors are evaluated the same way by all respondents.

Model 3 relaxes the restriction on the slope vector, so that each respondent can have both a unique intercept and a unique slope vector:

$$R_{iv} = \beta_{0i} + \sum \beta_{ki} X_{kiv} + \varepsilon_{iv}. \quad (3)$$

Model 3 assumes that within respondent the errors are distributed independently and with constant variance across vignettes.

模型 3 在模型 2 的基础上又进一步将斜率的限定放开，这时每个受访者的回归直线都具有独特的斜率和截距。

To address the question whether respondents have different intercepts and/or disparate views of the contextual features that condition the norm governing protest participation, we carry out three homogeneity tests. These tests first contrast Model 1 with Model 2; next Model 2 with Model 3; and finally, Model 1 with Model 3.

接下来执行了三个同质性检验，分别对比模型 1 和 2，模型 2 和 3，以及模型 1 和 3。

Three comments about specification and estimation are in order. First, preliminary analyses indicated that the number-of-participants vari-

对于模型的界定和估计，作者有三点评论。

able should be specified in logarithmic form, and that while perceived influence could be coded as a sign variable (−1, 0, +1, corresponding to the three categories), expected risk required two binary variables for its accurate representation.

第一，模型中“参加人数的预期”应采用对数形式，“感受的个人影响”变量编码为−1,0,+1的形式，“感受的个人风险”变量则使用的是两个虚拟变量。

Second, the dependent variable is an 11-category rating scale, and there has been some discussion concerning the appropriateness of least-squares estimation procedures for such cases (Winship and Mare, 1984). For example, Jasso (1988) estimates an ordered response model for a case in which the response variable can be interpreted as a 201-category extended rating scale. We are concerned, however, about the loss of information that arises from collapsing categories in order to estimate an ordered-response model, and we find cogent Bentler and Chou's (1987) reasonings in favor of applying procedures for continuous variables to ordinal variables when the number of categories is large. Hence, we use leastsquares estimation procedures.

第二，因变量的测量为一个 11 个类别的尺度，严格地说属于定序变量，作者经过考虑决定还是使用最小二乘法的估计程序。

Third, the operation of each variable is specified to be additive. It would be desirable to specify and estimate specifications with interactions between some of the conditioning factors. However, because each respondent rated only 10 vignettes, there are not enough degrees of freedom to include multiplicative terms.

第三，模型中应加入交互项，但考虑到样本量少，只采用了线性相加的形式。

Table 3 Summary of Estimated Rating Equations and Hypothessis Tests: Leipzig Sample, 1993

Mode/rest	R^2	F-Ratio
Model 1: Common intercept and common slopes (8 parameters) $R_{iv} = \beta_0 + \sum \beta_k X_{kiv} + \varepsilon_{iv}$	.29	247.4 (7;4,232)
Model 2: Differential intercepts and common slopes (431 parameters) $R_{iv} = \beta_{0i} + \sum \beta_k X_{kiv} + \varepsilon_{iv}$	.60	13.0 (430;3,809)
Model 3: Differential intercepts and differential slopes (3,392 parameters) $R_{iv} = \beta_{0i} + \sum \beta_{ki} X_{kiv} + \varepsilon_{iv}$	.96	5.7 (3,391;848)
Test of differential intercepts: Model 1 vs. Model 2 $\beta_{0l} = K = \beta_{424}$	—	6.8 (423;3,809)
Test of differential slopes: Model 2 vs.Model 3 $B_{k1} = K = \beta_{k424}$	—	2.5 (2,961;848)
Test of differential regressions: Model 1 vs.Model 3 $B_1 = K = \beta_{424}$	—	4.0 (3,384;848)
Number of respondents	424	
Number of ratings	4,240	

Note: Numbers in parentheses are degrees of freedom.

Table 3 reports the full three-model analysis. As shown, the common-intercept Model 1 is rejected in favor of the differential-intercept Model 2. The value of R^2 more than doubles, from .29 to .60, indicating that respondents differ in their "mean" view of the protest norm. Although contextual features affect the rating positively and negatively, nonetheless some respondents "start out" with a negative view of protest participation, others with a positive view. Both Model 1 and Model 2 are rejected in favor of the differential-intercept/differential-slopes Model 3. Thus, not only do respondents have a unique intercept, they also have a unique vector of slope coefficients. Model 3, which allows both differential intercepts and differential slopes, achieves a large magnitude of .96 on R^2.

从表 3 中的报告结果来看,模型 3 要优于模型 1 和 2。

Thus, there is substantial disagreement among the respondents. How are we to interpret this disagreement? There are several possibilities.

由此证明,受访者们对于抗议规范存有不同意见。作者给出了两个解释。一是可能反映

First, there may be distinct "social systems" or subgroups, each with distinctive norms; the norms we have measured may govern selected segments of the Leipzig population. Second, the normative order may be in transition, so that some of the norms we have measured may represent the remnants of once orderly and universal norms, while others may represent the beginnings of new norms. Of course, reality could be a mixture of both distinct social systems and transitional normative orders.

了莱比锡地区不同群体的规范差异；另一可能是捕捉到了规范变迁中新老规范的差异。当然也有可能二者兼而有之。

The Content of the Conditional Norms Governing the Obligation to Protest

Table 4 provides an initial glimpse of the respondents' aggregate views about how con-textual features condition the protest norm; it reports the mean and standard deviation of the ratings for each category of each vignette characteristic, together with the percentage of the ratings that are negative, zero, and positive. Although conclusive results must await exami-

作者进一步探讨了虚拟案例中的因素对受访者有关抗议规范的影响。在这部分他们用了多种方式来展现分析结果，值得我们借鉴。

首先，他们先用描述性分析来报告受访者们的总体情况。结果展示在表 4 里。报告的统计值包括不同人群对抗议义务打分的均值、标准差、负值的比例、零值的比例和正值的比例。

nation of the respondentspecific equations, a few preliminary features are worth noting here. First, while the mean rating is positive for both male and female prospective participants, nonetheless the obligation to protest is seen as stronger for males than for females-vignettes describing male prospective participants have, relative to vignettes describing females, (1) a higher mean rating, (2) a higher proportion with positive ratings, and (3) a lower proportion with negative ratings. Second, and in a similarly patterned result, both the mean rating and the proportions positive and negative suggest that the protest norm differs between economic and political discontent, with economic discontent producing a stronger held obligation to protest. Third, as expected, there are large differences in the protest norm between legal and illegal protests. Fourth, the "no mention" category in the perceived influence and expected risk factors operates as an intermediate category. Fifth, the greater the expected influence of participation,

在正文中对统计值所表现出的特征进行阐述。

the greater the held obligation to engage in the protest. Sixth, again as expected, the greater the personal risk, the lower the held obligation to protest. Seventh, the larger the expected number of participants, the greater the held obligation to participate in a protest.

Table 4　Characteristics of Vignette Ratings：Leipzig Sample, 1993

Vignette Characteristic	Vignette Ratings				
	Mean	Standard Deviation	Percent Negative	Percent Zero	Percent Positive
Gender					
Male	.207	3.429	34.8	17.8	47.4
Female	.108	3.438	36.0	18.9	45.1
Discontent					
Political	.080	3.452	36.2	18.7	45.1
Economic	.235	3.414	34.7	17.9	47.4
Kind of Protest					
Legal	1.596	3.042	19.0	15.9	65.2
Illegal	−1.425	3.130	53.6	21.0	25.4
Perceived Personal Influence					
Hardly make a difference	−.210	3.358	38.3	21.6	40.1
No mention	.122	3.431	35.5	18.8	45.6
Make a difference	.553	3.469	32.5	14.6	52.9

Continued

Vignette Characteristic	Vignette Ratings				
	Mean	Standard Deviation	Percent Negative	Percent Zero	Percent Positive
Expecred Personal Risk					
Violent police action	-1.105	3.222	50.5	19.3	30.2
No mention	.592	3.363	29.6	20.0	50.4
No problems	.928	3.366	26.9	15.7	57.4
Expected Number of Participants					
20	-.901	3.237	47.0	21.6	31.5
100	-.855	3.309	46.5	20.8	32.7
1,000	.133	3.484	36.4	17.5	46.1
10,000	1.133	3.189	24.1	15.8	60.0
100,000	2.616	2.701	9.6	13.5	76.9
Total(all vignettes)	.158	3.433	35.4	18.3	46.3

Note: Descriptive statistics are based on 424 perspondents and 4,240 ratings.

We turn now to examine the respondent-specific equations. For each respondent, we have estimates of seven coefficients, one intercept, and one value of R^2. The eight parameter estimates satisfy the conditions for unbiasedness. We summarize the results in two ways.

然后，作者考察具体应答者的等式模型，并且用两种方式来展示分析结果。

First, we present graphs of the quantile functions associated with each of these nine measures. The quantile function plots the value of a variable on its cumulative relative frequency, so that it is visually obvious what proportion of respondents have values of a coefficient (or R^2) smaller than the plotted values.'0 Figure 2 depicts the quantile function for each of the nine measures. To illustrate, the top left panel presents the quantile function for the coefficient of the prospective participant's gender; approximately one-half of the sample have negative coefficients, and one-half have positive coefficients. Many of the parameter estimates appear to be symmetric, almost approximating normal distributions. Of course, the medians vary, being close to 0 for the gender (a) and discontent (b) coefficients, negative for the risk/violent-action (e) coefficient and the intercept (h), and positive for the remaining coefficients.

第一种方式是对所有应答者等式的七个自变量的系数、等式的截距和 R^2 值做分位图，展示在图 2 中。分位图中用虚线标出参考线，可以比较直观地看出分布的比例。

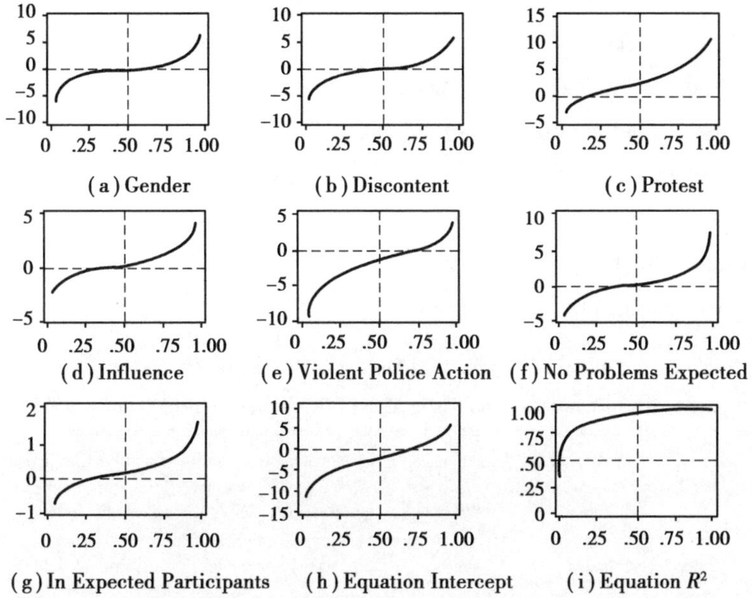

Figure 2　Quantile Plots of Respondent-Specific Parameter Estimates

Note: The x-axis shows the proportion of respondents; the y-axis shows parameter size.

Second, we present in Table 5, for each vignette characteristic, the proportion of the coefficients that were negative and positive, as well as the mean of the negative coefficients and the mean of the positive coefficients. Slightly over one-half of the respondents (51 percent) believe that men have a greater obligation to protest than do women, other things

第二种方式是用统计表展示模型 3 中每个自变量的回归系数中负值的比例和均值，以及正值的比例和均值。

the same; and slightly over one-half (also 51 percent) believe that the obligation to protest is stronger in the case of political discontent than in the case of economic discontent. Over three-fourths of the respondents believe that a legal protest carries a higher obligation to participate.

Table 5 Perentage of Sample with Positive and Negative Parameter Estimates in Model 3 Equations, and Their Mean Magnitude: Leipzig Sample, 1993

Vignette Characteristic	Negative Coefficient		Positive Coefficient	
	Percent	Mean	Percent	Mean
Gender (1=female)	51.4	−1.663	48.6	1.800
Discontent (1=economic)	50.7	−1.953	49.3	1.846
Kind of protest (1=legal)	23.6	−1.925	76.4	4.135
Perceived personal influence	38.2	−.989	61.8	1.274
Expected personal risk−1 (1=violent)	70.5	−3.123	27.4	1.620
Expected personal risk−2 (1=no problems expected)	41.3	−1.606	56.8	2.110
Expected number of participants (logged)	35.1	−.300	64.9	.479
Constant	68.4	−4.458	31.6	2.500

Notwithstanding respondents' personal idiosyncrasies, it is useful to examine the pooled effects. After all, it is the amalgam of personal views

虽然受访者的个体特征很重要，但对于抗议这种集体性行动来说，受访者们的共性也

that leads to collective action. Table 6 reports the parameter estimates for Models 1 and 2. The Model 1 estimates are corrected for heteroskedasticity due to the clustering of observations by respondent; Model 2 provides for respondent clustering via the respondent-specific intercepts. The Model 1 and Model 2 results are similar; all signs are the same, the magnitudes are similar, and only the gender coefficient has appreciably different observed significance levels in the two Models. All the estimates are highly statistically significant (beyond the .0005 level), except the estimates for discontent, which are not significant, and the estimates for gender, whose observed significance levels are .06 in Model 1 and .01 in Model 2. Of course, it should be kept in mind that both Models 1 and 2 are rejected by Model 3.

…

值得关注。于是作者通过模型 1 和 2 来分析自变量的作用方式。

Table 6 Parameter Estimates for Model 1 and Model 2 Protest Norm Equations: Leipzig Sample, 1993

Vignette Characteristic	Model 1	Model 2
Gender	-.175	-.201
(1=female)	(1.86)	(2.70)
Discontent	.065	.059
(1=economic)	(.69)	(.79)
Kind of protest	2.575	2.606
(1=legal)	(17.40)	(31.99)
Perceived personal	.364	.389
influence	(6.09)	(8.52)
Expected personal risk-1	-1.731	-1.823
(1=violent)	(12.85)	(19.90)
Expected personal risk-2 (1=no problems	.323	.311
expected)	(3.32)	(3.48)
Expected number of	.230	.195
participants (logged)	(10.50)	(12.77)
Constant	-2.037	—
	(10.67)	
R^2	.29	.60
Number of respondents	424	
Number of ratings	4,240	

Note: Numbers in parentheses are absolute values of *t*-ratio, Model 1 *t*-ratios are based on Huber standard errors and are corrected for heteroskedasticity due to clustering.

SUMMARY AND DISCUSSION

…

Many other questions were raised by this research. A methodological issue concerns the feasibility of fielding in East Germany and in eastern Europe factorial survey instruments that (1) include more information in the vignettes, (2) ask respondents to rate a larger number of vignettes, and (3) introduce more sophisticated rating tasks, such as the Stevens-type magnitude estimation techniques. Substantively, it will be important to investigate the effects on protest norms of additional features of protest situations and of characteristics of potential participants (e.g., health status and familial and occupational responsibilities), as well as external factors such as weather.

The theoretical challenge is to develop accounts of the emergence and operation of norms, accounts that yield many and refined predictions linking the precise character of norms

在总结部分，作者首先重申了研究的两个目标，然后概述了研究方法，最后介绍了研究发现。他们也提出了一些有待进一步探讨的理论、实证或方法上的问题。

在方法上作者关心的是在德国或东欧地区是否可能使用更复杂的调查-实验工具，如(1)虚拟案例包括更多的信息；(2)受访者给更多的虚拟案例打分；(3)采用更复杂的打分方法。

to characteristics of the population and the social context. The measurement procedures developed in this paper should prove useful in the task of testing the predictions derived from such theories.

析因调查-实验对于研究规范、信念和判断具有优势(Jasso, 2006),因为人们做出的决定是在特定的情境下,综合考虑各方面因素的结果。常规的析因调查-实验就是要通过虚拟案例构建这种特定的情境,同时通过数据分析从交织在一起的多种因素的作用中确定某个特定因素的独立作用。

Jasso 和 Opp 的这项研究虽然也采用析因调查-实验的方法,但其目的不是探究影响人们做出参与政治行动的因素的作用,而是为了测量决定人们参与政治行动的规范的特征,所以建构效度对于本项研究来说尤为重要,而这个建构效度是建立在析因调查-实验的效度之上的。

Jasso 是析因调查-实验的先行者,早在 1977 年他就和 Rossi 合作利用调查-实验研究分配公平的问题,在调查-实验的设计和分析上经验丰富。对于此项调查-实验,Jasso 的遗憾是每个受访者仅对 10 个虚拟案例打分,而在她以前的研究中曾经有过一个受访者对 60 个或 40 个虚拟案例打分。另外,虚拟案例的维度也可以再增加一些,打分的方法也可以再复杂一些。

析因调查-实验的方法在中国的社会科学研究中有很好的应用前景,实际上大多数国外析因调查-实验所涉及的主题都适用于中国背景,如对家庭或个人社会地位的判断、对分配公平的信念、堕胎或生育的情境抉择,以及专业人士的实务处理等。这种方法不仅可以对中国问题进行深入分析,也可以提高已有研究成果的外部效度。

3.4　政治学案例

Meng 等(2014)的论文是列举调查-实验的一个代表,研究的主题是省和市级地方领导对体制内渠道和网络渠道市民反映意见的回应行为。研究者基于已有的知识和预调查的验证,发现如果直接就这一问题提问地方领导,几乎所有人都会回答考虑通过这些渠道反映上来的意见。而在实际调查中采用列举调查-实验的方法却发现,只有略多于一半的受访者愿意考虑这些意见。可见,列举调查-实验的方法对于这项研究十分重要。

政治学研究常常会触及一些敏感性问题,得到真实回答往往是研究成功的先决条件,因此,列举调查-实验在政治学研究中的应用较多。孟天广及其合作者的这篇文章是目前少有的用列举调查-实验的方法研究中国政治问题的学术文章之一,显示了我国政治学研究在方法上的前沿性。而且这篇文章对列举调查-实验的设计、实施和分析方法均有详细介绍,对调查-实验中常遇到的一些问题也有论述,因此非常适宜作为范例评析。

Abstract

… In this article, we develop and test the concept of "receptivity," that is, whether autocrats are willing to incorporate citizen preferences into policy, using a list experiment of 1,377 provincial-and city-level leaders in China. Contrary to expectation, we find that leaders are similarly receptive to citizen suggestions obtained through either formal institutions or the Internet unless they perceive antagonism between the state and citizens, in which case receptivity to input from the Internet declines, while receptivity to formal institutions remains unchanged. Our findings show that whether quasi-democratic institutions are mere window dressing or true channels of responsiveness depends on the perceived quality of state-society relations.

作者在摘要中首先介绍了研究的背景和价值，并且提出了"回应性"的概念，即统治者是否愿意在决策中汲取民众的偏好。为测量中国地方领导在回应性上的态度，作者采用了列举调查-实验的方法。数据分析发现地方领导们对国家与社会关系的感受是影响其回应民意的一个重要条件。

Introduction

…

In this article, we focus on two questions related to the conditions for nondemocratic responsiveness: first, is there variation in responsiveness to

在文章的介绍部分点明两个研究问题，并简要介绍了研究思路。

different types of quasi-democratic institutions that provide citizens with opportunities for voice? Second, under what conditions will such channels be mere window dressing as opposed to true channels of responsiveness? ... We focus on one component of responsiveness, what we call "receptivity," that is, the willingness of political leaders to incorporate citizen preferences into policy.

Using an original survey experiment of 1,377 government and Party leaders in China, through indirect questioning, we find that when making policy and expenditure decisions, slightly over one-half of provincial-and city-level leaders are receptive to suggestions from citizens expressed through formal institutional channels or through the Internet. However, we find that receptivity to citizen feedback is conditional on perceptions of social contention. In localities where officials attribute poor government performance and public disobedience to antagonism between leaders and citizens, receptivity to

接下来，作者介绍了研究的方法和发现。在对 1337 名地方领导的调查中发现这些领导在回答回应性的问题时存在社会期许的现象，直接提问时几乎所有受访者都表示愿意回应正规和网络渠道反映的民意，而当采用列举调查-实验的非直接提问方法时，愿意回应的人数比例仅略超过一半。

citizen feedback obtained from the Internet declines. Our results also suggest that respondents may be less receptive to feedback from the Internet than input from formal institutions when faced with social contention. In Chinese, antagonism between leaders and citizens is ganqun guanxi jinzhang（干群关系紧张）, a concept that the Chinese Communist Party (CCP) connects with social instability in the form of protests and collective action (see "Quasi-Democratic Institutions to Mitigate Social Contention" section for more details). Our experimental design also reveals very high levels of social desirability bias whereby in direct questioning, nearly all respondents appear to be receptive to both formal and Internet channels.

…

Receptivity: A Precondition for Responsiveness

…

The Survey Experiment

To determine whether leaders in China are receptive to citizen sugges-

本部分阐述了"回应性"的概念,并且回顾了相关的研究成果。

tions obtained through the country's quasi-democratic institutions and the Internet, we conduct a survey experiment of provincial-and city-level officials. We measure receptivity using a list experiment to determine whether, when making policy and expenditure decisions, leaders are willing to seriously consider suggestions from residents obtained through these channels. …

…

List experiments are a form of indirect questioning that ask respondents how many items on a list of responses apply to them. The list includes a treatment, or sensitive, item. As long as the respondent does not select either none or all of the items on the list, the respondent knows that her privacy is protected because the researcher will not know which specific items apply. 8 Then, by varying the items on the list across randomly selected groups of respondents, list experiments allow us to estimate the proportion of respondents who are more likely to answer each

作者详细介绍了本项研究所采用的调查-实验的方法。首先指出具体采用了列举调查-实验的方法来测量回应性，然后对列举调查-实验做了简要的介绍。

treatment item in the affirmative.

We pretested the components of our list experiment with government and Party officials prior to implementation of the survey. We asked the following question of the control group:

> Several factors are listed below. How many of these factors do you think should be seriously considered when making local policy and expenditure decisions related to the needs of the people? You do not need to say which factors you agree with, only how many factors you think should be seriously considered.
>
> (1) Local administrative expenditures (本地行政管理支出)
>
> (2) Influence in attracting foreign investment (吸引外资的需要)
>
> (3) Scope of the migrant population (流动人口规模)
>
> …

Based on prior knowledge as well as survey pretesting, we believed that the chosen control items

作者展示了研究中所用列举实验的设计结果。该列举实验的问题是请受访者回答在制定有关民生的地方政策和支出决定时要考虑的因素有几个。控制条目设计了三个，分别为本地行政管理支出、吸引外资的需要和流动人口规模。基于先前的知识和预调查的发现，证实这些条目之间彼此负相关，这样可以避免列举调查-实验设计时可能存在的“天花板”或“地板”效应（参看 2.2.1 处理操纵设计）。

were negatively correlated. Local leaders who are focused on administrative expenditures are more likely to be from localities with less fiscal revenue and are less likely to have significant resources to spend on the welfare needs of migrants (Shue & Wong, 2007). Similarly, a focus on economic issues, such as foreign investment, is often an alternative strategy to one that focuses on social policy issues, such as migrant welfare. This trade-off in terms of emphasizing economic policies versus welfare policies is embodied in divergent policy positions of top leaders. ...

Treatment Conditions

To measure and compare the receptivity of state officials to citizen participation through formal and Internet channels, we divided the sample of provincial-and city-level officials into two treatment groups. One treatment group tests receptivity to suggestions from formal institutions, including a community-based institution (a residential committee), a Party-

此列举实验有两个处理，因而将受访者分为两个实验组。一个处理检测对体制内渠道民意的回应性；另一个则是对网络渠道民意的回应性。第一个处理条目是"市民通过居委会、党委会、人大代表等渠道反映的意见"。第二个处理条目是"市民通过网络反映的意见"。这样，

based institution (a Party committee), and a legislative institution (a people's congress), to reflect a range of quasi-democratic institutions adopted by the CCP. The second treatment group tests receptivity to suggestions from the Internet.

…

For the first treatment group, we asked a question identical to that of the control group, with the exception that a treatment item concerning suggestions of residents obtained from formal state institutional channels is appended to the list:

Several factors are listed below. How many of these factors do yo think should be seriously considered when making local policy and expenditure decisions related to the needs of the people? You do not need to say which factors you agree with, only how many factors you think should be seriously considered.

(1) Local administrative expenditures

(2) Influence in attracting foreign investment

实验组的受访者有四个条目可选，其中三个条目和控制组的条目完全相同，有一个条目是实验组所特有。

(3) Suggestions from residents expressed through the residential committee, local party organization, or people's congress representative(市民通过居委会、党委会、人大代表等渠道反映的意见)

(4) Scope of the migrant population

The second treatment condition focused on examining receptivity to suggestions obtained through the Internet. ...

For the second treatment group, the question again is identical to the control condition, with the exception that a treatment item concerning suggestions from residents obtained through the Internet is appended to the list:

Several factors are listed below. How many of these factors do yo think should be seriously considered when making local policy and expenditure decisions related to the needs of the people? You do not need to say which factors you agree with, only how many factors you think should be seriously considered.

(1) Local administrative expenditures

(2) Influence in attracting foreign investment

(3) Suggestions from residents expressed through the Internet(市民通过网络反映的意见)

(4) Scope of the migrant population

Measuring Antagonism

Our measure of antagonism between the state and citizens represents the respondents' perceptions of tensions between the state and citizens. Antagonism (干群关系紧张) is one of seven possible responses to the question: "In the course of governing, there may be obstacles to governance and public disobedience at the local level. What do you think are the main reasons for these problems?" (See Online Appendix C for the survey instrument in Chinese and English.) Other possible responses to this question include low

本项研究中的一个重要的自变量就是干群关系紧张(antagonism)，文章也展示了用来测量这一变量的问题形式。在一般的社会调查中，由于受访者使用的是相同的调查问卷，研究者不必担心不一致的启动效应。但对于搭载了调查-实验的社会调查，研究者就要十分小心不同的处理对其他调查问题应答的影响。对此作者也有周全的论述，从问卷间隔的时间、问题的顺序上来说明对"干群

public competence（公众素质不高）, inappropriate policies（政策不合理）, and poor policy implem-entation（执行方式不当）.

…

Our measure of antagonism is taken after the survey experiment. As a result, we must discuss the possibility that the treatment items in the list experiment are directly affecting the respondents' reported perceptions of social antagonism. We believe it is extremely unlikely that our experiment affects the respondents' reported perceptions of antagonism. The question measuring antagonism (Question C9) occurs 10 min (32 responses) after the survey experiment (Question B5). Because of this distance, we expect that any priming effect of the survey experiment would be very small. Furthermore, immediately before the question measuring antagonism, the respondents are asked how they obtain information about citizen preferences (Question C8). Answers to

关系紧张"变量的测量没有受到列举调查-实验的影响。

this question include in-person communications, focus groups, research, phone, email, online, and petitions. Because respondents in all treatment groups (and the control group) see this question immediately before our measure of antagonism, we believe any effect the survey experiment has in priming respondents is negated prior to our assessment of the antagonism variable.

Sampling and Balance

Our list experiment was conducted as part of the Local Governance and Public Goods Survey, which took place from May to August 2013 (P. Yang & Meng, 2014). To our knowledge, this survey is the first large-scale academic survey of government and Party leaders in China. Survey respondents are provincial-and city-level leaders who make and implement policy and expenditure decisions; they preside over Party organs and legislative bodies; and they have the authority to remove lower level officials.

本部分介绍了调查对象的来源、样本的选取方法和实验分组的方法。首先要报告的是调查的执行时间和项目名称，然后定义目标总体。继续报告的是抽样方法：将全国分为东部和中西部两大区域，每个大区选取 3 个省级行政单位，在每个省级行政单位内选取 2 至 3 个市级行政单位，最后一共选取 15 个市级行政单位，6 个在东部，9 个在西部。从以上描述中可

The sampling method for the Local Governance and Public Goods Survey divided China into an eastern region and a west-central region, and three provinces (or provincial-level municipalities) were selected from each region. In the eastern region, the provinces of Beijing, Shandong, and Zhejiang were selected, and in the west-central region, the provinces of Henan, Sichuan, and Guangxi were selected. Within each province, two to three city-level administrative units were selected, resulting in six city-level units in eastern China and nine city-level units in west-central China. Figure 1 compares the population and per capita GDP of the cities in the survey sample against all Chinese cities, and shows that the sample cities are representative of Chinese cities in terms of population size and level of economic development.

The surveys were distributed to officials in all 15 of the cities as well as the two provinces based on a quota sampling method aimed at reaching a

以判断这个调查在初级和二级单元的选取上采用了非概率的目的抽样方法。文章在图 1 展示了这些市级样本在人口规模和经济发展指标上与全国总体的比较，虽然目测比较相近，但文章认为这并不能证明这是一个中国城市的代表性样本。但是对于本项调查来说，因为抽样框难以获取，目的抽样的方式是最为适合的样本选取方法。此调查的末端抽样采用了配额抽样的方法，依据的指标是调查对象所在的单位性质和本人的行政级别。三种不同性质的单位按照6∶2∶2的比例配额，同时保证不同地区调查对象的行政级别分布相似。调查地点是受访者的工作地点，方式是自填。由于采用纸版问卷，执行中调查者随机排列不同版本的问卷，并且按照排列顺序发放给受访者。

certain number of respondents by the type of state unit and the rank of the respondent. Every effort was made to ensure that respondents across localities belonged to a similar mix of state entities and represented a similar mix of seniority rankings. In each selected locality, we provided local government collaborators with the following list of state units by category:

(1) Government administrative units: office of the local government (政府办公室), development and reform commission (发改委), finance (财政), education (教育), human resources and social security (人力资源和社会保障), public security (公安), health (卫生), taxation (税务), state-owned asset supervision and administration (国资委).

(2) CCP units: office of the party committee (党委办公室), organization department (组织部), propaganda department (宣传部).

(3) Other units: people's congress (人民代表大会), people's political consultative conference (人民政治协商会议), court (法院), procuratorate (检察院), Communist Youth League (共青团), Federation of Trade Unions (工会), Women's Federation (妇女联合会), Federation of Industry and Commerce (工商业联合会).

The local collaborator then enrolled officials from the listed organizations in each of the three categories based on a ratio of 6∶2∶2.

In addition to the category of the work unit, respondents were also enrolled to ensure a similar distribution in the government rank of the respondents across localities. Respondents included vice section chiefs and below (副科长级及以下), section chiefs (科长级), vice department chiefs (副处长级), and department chiefs and above (处长级及以上).

The surveys were distributed at the respondents' place of work, and randomization was achieved through the randomized ordering of the surveys. The surveys were completed by the respondents in private, and no personal identifiers were collected. The human subjects aspect of our experimental protocol was preapproved by our university's Institutional Review Board.

A total of 1,800 survey experiments were distributed, with 500 surveys containing the control condition and 650 surveys for each of the two treatment conditions. Of the 1,800 surveys distributed, 1,377 survey experiments were completed (76.5%). Of the completed surveys, 843 (61%) came from government administrative units, 211 (16%) from CCP units, and 313 (23%) from other units...

We find that the response rate for the control condition (75%) is similar to the response rate for the treatment conditions: 78% for formal institutions and 76% for the Internet.

本次调查最终发放了1800份问卷，其中控制组问卷500份，两个实验组问卷各650份。文中报告了访到率为76.5%，以及应答样本其他特征上的分布情况。作者特别强调无应答现象对实验结果的影响可以忽略。一是因为控制组和两个实验组内的应答率基本相同；二是不同的处理手段不大可能会影响到受访者是否应答。

We believe it is very unlikely that differences in the response rate between treatment and control groups resulted in a selection bias because the response rates are similar and because the respondents have already spent a few minutes on the survey answering demographic and background questions before encountering the list experiment; they are thus invested in the survey and are unlikely to stop completing the survey because they have encountered the control condition, which had the lowest response rate.

Table 1 shows the preintervention characteristics of the respondents by treatment group: …

作者对随机化分组的操控结果进行了检验，证明控制组和两个实验组在六个特征上没有显著差异。不过 Mutz (2011) 认为这种检验是没有必要的。

Results

First, we present the observed data and mean results by treatment group from the list experiment to compare the receptivity between the formal and Internet channels. Then,

本项研究的数据分析分为两步：首先对列举实验中观测到的数据进行分析，以比较对正规渠道和网络渠道反映

to evaluate whether receptivity is conditional on antagonism, we present the results using difference-in-means estimators with subsets of data and maximum likelihood estimators with an array of model specifications ...

Overall Receptivity

Table 2 summarizes the observed data for the control group and each treatment group in our survey experiment. More than 40% of the respondents in the control group answer affirmatively to all three control items. While this indicates a potential risk of ceiling effects, we find that when modeling ceiling and floor effects, the estimated population proportion of ceiling liars and floor liars is close to zero and does not alter our substantive conclusions. The left panel of Figure 2 shows the mean response rate for each group—2.3 items for the control group, 2. 8 items for the formal institutions treatment group, and 2.9 items for the Internet channel treatment group.

的意见的回应性。然后采用均值差和最大似然估计的方法分析干群关系紧张的感受对于回应性的影响。

在报告列举实验分析结果时有必要首先展示观测数据的分布情况，见表 2。然后基于这个分布情况，计算两个实验组中选取处理条目的比例和置信区间。这个结果用带有估计值和置信区间的箱图或线段图展示较为直观，如图 2 所示。

Based on these mean responses, the right panel of Figure 2 shows that the estimated proportion of respondents who are receptive to citizen suggestions from formal channels is 53% (95% confidence interval of 42% ~ 65%) and the estimated proportion of respondents who are receptive to citizen suggestions from the Internet is 57% (46% ~ 69%). This shows that, on average, receptivity to formal and Internet channels is very similar...

...

Table 2 Observed Data From the List Experiment on What Factors Should Be Considered When Making Policy and Expenditure Decisions Related to the Needs of the People

Response value	Control		Treatment			
			Formal		Internet	
	Frequency	Proportion	Frequency	Proportion	Frequency	Proportion
0	3	0.8%	7	1.4%	3	0.6%
1	46	12.3%	52	10.2%	52	10.5%
2	162	43.3%	122	24.0%	116	23.5%
3	163	43.6%	168	33.0%	159	32.2%
4			160	31.4%	164	33.2%
Total	374		509		494	

The table displays the number of respondents for each response value and its proportion for each of the treatment groups as well as control group.

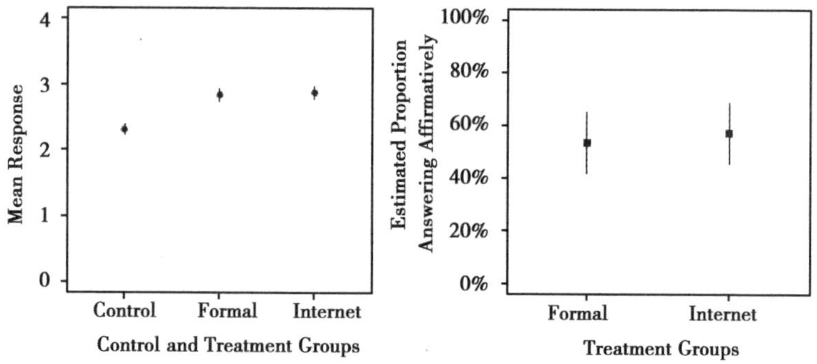

Figure 2　Mean response to control and treatment items (left panel). Estimated proportions of respondents answering treatment items in the affirmative (right panel).

"Formal" refers to whether or not "suggestions from local residents expressed through the residential committee, local party organization, or people's congress representative" should be seriously considered when making policy and expenditure decisions. "Internet" refers to whether or not "suggestions from local residents expressed through the Internet" should be seriously considered when making policy and expenditure decisions. 95% confidence intervals are shown.

Even though slightly over one-half of the respondents say they would seriously consider suggestions from residents through our list experiment, in direct questioning of the respondents in the control group, 98% (96%~100%) report they would be receptive to suggestions obtained through formal channels and 96% (93%~98%) report they would be receptive to suggestions obtained from

列举调查-实验中在控制组中直接提问受访者关于敏感条目的问题是检测社会期许的有效办法。本项研究就采用这种方法，证明了省级和市级地方领导们对于回应性问题的应答存在社会期许的行为，而列举实验的办法则获得了相对真实的答案。

the Internet. This shows that social desirability bias is large and is present for both treatment items… In other words, receptivity is a socially desirable behavior for provincial and city-level leaders.

…

Antagonism Between Citizens and Officials

To evaluate whether the receptivity of leaders to citizen suggestions is conditional on perceptions of antagonism between state and society, we employ a difference-in-means analysis as well as a maximum likelihood estimator. These estimators provide different trade-offs in terms of statistical efficiency and consistency. Even though the difference-in-means estimator is consistent, it is statis-tically inefficient due to the aggregation of responses, and even though the maximum likelihood estimator is more efficient, it may be less consistent (Blair & Imai, 2012; A. Glynn, 2010).

作者介绍了这部分所采用的分析方法及各自的优劣，即均值差的方法得到估计值稳定但统计功效差，而最大似然法得到的估计值统计功效好但不稳定。

Using the difference-in-means estimator, we compare the mean response with our list experiment between the formal and Internet channels for (a) all respondents, (b) respondents who do and do not perceive antagonism, and (c) matched subsets of respondents who do and do not perceive antagonism. For the difference-in-means analysis of matched respondents, we use coarsened exact matching to divide the respondents into two data sets: those who do report antagonism and those do not report antagonism, which are similar in terms of the preintervention covariates of age, gender, level of education, government rank, whether they belong to a CCP unit, years in government, and the local level of economic development (Iacus, King, & Porro, 2012). The right panel of Figure 3 shows the covariate balance for the matched subset of respondents.

The left panel of Figure 3 shows the results of the difference-in-means analysis. This figure shows the mean response to the Internet channel

作者将应答者分为几个人群，然后利用均值差的分析比较了他们对于正规渠道和网络渠道反映意见的回应性的差异。这几个人群分别为：

(1)所有应答者；

(2)感受到干群关系紧张的应答者；

(3)没有感受到干群关系紧张的应答者；

(4)粗化精确匹配后的感受到干群关系紧张的应答者；

(5)粗化精确匹配后的没有感受到干群关系紧张的应答者。

采用粗化精确匹配的目的在于控制住一些协变量对于分析结果的影响。这几组的均值差及其95%的置信区间展示在图3的左图中。可以非常直观地看出图中最后一组，即粗化精确匹配后的感受到干群关系紧张的应答者对于两种不同渠道反映意见的回应性有显著差别。文章对这一分析结果作了详细解释。

treatment minus the mean response to the formal channel treatment. Positive estimates denote respondents are more receptive to the Internet channel treatment, and negative estimates denote they are more receptive to the formal channel treatment. Looking at all respondents, as expected, there is no statistical difference in receptivity to formal and Internet channels. Similarly, when examining all respondents who do not report antagonism as well as the matched subset of respondents who do not report antagonism, the respondents do not reveal more receptivity to formal or Internet channels. However, when examining all respondents who do report antagonism as well as the matched subset of respondents who do report antagonism, we see a negative difference in the means estimates, which shows respondents are more receptive to formal channels than to the Internet channel. For respondents who perceive antagonism, the mean response to the formal institutions treatment is 2.8, and the mean response to the Internet treatment is 2.6. Due to the lack of statistical efficiency, this difference-in-means estimate is not statistically significant at the 95% level. However, among the respondents who perceive antagonism in the matched subset of data, the average response to the formal institutions treatment is 2.8, the average response to the Internet treatment is 2.4, and the difference in the average responses is statistically significant at the 95% level. This difference-in-means analysis shows that among respondents who perceive antagonism between state and society, receptivity to the Internet channel is lower than receptivity to formal channels, whereas among respondents who do not perceive antagonism, there is no difference in receptivity to these two types of channels.

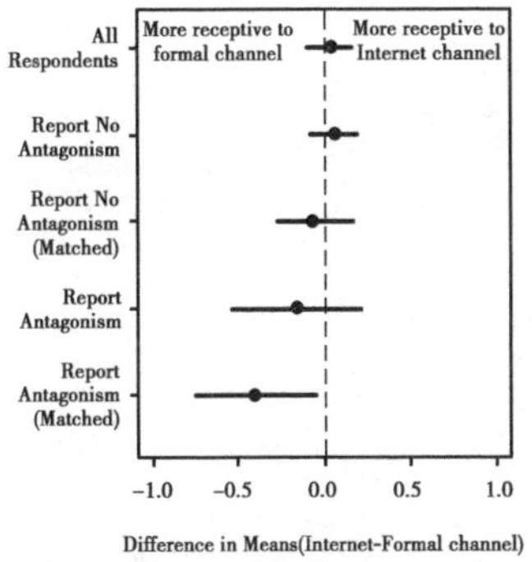

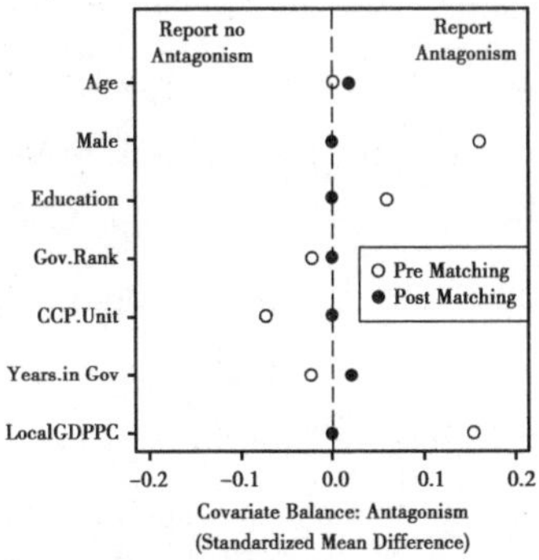

Figure 3　Difference-in-means estimator between Internet and formal channels for all respondents and subsets of respondents who do and do not report antagonism (left panel). Covariate balance of preintervention variables for respondents who do 95% confidence intervals are shown.

In the above analysis, we only examine the difference between receptivity to formal and Internet channels. To examine the effect of antagonism on the difference in receptivity to Internet versus formal institutional channels, we compare the difference-in-means results between the matched set of respondents who do perceive antagonism and those who do not (rows 3 and 5 of Figure 3). The difference in the average response to Internet versus formal institutions among matched respondents who report antagonism is −0.408 (SE = 0.176),

文章对于匹配后感受和没有感受到干群关系紧张的两组应答者的回应性进行均值差分析，发现两组人群的应答差异在0.10水平上显著，意味着感受到干群关系紧张会降低应答者对网络渠道民意的回应。

whereas the difference in mean response to Internet versus formal institutions among matched respondents who do not report antagonism is-0.064 (SE=0.111). This implies we can reject the null hypothesis of no difference in the effect of antagonism on the mean response between Internet and formal institutions treatment items at the 10% level (90% confidence interval [CI] = [-0.687, -0.001]). In other words, the data suggest that receptivity to input obtained through the Internet may be lower than receptivity to input from formal institutions when there is social antagonism.

We employ two additional estimators proposed by Blair and Imai (2012) and Imai (2011) to further test the robustness of our finding—a nonlinear least squares estimator and a maximum likelihood estimator. ...

作者又采用第二种方法，及 2.4.2 节中提及的 Blair and Imai (2012) 和 Imai (2011) 提出的方法进一步验证分析结果的稳健性。

Table 3　Maximum Likelihood Estimator for Formal Channels

	Model 1	Model 2	Model 3	Model 4	Model 5	Model 6
Intercept	0.353	1.135	−0.853	−2.357	35.432	7.623
	(0.989)	(1.343)	(4.834)	(4.574)	(17.553)	(11.717)
Antagonism with residents	−0.118	0.107	0.007	−0.078	0.131	0.236
	(0.546)	(0.664)	(0.646)	(0.616)	(1.006)	(0.667)
Control variables						
Age		−0.027	−0.022	−0.029	−0.028	−0.022
		(0.044)	(0.045)	(0.044)	(0.049)	(0.046)
Male		−0.319	−0.267	−0.298	−0.391	−0.395
		(0.47)	(0.469)	(0.454)	(0.605)	(0.47)
Education		0.351	0.310	0.230	0.273	0.167
		(0.423)	(0.424)	(0.429)	(0.471)	(0.434)
Gov rank		−0.319	−0.351	−0.406	−0.744	−0.506
		(0.302)	(0.297)	(0.315)	(0.352)	(0.324)
CCP unit		0.476	0.403	0.586	0.942	0.521
		(0.591)	(0.609)	(0.63)	(0.956)	(0.72)
Years in gov		0.027	0.022	0.038	0.035	0.031
		(0.043)	(0.044)	(0.043)	(0.049)	(0.047)
Local GDP per capita			0.190	0.413	−2.924	−0.372
			(0.456)	(0.45)	(1.545)	(1.096)
Fixed effects City				−0.665		−0.496
				(0.508)		(0.554)
Guangxi					−3.372	−1.855
					(1.433)	(1.278)
Sichuan					−3.351	−2.475
					(1.555)	(1.542)
Shandong					−6.519 1	−3.578
					(2.274)	(1.677)
Zhejiang					−0.054	−1.642
					(1.423)	(1.423)
Henan					−4.944	−2.285
					(2.185)	(1.706)

Estimated coefficients based on a maximum likelihood estimator where the outcome variables are whether or not "suggestions from residents obtained through channels such as residential committees, local party organizations, and people's congress representatives" are factors respondents will seriously consider when making policy and expenditure decisions, CCP = Chinese Communist Party. Standard error in parentheses.

Table 3 shows the coefficient estimates of the maximum likelihood estimator for six model specifications where the dependent variable is receptivity to formal channels, and Table 4 shows the coefficient estimates of the same model specifications where the dependent variable is receptivity to the Internet channel. The first model specification examines the effect of antagonism on receptivity. The second model specification includes as controls the preintervention variables of age, gender, level of education, government rank, whether the respondent belongs to a CCP unit, and the number of years the respondent has worked in government. The third model adds local per capita GDP in 2012. The fourth model adds fixed effects for city-level respondents, the fifth model adds provincial fixed effects, and the sixth model includes all preintervention covariates as well as the city and provincial fixed effects.

Table 3 shows that across all six model specifications, perceptions of

作者分别以对正规渠道和网络渠道的回应性为因变量，采用最大似然法，通过 6 个模型来估计干群关系紧张的感受对因变量的影响。并在表 3 和表 4 中展示了分析结果。这些分析结果再次证明当应答者感受到干群关系紧张时，其对于正规渠道反映意见的回应没有显著变化，但对于网络渠道反映的意见会倾向于不理会。

state-society antagonism do not predict whether or not the respondents would seriously consider "suggestions from residents obtained through channels such as residential committees, local party organizations, and people's congress representatives" when making policy and expenditure decisions related to the livelihood of the people. Three coefficient estimates are positive, two are negative, one is near zero, and none are statistically significant.

Table 4　Maximum Likelihood Estimator for the Internet Channel

	Model 1	Model 2	Model 3	Model 4	Model 5	Model 6
Intercept	−0.337	1.515	5.210	5.029	27.486	30.283
	(1.039)	(1.721)	(4.342)	(4.479)	(12.769)	(14.746)
Antagonism with	−0.776	−0.927	−1.021	−1.034	−1.019	−1.089
residents	(0.534)	(0.55)	(0.547)	(0.552)	(0.583)	(0.593)
Control variables						
Age		−0.065	−0.058	−0.059	−0.094	−0.103
		(0.049)	(0.051)	(0.05)	(0.057)	(0.059)
Male		0.039	−0.001	−0.015	−0.069	−0.080
		(0.439)	(0.447)	(0.455)	(0.484)	(0.498)
Education		0.436	0.473	0.498	0.447	0.473
		(0.476)	(0.488)	(0.494)	(0.488)	(0.51)

Continued

	Model 1	Model 2	Model 3	Model 4	Model 5	Model 6
Gov rank		−0.377 (0.339)	−0.458 (0.345)	−0.460 (0.344)	−0.424 (0.359)	−0.405 (0.364)
CCP unit		0.002 (0.592)	0.050 (0.601)	−0.032 (0.582)	0.270 (0.683)	0.198 (0.721)
Years in gov		0.101 (0.051)	0.101 (0.052)	0.105 (0.053)	0.130 (0.059)	0.138 (0.061)
Local GDP per capita			−0.369 (0.394)	−0.352 (0.425)	−2.266 (1.094)	−2.515 (1.286)
Fixed effects City				−0.030 (0.525)		0.180 (0.611)
Guangxi					−2.000 (1.281)	−2.135 (1.34)
Sichuan					−1.142 (1.431)	−1.216 (1.484)
Shandong					−2.698 (1.886)	−2.994 (2.07)
Zhejiang					0.384 (0.988)	0.453 (1.002)
Henan					−3.117 (1.727)	−3.433 (1.875)

Estimated coefficients based on a maximum likelihood estimator where the outcome variables are whether or not "suggestions from residents obtained through the Internet" are factors respondents will seriously consider when making policy and expenditure decision, CCP = Chinese Communist Party. Standard error in parentheses.

In contrast, Table 4 shows that across all six model specifications, perceptions of state-society antagonism negatively predict whether respondents would seriously consider "suggestions from residents obtained through the Internet" when making policy and expenditure decisions related to the livelihood of the people. The coefficient estimates are all negative, and results in Models 2 through 6 are statistically significant at the 90% level.

Although we know from Tables 3 and 4 that antagonism predicts decreased receptivity to the Internet channel but not to the formal channel, we hone in on our quantity of interest—the difference in the estimated percentage of respondents who are receptive to each type of channel conditional on antagonism by estim-ating the mean difference in predicted values in Figure 4.

为了使分析结果更为直观，文章再次使用图形来展示。图 4 中的数据基于表 3 和表 4 中的第 3 个模型的预测值的均值差异及 95% 的置信区间。从图中可以更为清晰地读出是否感受到干群关系紧张的两组人回应正规渠道的预测比例差为 0%，95% 的置信区间在正负 25% 之间。而对于回应网络渠道的预测比例差接近 -25%，95% 的置信区间不包含 0%。

Figure 4 shows the mean difference in predicted values across two data sets, one data set of respondents reporting antagonism and one data set of respondents reporting no antagonism, where all other covariates are set to the observed values of each respondent. This figure shows that for formal channels, there is no difference between those who perceive antagonism and those who do not perceive antagonism in the estimated proportions of respondents who are receptive. The difference in the estimated percentage of resp-ondents who are receptive to formal channels between those who do and those who do not perceive antagonism is 0%, with 95% CIs of −24% to 25%. In contrast, for the Internet channel, Figure 4 shows that respondents are less receptive to the Internet channel when they perceive antagonism. Specifically, the difference in the estimated percentage of respondents who are receptive to the Internet channel between those who do and those who do not perceive antagonism is −23%, with 95% CIs of −46% to −1%.

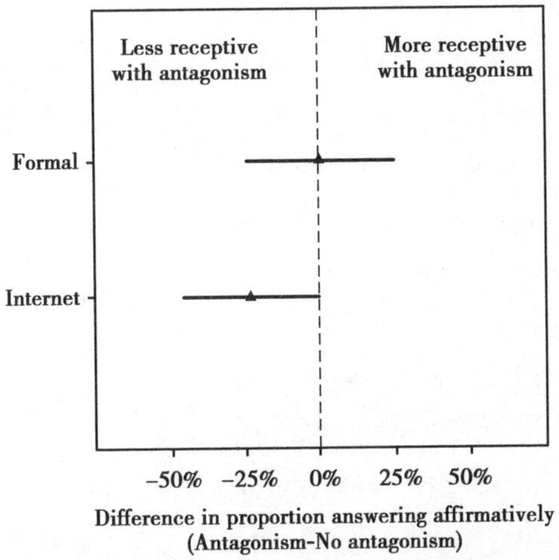

Figure 4　Difference in estimated proportions of respondents answering the treatment item in the affirmative based on respondents who do and do not report antagonism.

Represents the mean difference in predicted values of the maximum likelihood estimator Model 3 from Table 3 and 4, where all other covariates are set to observed values. 95% confidence intervals are shown.

Other model specification produces extremely similar results.

To compare the effect of antagonism on the Internet channel and the formal institutions channel, we examine the statistical significance of the difference in mean predicted values of the maximum likelihood estimator based on Model 3 from Tables 3 and 4. In other words, we compare

作者也对图 4 中展示的结果进行了统计检验，证明感受到干群关系紧张的影响在 10%的统计水平上显著。

the difference in the two statistical estimates presented in Figure 4. The effect of antagonism on the proportion of respondents answering the Internet treatment versus the formal institutions treatment items in the affirmative is −0.235 with standard error of 0.142. This means we can reject the null hypothesis of no difference in the effect of antagonism on the estimated proportion of respondents answering the Internet channel and the formal institutions treatment items in the affirmative at the 10% level. In other words, similar to the difference-in-means analysis, receptivity to citizen feedback from the Internet is lower than receptivity to citizen feedback from formal institutions when respondents perceive antagonism between the state and citizens.

…

Concluding Remarks

In this article, we seek to expand our understanding of responsiveness under authoritarianism. … As such, the concept of receptivity—

文章的最后一部分是结语。此部分总结了此项研究对于"回应性"概念的界定，基于调查-实验数据分析的发现，

and, by definition, responsiveness—should not be applied wholesale to all authoritarian, competitive authoritarian, or even transitional regimes.

…

Our finding reveals that for many (though not all) local leaders, these quasi-democratic institutions are more than mere window dressing. Because our research is focused at the subnational level, our findings cannot automatically be extended to Chinese national institutions, "Chinese governance" writ large, or to other nondemocratic regimes. Receptivity may be present in local government institutions because expressed preferences at these levels may be less threatening politically, while recep-tivity may be nonexistent at the national level, or the conditions for responsiveness may be qualitatively different at the national level. Finally, although we show that local leaders are receptive to citizen suggestions, we do not know whether they actually incorporate these suggestions into policy decisions. And, as noted in

以及研究结果的意义和局限。

the "Receptivity: A Precondition for Responsiveness," because of explicit and implicit limits on citizen expression, even if subnational leaders in China do incorporate suggestions into action, the scope of their responsiveness is truncated, and "responsiveness" in China's authoritarian context differs from responsiveness in a democratic setting. Finally, these findings point to several potential avenues for future research, including examination of the reasons for the conditional receptivity we observe and how actual levels of social contention and collective action influence responsiveness to different types of quasi-democratic institutions.

列举调查-实验在美国多应用于对种族态度和投票行为的研究中,因为在美国的政治文化氛围下这方面的调查问题最容易引发社会期许的应答。在中国也同样存在一些敏感问题以至于受访者在应答时会有所顾忌,不愿说出真实想法。孟天广等在对中国地方官员回应性的研究中就遇到了这个问题,理论上认为这些地方官员没有必然的动机去回应市民意见,但如果在调查中直接询问,他们则可能会给出"政治正确"的答案,表示会认真考虑民意。于是,他们在研究中采用了列举调查-实验的方法。

列举调查-实验的设计看似很简单,然而高质量的设计需要有周全的考虑。对于本项研究的调查-实验,为避免条目设计时可能存在的“天花板”或“地板”效应做了预调查,证实这些条目之间彼此负相关。在问题的顺序上,把对“干群关系紧张”变量的测量和列举条目的问题隔开,以避免启动效应。此文中讨论了样本的代表性和问题无应答对研究的影响,还对样本的随机化分配做了统计检测。

在对调查-实验数据的分析上,作者首先证明了列举调查-实验对于本项研究的必要性,直接提问有接近 100%的受访者回答会考虑从正规渠道或网络渠道反映的民意,但调查-实验数据却证明仅有大约一半的人真的这么认为。当用常规的均值差方法没有发现对正规渠道和网络渠道反映民意的回应比例上存在显著差异时,作者先是应用了粗化精确匹配技术,比较感受不同干群关系的受访者子群体间的差异,然后采用了 Imai(2011)提出的多元回归模型方法,在控制受访者一些特征的情况下,分析地方干群关系紧张对于地方官员回应性的影响,并得出了有意义的结论。

总而言之,这篇文章在列举调查-实验的设计、分析,还有结果报告和讨论方面都值得学习者们借鉴。中国的调查研究数据中存在诸多社会期许或政治正确的应答,对此研究者们要保持谨慎和清醒,并且可以考虑运用列举调查-实验的方法来获取真实的数据信息。

/ 第 4 章 /

调查-实验分析的统计软件应用

大多数统计软件都可用于对调查-实验数据的分析。一般认为,SAS 统计软件对于实验数据的分析能力最强,因而广泛应用在医药卫生行业,但由于其价格较高,编程语言较为复杂,在社会科学研究领域应用不多。这里重点介绍社会科学研究者们较为常用的统计软件:SPSS 和 STATA,主要介绍如何在这两个软件上实现对调查-实验数据的基本分析。不过,对列举实验数据的多元回归分析,由于方法较新,在 SPSS 和 STATA 上还未能实现,本部分将基于 Imai 等作者提供的 R 程序包来进行实例讲解。

用来分析的软件版本分别为:SPSS20、STATA13 和R3.2.3。

4.1 常规调查-实验的数据分析

在此部分主要介绍使用 SPSS 和 STATA 执行常规的数据分析,包括均值差的 T 检验,方差分析,以及回归分析。所用调查-实验原始数据来自社会科学分时实验室(Time-sharing Experiments in the Social Sciences, TESS),示例数据经由 SAGE 研究方法数据集(SAGE research methods dataset)整理并获取。[①]

4.1.1 均值差

这个调查-实验的研究目的是发现美国人的国家认同感是否与其对亚群体的态度显著相关。实验中将受访者随机分为两组,一组在回答态度问题前展示美国国旗的图像,作为实验组;另一组

① 本章示例所用数据集,请发邮件至"万卷方法"书友会邮箱 wjffsyh@ foxmail.com 索取,注明书名即可。

则没有展示,直接回答态度问题,作为控制组。本示例考察美国人对其中一组亚群体——外国移民的态度。测量尺度为 1 到 10,"1"代表完全没有好感,"10"代表非常有好感。

示例数据集命名为 Exdata1,共包括两个变量,3064 个观测值。具体变量描述见表 4.1,数据集中 immigrant 为结果变量,flag 为处理变量。

表 4.1　Exdata1 数据集中的变量

变量名称	变量描述	取值范围
immigrant	受访者对于外国移民的态度	1~10
flag	是否展示给受访者美国国旗图像	0~1

SPSS 软件

在做数据分析前,首先要掌握变量的分布情况。均值差的 T 检验需要满足三个假定:

①两组的观测样本彼此独立抽选;

②两组观测样本均选自正态分布的总体;

③两组样本观测到的研究变量的方差相等。

在此调查-实验中,控制组和实验组随机分配,满足第一个假定。下面我们从统计角度来检验第二和第三个假定。SPSS 软件中的[探索]功能可以完成这个任务。具体操作是在菜单中选择:

[分析]→[描述统计]→[探索]

在弹出的窗口里将 immigrant 变量选入[因变量列表]对话框内,将 flag 变量选入[因子列表]对话框内。然后单击窗口右侧[绘制]按钮,在弹出的窗口勾选[直方图][带检验的正态图],以及 Levene 检验下的[幂估计]，如图 4.1 所示。

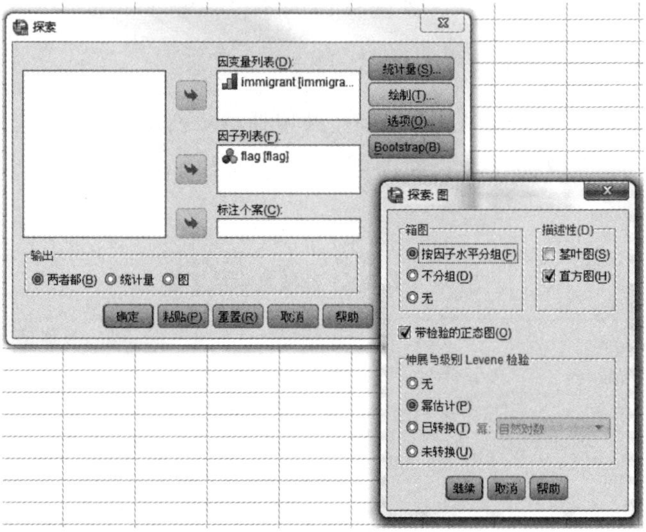

图 4.1　SPSS[探索]分析操作示意图

输出结果中首先查看各组的样本个数及数据值缺失情况(图 4.2)。没有展示国旗图像的控制组样本数为 1528 个，展示了国旗图像的实验组样本数为 1536 个，两组样本个数比较平衡，并且在 immigrant 变量上没有出现变量值缺失。

案例处理摘要

		案例					
		有效		缺失		合计	
	flag	N	百分比	N	百分比	N	百分比
immigrant	no flag (control group)	1528	100.0%	0	0.0%	1528	100.0%
	flag (treatment group)	1536	100.0%	0	0.0%	1536	100.0%

图 4.2　SPSS 输出(案例处理摘要)

接下来的常规操作是查看直方图(图 4.3)，这样可以对数据分布有直观的了解。可以观察到控制组和实验组中选择量表的中间位置“5”的受访者人数最多，并且选择“5”以上量表数值的受访者数目较多。两组受访者的应答特征比较相似。

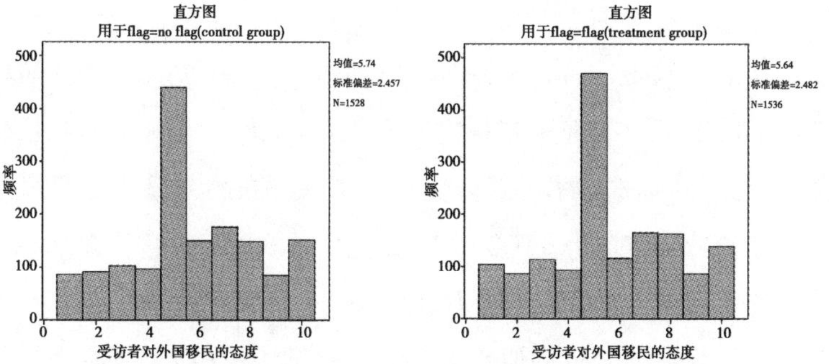

图 4.3　SPSS 输出(直方图)

从统计值的描述和检验上可以进一步了解数据的特征。如图 4.4 所示,在对外国移民的态度上,控制组受访者的量表均值为 5.74,方差为 6.035;实验组受访者的量表均值为 5.64,方差为 6.161。均值差为 0.10,方差比较接近。此外,两组数据的偏度和峰度均小于 1,可认为近似于正态分布。

描述

	flag			统计量	标准误
immigrant	no flag (control group)	均值		5.74	.063
		均值的 95% 置信区间	下限	5.61	
			上限	5.86	
		5% 修整均值		5.76	
		中值		5.00	
		方差		6.035	
		标准差		2.457	
		极小值		1	
		极大值		10	
		范围		9	
		四分位距		3	
		偏度		.005	.063
		峰度		-.624	.125
	flag (treatment group)	均值		5.64	.063
		均值的 95% 置信区间	下限	5.51	
			上限	5.76	
		5% 修整均值		5.65	
		中值		5.00	
		方差		6.161	
		标准差		2.482	
		极小值		1	
		极大值		10	
		范围		9	
		四分位距		4	
		偏度		.011	.062
		峰度		-.655	.125

图 4.4　SPSS 输出(统计描述)

正态性检验有两种方式：一种是采用正规的统计检验，SPSS 中采用的是 Kolmogorov-Smirnov（K-S）和 Shapiro-Wilk（S-W）的检验（图 4.5）；另一种是通过标准 Q-Q 图（图 4.6）。K-S 和 S-W 检验的零假设是“抽选样本的总体数据是正态分布的”，输出结果显示两个检验的 p 值均为 0.000，意味着至少在 0.001 的显著性水平上要拒绝零假设。而在标准 Q-Q 图上，数据点基本在一条直线上，由此可以认为数据分布近似正态分布。根据中央极限定理，当样本量较大时，即使样本的总体数据出现非正态分布，T 检验仍然适用。但对于小于 50 的样本量，如果出现非正态的情形，T 检验则可能给出错误的检验结果。本调查-实验的各组样本量接近 2000，并且没有表现出严重的偏态，因此可以用 T 检验来分析实验结果。

正态性检验

flag		Kolmogorov-Smirnov[a]			Shapiro-Wilk		
		统计量	df	Sig.	统计量	df	Sig.
immigrant	no flag (control group)	.152	1528	.000	.951	1528	.000
	flag (treatment group)	.166	1536	.000	.948	1536	.000

a. Lilliefors 显著水平修正

图 4.5　SPSS 输出（正态性检验）

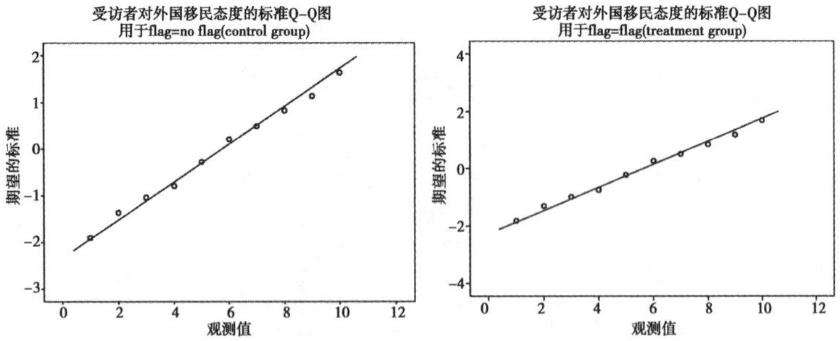

图 4.6　SPSS 输出（标准 Q-Q 图）

针对均值差 T 检验的第三条假定，做方差齐性检验。SPSS 输出上展示基于均值的 Levene 统计值为 0.205，p 值为 0.651，因此不能拒绝零假设,可以断定 immigrant 变量在两组上的方差均等,如图 4.7 所示。

方差齐性检验

		Levene 统计量	df1	df2	Sig.
immigrant	基于均值	.205	1	3062	.651
	基于中值	.015	1	3062	.902
	基于中值和带有调整后的 df	.015	1	3061.963	.902
	基于修整均值	.208	1	3062	.648

图 4.7　SPSS 输出(方差齐性检验)

了解了数据的基本情况并判断均值差 T 检验的假定条件基本满足后,就可以进行 T 检验。SPSS 中的操作方法也很简单,步骤如下:

[分析]→[比较均值]→[独立样本 T 检验]

这时会弹出[独立样本 T 检验]窗口,将 immigrant 变量放入[检验变量]对话框,将 flag 变量放入[分组变量]对话框中,然后单击[定义组],在弹出的窗口里[组 1]位置录入 0,[组 2]位置录入 1(图 4.8)。

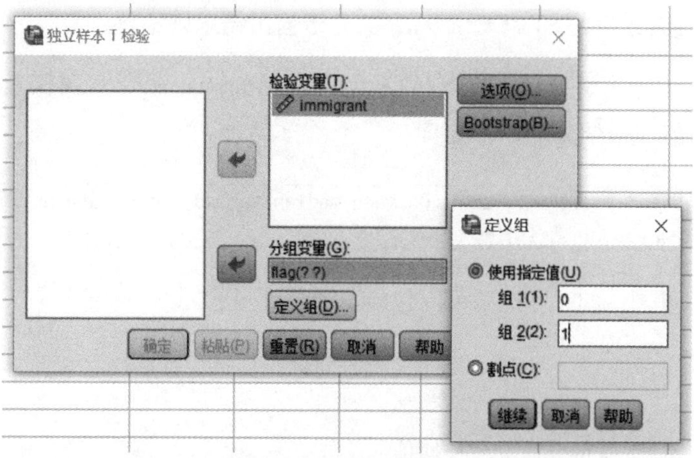

图 4.8　SPSS"独立样本检验"操作示意图

操作后的输出结果如图 4.9 所示。第一个表格中展示的是 immigrant 变量在各组的基本统计描述值；第二个表格展示的是均值差及其检验结果，其中也包含了方差齐性检验。从输出结果上看，均值差为 0.099，t 值为 1.108，在自由度为 3062 的情形下，p 值为 0.268，解释为控制组和实验组的受访者在对外国移民态度上仅存在着微小差别，并且这个差别在统计上不显著。这意味着是否看到美国国旗的图像没有影响到受访者对外国移民的态度。

组统计量

flag		N	均值	标准差	均值的标准误
immigrant	no flag (control group)	1528	5.74	2.457	.063
	flag (treatment group)	1536	5.64	2.482	.063

独立样本检验

		方差方程的 Levene 检验		均值方程的 t 检验						
		F	Sig.	t	df	Sig.(双侧)	均值差值	标准误差值	差分的 95% 置信区间	
									下限	上限
immigrant	假设方差相等	.205	.651	1.108	3062	.268	.099	.089	-.076	.274
	假设方差不相等			1.108	3061.919	.268	.099	.089	-.076	.274

图 4.9　SPSS 输出(独立样本检验)

STATA 软件

以上 SPSS 的分析结果也可以用 STATA 软件实现。此处仅列出对应分析的 STATA 命令语句，对于输出结果则不再讲解。

(1)探索分析。在 STATA 中可以用 tabstat 命令实现探索分析，语句示例如下：

```
tabstat immigrant, stats(n mean median var sd max min range iqr
skewness kurtosis) by (flag)
```

其中 stats( )选项可以包括下列统计量：

n	非缺失观测值总数
sum	总和
mean	平均值

median	中位值
max	最大值
min	最小值
range	极差=最大值-最小值
p1	第 1 百分位数(其他分位数同理)
iqr	四分位距=第 75 百分位数-第 25 百分位数
var	方差
sd	标准差
semean	均值的标准误
skewness	偏度
kurtosis	峰度

(2)绘制直方图。STATA 中绘制直方图的命令语句为:

```
hist (immigrant) if flag= =0, freq
hist (immigrant) if flag= =1, freq
```

逗号后选项中的 freq 也可换作 percent 或者 density,这样直方图的纵轴表示的就不是频数,而是百分比或密度。

(3)正态性检验。STATA 软件中常用的正态性检验有基于偏度和峰度的 Skewness-Kurtosis 和 Shapiro-Wilk 检验,STATA 命令分别为 sktest 和 swilk。对控制组和实验组进行检验命令语句示例如下:

```
sktest immigrant if flag= =0
sktest immigrant if flag= =1

bysort flag: swilk immigrant
```

绘制标准 Q-Q 图的命令语句为：

```
qnorm (immigrant) if flag = =0
qnorm (immigrant) if flag = =1
```

(4)方差齐性检验。STATA 中运行 Levene 检验的命令为：

```
robvar immigrant, by (flag)
```

输出结果中 W0 是基于平均值,W50 是基于中位数,W10 是基于修整 10%数值后的均值。

(5)均值差的 T 检验。STATA 中对于两个独立样本的 T 检验的命令为：

```
ttest immigrant, by (flag) # 假设方差相等
ttest immigrant, by (flag) unequal # 假设方差不等
```

输出结果会提供单边和双边的检验结果。

4.1.2 方差分析

用于方差分析的调查-实验案例是想检测人们对于患有某些严重疾病的亲属是否会感到羞耻。实验中选取了三种疾病:精神分裂症、药物依赖和肺气肿。前两种疾病属于精神疾病,而第三种属于器质性疾病。实验处理采用虚拟案例的形式,描述一个家庭成员得了以上三种疾病之一,虚拟案例示例如下：

琼是弗兰克的妻子。弗兰克今年 30 岁,患有精神分裂症。弗兰克和家人一起住在公寓里,在公寓附近的商店做售货员。弗兰克多次因病住院,疾病已经严重影响了他的生活。

然后询问受访者在多大程度上同意“琼应该为弗兰克的疾病

感到羞耻”。测量尺度为 1 到 7,“1”代表完全不同意,“7”代表非常同意。

示例数据集命名为 Exdata2,共包括两个变量,960 个观测值。具体变量描述见表 4.2,数据集中 shame 为结果变量,condition 为处理变量。

表 4.2　Exdata2 数据集中的变量

变量名称	变量描述	取值范围
shame	“应该感到羞耻”的同意程度	1~7
condition	疾病类型	1~3

本案例也只有两个变量,但处理变量包含三个类别,也就是要比较这三个实验组的结果变量均值,因此无法使用比较两组样本的 T 检验,而采用单因素方差分析(One-way ANOVA)。

同样,在做数据分析前,要了解变量的分布情况,并要对方差分析的一些基本假定进行验证,具体方法前面已经介绍过,此处不再赘言。

SPSS 软件

在 SPSS 中进行单因素方差分析的操作步骤为:

[分析]→[比较均值]→[单因素 ANOVA]

在弹出的窗口里将 shame 变量选入[因变量列表]对话框内,将 condition 变量选入[因子]对话框内。然后单击窗口右侧[两两比较]按钮,在弹出的窗口中勾选[Bonferroni]选项,如图 4.10所示。如果想了解数据的基本情况，也可单击右侧[选项]按钮，然后勾选[描述性]选项。

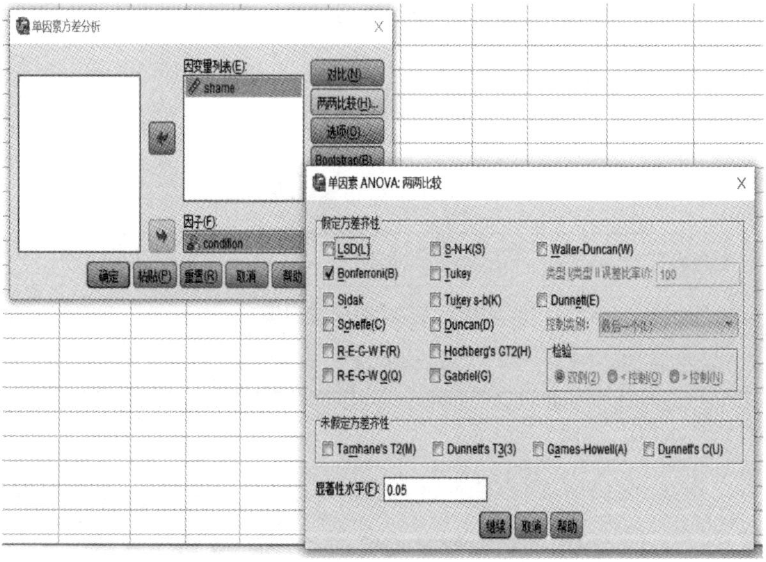

图 4.10　SPSS“单因素方差分析”操作示意图

运行后 SPSS 的输出结果包括三个表格（图 4.11）。第一个表格中报告 shame 变量的分布情况，包括应答不同病种的虚拟案例的样本数、应答均值和标准差、均值的标准误及 95%的置信区间，还有应答的极小值和极大值。从这个表格中的数据可以观察到，三个随机组的样本量基本均衡，对精神分裂症和肺气肿的应答均值比较接近，分别为 1.87 和 1.78，而对药物依赖的应答均则略高一些，为 2.72。三组应答的标准差目测也差异不大。

描述

shame

	N	均值	标准差	标准误	均值的 95% 置信区间		极小值	极大值
					下限	上限		
精神分裂症	312	1.87	1.211	.069	1.73	2.00	1	7
药物依赖	326	2.72	1.443	.080	2.57	2.88	1	7
肺气肿	322	1.78	1.171	.065	1.65	1.90	1	7
总数	960	2.13	1.351	.044	2.04	2.21	1	7

单因素方差分析

shame

	平方和	df	均方	F	显著性
组间	177.096	2	88.548	53.858	.000
组内	1573.400	957	1.644		
总数	1750.496	959			

在此之后检验

多重比较

因变量: shame

Bonferroni

(I) condition	(J) condition	均值差 (I-J)	标准误	显著性	95% 置信区间	
					下限	上限
精神分裂症	药物依赖	-.859*	.102	.000	-1.10	-.62
	肺气肿	.089	.102	1.000	-.16	.33
药物依赖	精神分裂症	.859*	.102	.000	.62	1.10
	肺气肿	.948*	.101	.000	.71	1.19
肺气肿	精神分裂症	-.089	.102	1.000	-.33	.16
	药物依赖	-.948*	.101	.000	-1.19	-.71

*. 均值差的显著性水平为 0.05。

图 4.11　SPSS 输出(单因素方差分析)

第二个表格报告了单因素方差分析的 F 检验结果。F 检验的零假设是各组之间的应答均值没有差异。统计结果显示 F 统计值为 53.858,自由度是 2 和 957,由此计算出 p 值小于 0.001。因此判定零假设成立的可能性非常小,于是认为受访者对这三个病种案例的应答上存在显著差异。

F 检验只是验证了三组样本的应答结果不同,具体差异表现可以通过解读第三个表格来了解。Bonferroni 多重比较法在一定程度上校正了两两比较均值上的差异,其零假设是对前个病种(I)

案例的应答均值和对后个病种(J)案例的应答均值没有差异。从第三个表格的第三和第四行,即药物依赖分别与精神分裂症和肺气肿相比,可以发现均值差异的显著性 p 值都在 0.001 以下,这意味着相对于精神分裂症和肺气肿,受访者认为当家人患有药物依赖这种疾病时更应该感到羞耻。

STATA 软件

在 STATA 中,单因素方差分析可以用 oneway 命令来执行,语句示例如下:

```
oneway shame condition, tabulate bonferroni
```

输出结果与 SPSS 输出结果基本相同,此处也不再讲解。

4.1.3 回归分析

在上述的虚拟案例中再补充加入患病者的年龄信息,考查这种羞耻感是否会因患病者的年龄不同而有所差异。因为在虚拟案例中不能用连续变量,因此将年龄从 25 到 70 岁,每 5 岁为一个水平,共分为 10 个水平[①]。

示例数据集命名为 Exdata3,共包括三个变量,960 个观测值。具体变量描述如表 4.3,数据集中 shame 为结果变量,或因变量;condition 和 age 为处理变量,或自变量。

① 此变量为示例编制,而非来自原始实验数据。

表 4.3　Exdata3 数据集中的变量

变量名称	变量描述	取值范围
shame	“应该感到羞耻”的同意程度	1~7
condition	疾病类型	1~3
age	年龄水平	1~10

SPSS 软件

在本数据集中，shame 和 condition 属于定序变量，本分析中作为连续的定距变量来处理。condition 变量是定类变量，在进行回归分析前，需要将其转换为三个存储值为 0 或 1 的二分变量。在 SPSS 中转换的方法是：

[转换]→[重新编码为不同变量]

在弹出的窗口上将左边对话框中的 condition 选入中间的对话框，然后在最右边[输出变量]的名称处输入新的变量名，如 cond 1，在标签中输入[精神分裂症]，然后单击[更改]。接下来单击中间对话框下的[旧值和新值]，会弹出一个新的窗口，点选左边[旧值]中的[值]，在对话框处录入“1”，然后点选右边[新值]中的[值]，在对话框中录入“1”，然后单击下面对话框左侧的[添加]，这时对话框里就会出现[1—>1]。接下来将 1 以外的其他值赋值为 0，左边点选[所有其他值]，右边[值]的对话框内录入“0”，之后单击添加，就出现如图 4.12 展示的情形。单击[继续]和[确定]后就生成新的变量 cond 1，其变量值 1 代表精神分裂症，0 代表其他疾病。

按照此种方法将 condition 变量重新编码，生成新的变量 cond 2(药物依赖)和 cond 3(肺气肿)。注意在填写[旧值和新值]

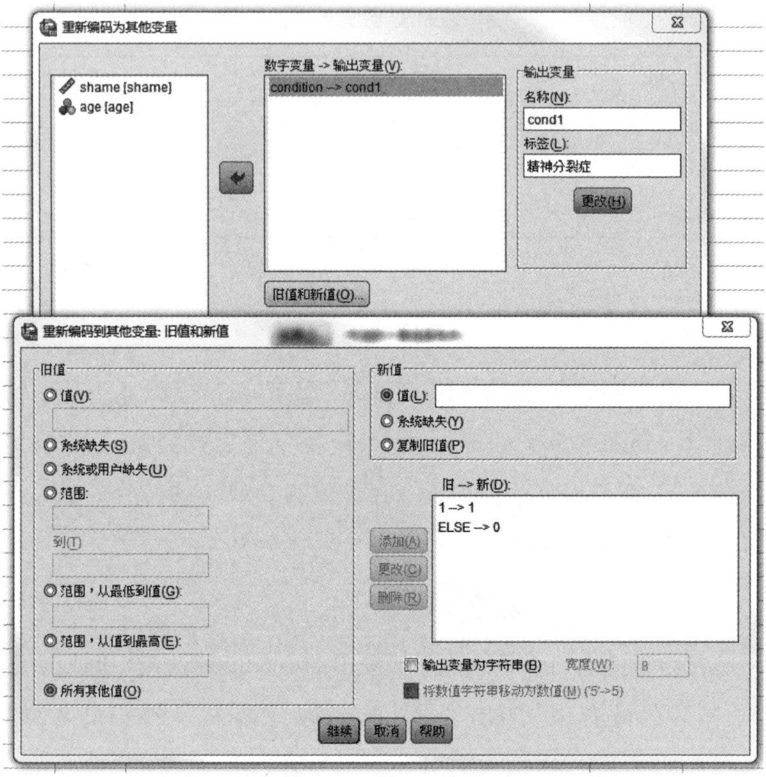

图 4.12　SPSS“重新编码为其他变量”操作示意图

窗口时，左边的[值]对话框内应该填写相应的“2”或“3”，右边[新值]对话框则均填写“1”。

在回归分析中，由于 condition 变量重新编码形成的三个新的二分变量具有多重共线的特征，也就是知道其中两个变量，就可以确定第三个变量，所以只能选取其中两个变量带入模型中。研究者可以根据模型解释的需要取舍，本示例选取 cond 1(精神分裂症)和 cond 3(肺气肿)作为自变量。

SPSS 中回归分析的操作步骤是：

[分析]→[回归]→[线性]

在[线性回归]窗口将左边对话框内的 shame 变量选入[因变量]的对话框,将 cond 1,cond 3 和 age 变量选入[自变量]的对话框,如图 4.13 所示,然后单击[确定]。

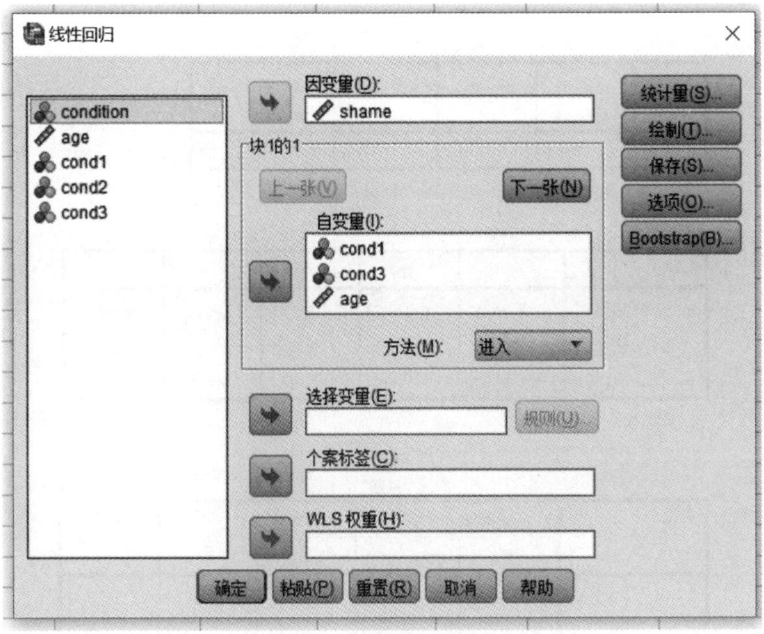

图 4.13　SPSS"线性回归"操作示意图

输出结果包括四个表格(图 4.14)。第一个表格报告了回归模型中包括的自变量,包括 age,精神分裂症(cond 1)和肺气肿(cond 3)三个变量。第二个表格报告的是模型拟合的评价系数 R^2 及相关指标,R^2 测量的是因变量的方差能被模型所解释的比例。在这个例子中的 R^2 值为 0.102,意味着 shame 变量大约 10%的变异可以被这几个自变量解释。第三个表格是方差分析的结果,F 统计值为 36.062,在 3 和 956 的自由度上显著性水平小于

0.001，意味着回归模型中至少有一个自变量的系数不为0。

输入/移去的变量[a]

模型	输入的变量	移去的变量	方法
1	age，cond1，cond3[b]	.	输入

a. 因变量：shame

b. 已输入所有请求的变量。

模型汇总

模型	R	R 方	调整 R 方	标准 估计的误差
1	.319[a]	.102	.099	1.283

a. 预测变量：(常量)，age，cond1，cond3。

Anova[a]

模型		平方和	df	均方	F	Sig.
1	回归	177.957	3	59.319	36.062	.000[b]
	残差	1572.539	956	1.645		
	总计	1750.496	959			

a. 因变量：shame

b. 预测变量：(常量)，age，cond1，cond3。

系数[a]

模型		非标准化系数		标准系数	t	Sig.
		B	标准 误差	试用版		
1	(常量)	1.808	.108		16.754	.000
	cond1	.856	.102	.300	8.422	.000
	cond3	-.086	.102	-.030	-.846	.398
	age	.010	.014	.022	.723	.470

a. 因变量：shame

图4.14 SPSS输出结果(线性回归分析)

第四个表格报告了回归分析的结果。首先，在表格的第一行是“常量”，指的是当模型中所有自变量均取值为0时因变量的平均值。因为自变量age的取值范围是从1到10，不包含0，所以在本例中对于常量的解读是没有意义的。表格的第二和第三行报告的是自变量 cond 1(精神分裂症)和 cond 3(肺气肿)的回归系数和检验结果。可以看到,cond 1 的非标准化系数为-0.856,cond 3 的非标准化系数为-0.942,对两个系数的 T 检验所得 p 值均小于 0.001。因为 cond 1,cond 2 和 cond 3 是从 condition 衍生出的二分变量,所以对 cond 1 和 cond 3 回归系数的解读要基于和 cond 2 的比较。如 cond 1 的回归系数意味着,在控制虚拟案例中患病者年龄不变的情况下,受访者认为对患有精神分裂症的病人所应该有的羞耻程度比患有药物依赖的病人的羞耻程度少 0.856 个数值。cond 3 的回归系数也是表明受访者认为和肺气肿病相比,更应该为患有药物依赖的家人感到羞耻。表格的最后一行是 age 变量的回归系数和检验结果,因为 T 检验不显著,这个系数是 0 的可能性较大,因此可以断定 age 变量对因变量没有显著影响,也就是说,在同一种病种下,受访者对于羞耻程度的判断没有受到患病人年龄的影响。

对于整个研究来说,患病者的年龄是否会影响到受访者对羞耻程度的判读还不能定论,需要对上述模型进行诊断。年龄的影响也许是非线性的,年龄和病种之间也许存在交互作用,因此还需要对模型进行改进。

STATA 软件

STATA 中将定性变量重新编码为二分变量可以采用以下方法:

```
tab condition, gen(cond)
```

运行后会自动生成 cond 1,cond 2 和 cond 3 三个二分变量。然后根据需要选用其中两个变量放入回归模型,命令为:

```
reg shame cond1 cond3 age
```

如果对进入模型的二分变量不予控制，也可以采用下面命令一步完成回归分析：

```
xi: reg shame i.condition age
```

前缀 xi 表示回归模型中包含需要分解为二分变量的定性变量，在自变量 condition 前加上 i 并以“.”隔开，指示 condition 变量需要进行转换。运行这个程序，软件会默认将 condition 变量值为 1 的类别作为比较类别，不放入模型中。输出结果和 SPSS 输出结果基本相同。

4.2 析因调查-实验的多水平模型分析

在析因调查-实验中，如果一个受访者就多个虚拟案例做判断，这时建议采用多水平模型分析，通常把虚拟案例看作个体层面，即水平 1 上的元素，而把应答者看作组层面，即水平 2 上的元素。

4.2.1 数据介绍

这里用作示例的析因调查-实验数据改编自美国 1986 年综合社会调查(General Social Survey)。该调查中采用虚拟案例的方法询问受访者对贫困家庭获取政府资助的意见。原始虚拟案例中共设计了 10 个维度，本示例选取其中四个维度，分别为①孩子的个数；②父母婚姻状态；③父亲就业情况；④家庭周收入。调查共采

访了 1470 个受访者,每个受访者要阅读 7 个虚拟案例,然后回答下列问题:

这个家庭每周的收入应该是多少?包括该家庭已有的收入和你认为这个家庭应该得到的政府资助。

示例数据集命名为 Assistance,共包括 7 个变量,9709 个观测。其中受访者层面的变量包括受访者的代码和种族,虚拟案例层面的变量包括上述四个维度的处理变量和结果变量。各变量的情况见表 4.4。

表 4.4　Assistance 数据集中的变量

变量名称	变量描述	取值范围
id	受访者代码	1~1470
race	受访者种族	1.白人;0.非白人
amount	该家庭应该得到的周收入	0~600 美元,间距为 50 美元
children	该家庭 8 岁以下孩子个数	1. 一个孩子(child1) 2.两个孩子(child2) 3.三个及以上个孩子(child3)
maristat	父母婚姻状态	1.在婚(maristat1) 2.离异(maristat2) 3.未婚(maristat3)
fathersitu	父亲就业状况	1.全职就业(fathersitu1) 2.失业,在找工作(fathersitu2) 3.失业,没找工作(fathersitu3) 4.服刑(fathersitu4) 5.残疾(fathersitu5)
faminc	家庭周收入	1.每周 50 美元(faminc1) 2.每周 100 美元(faminc2) 3.每周 200 美元(faminc3) 4.每周 300 美元(faminc4)

虚拟案例中的处理变量均为定类变量，在采用回归模型分析前需要将其转换为二分变量，对这些变量进行重新编码后新生成的变量名附在表 4.5 最后一列的括号里。

4.2.2 SPSS 软件

使用 SPSS 进行多水平回归分析的菜单操作步骤是：

[分析]→[混合模型]→[线性]

然后在弹出的[线性混合模型]的窗口中设定各种选项。多水平回归分析的一般步骤是先建构空模型，考察组间是否有显著的差异，从而确定多水平模型分析的方法是否适用，然后确认高水平上的变量对因变量的效应。就本例而言，是指应答者特征变量对于因变量的效应。最后联合考察：两个水平上的变量对于因变量的效应，即应答者特征和虚拟案例中的处理变量对于因变量的效应。此部分也将按照这三个步骤介绍在 SPSS 上的操作。

建构空模型，考察是否适用多水平模型分析方法

空模型就是在模型中不加入任何自变量，在 SPSS[线性混合模型]的窗口中设置如下：

①选取 id 变量，将其送入[主题]的对话框，然后单击[继续]（图 4.15）。id 即是第二水平的标示变量。

②在新弹出的[线性混合模型]的窗口将 amount 送入[因变量]对话框（图 4.16）。因为是空模型，[因子]和[协变量]对话框中不要放入任何变量。

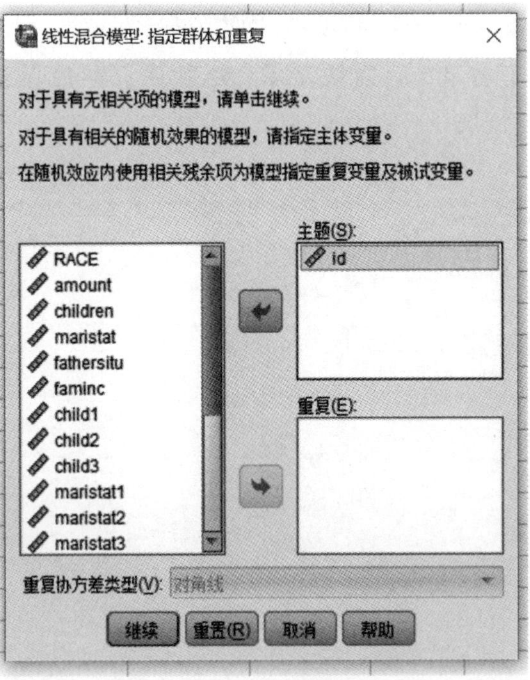

图 4.15　SPSS“线性混合模型”操作示意图：指定群体和重复（空模型）

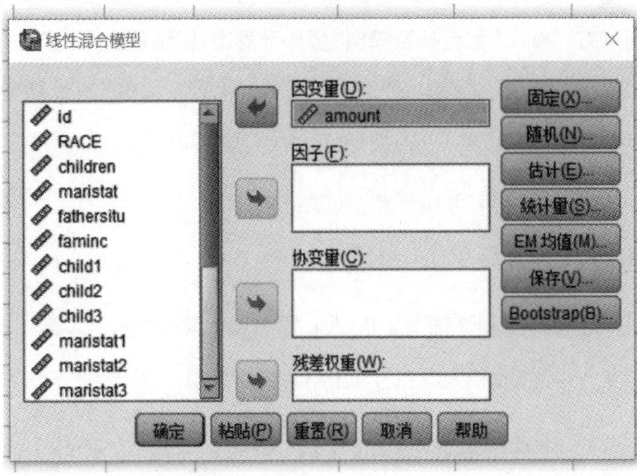

图 4.16　SPSS“线性混合模型”操作示意图：指定因变量（空模型）

③单击[固定]按钮，进入[固定效应]对话框，勾选[包括截距]，在[平方和]后确认显示[类型Ⅲ]，然后单击[继续]（图 4.17）。

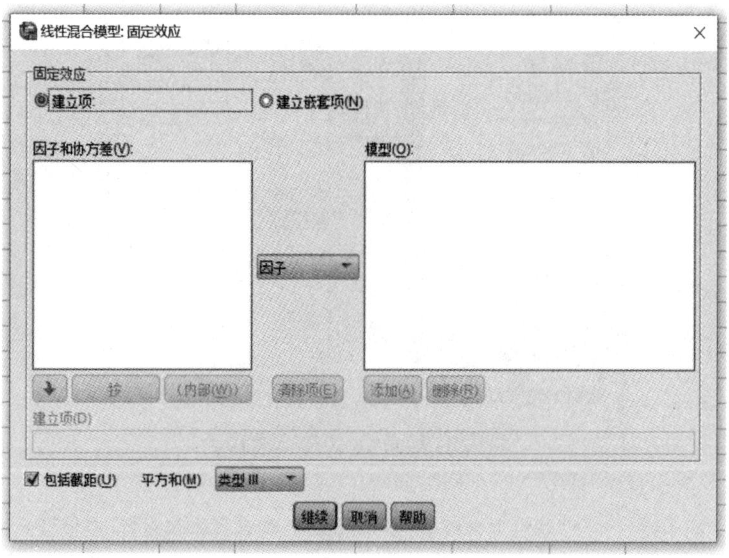

图 4.17　SPSS“线性混合模型”操作示意图：固定效应（空模型）

④单击[随机]按钮，进入[随机效果]对话框，在[协方差类型]框选择[未结构化]，是对协方差矩阵不设定任何约束。然后勾选[包括截距]，并将[主题]对话框中的 id 送入[组合]对话框中（图 4.18），完成后单击[继续]。

⑤单击[统计量]按钮，进入[统计量]对话框，勾选[参数估计]和[协方差参数检验]（图 4.19），然后单击[继续]。

⑥回到[线性混合模型]的窗口，单击[确定]，SPSS 开始运行并输出分析结果。

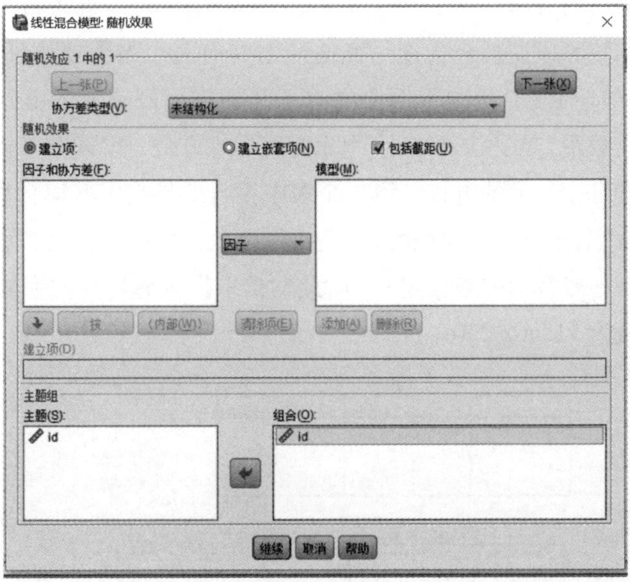

图 4.18　SPSS"线性混合模型"操作示意图：随机效果(空模型)

图 4.19　SPSS"线性混合模型"操作示意图：统计量(空模型)

输出的分析结果分为三部分内容(图 4.20)。首先报告的是模型维数和模型拟合优度。此空模型共有三个参数要估计,其中“固定效应截距”是本示例中的虚拟案例层面回归线的截距,“随机效应截距”是受访者层面回归线截距的方差,而“残差”代表受访者自身应答上的方差。第二个表中报告的是空模型拟合优度的多个指标,比较不同模型时,这些指标上数值较小的模型拟合优度较好。一般常用的指标是-2LL,此输出中报告的是有约束的-2LL统计值为 113362.230。

模型维数[a]

		水平数	协方差结构	参数的数目	个体变量
固定效应	截距	1		1	
随机效应	截距	1	标识	1	id
残差				1	
合计		2		3	

a. 因变量: amount。

信息条件[a]

-2 受约束的对数似然值	113362.230
Akaike 的信息条件 (AIC)	113366.230
Hurvich 和 Tsai 的条件 (AICC)	113366.232
Bozdogan 的条件 (CAIC)	113382.560
Schwarz 的 Bayesian 条件 (BIC)	113380.560

以“较少为较好”的格式显示信息条件。

a. 因变量: amount。

有约束的-2LL

固定效应

固定效应的检验类型 III[a]

源	分子 df	分母 df	F	显著性
截距	1	1379.430	14527.509	.000

a. 因变量: amount。

虚拟案例层面的回归线截距

固定效应估计[a]

参数	估计	标准误差	df	t	显著性	95% 置信区间	
						下限	上限
截距	256.116392	2.124916	1379.430	120.530	.000	251.947975	260.284808

a. 因变量: amount。

协方差参数

应答者自身在因变量(amount)上的方差

协方差参数估计[a]

参数	估计	标准误差	Wald Z	显著性	95% 置信区间	
					下限	上限
残差	6306.247844	98.654731	63.922	.000	6115.822418	6502.602454
截距 [个体 = id] 方差	5319.263145	237.983900	22.351	.000	4872.689161	5806.764903

a. 因变量: amount。

应答者之间在因变量(amount)上的方差

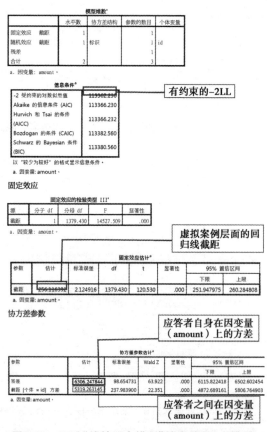

图 4.20　SPSS“线性混合模型”输出结果(空模型)

输出的第二部分报告参数的估计和统计检验。由“固定效应”的两个表格中可以得知,虚拟案例层面的回归线截距为 256.12,在 1%的置信水平上统计显著。“协方差参数”的表格中报告了另外两个参数的估计结果:受访者层面回归线的截距的方差为 5319.26,受访者自身应答上的方差为 6306.25。SPSS 软件没有直接给出组内相关系数(ICC)的统计值,但根据 4.1 节 ICC 的计算公式,可以很容易地算出

$$\text{ICC} = \frac{5319.26}{5319.26 + 6306.25} = 0.4576$$

ICC 远大于 0,因此采用多水平模型分析是适宜的。SPSS 提供的 Wald 检验也证实了这一点,两个方差的估计值都是统计显著,说明方差为 0 的可能性非常小。

加入应答者种族变量,考察是否对因变量有影响

对此模型的分析需要在空模型的 SPSS 设置基础上补充对应答者种族变量的设置。

①选取 id 变量,将其送入[主题]的对话框,然后单击[继续](同图 4.15)。id 即是第二水平的标示变量。

②在新弹出的[线性混合模型]的窗口将 amount 送入[因变量]对话框,将 RACE 放入[协变量]对话框(图 4.21)。

③单击[固定]按钮,进入[固定效应]对话框,将 RACE 送入[模型]对话框,勾选[包括截距],在[平方和]框内选择[类型Ⅲ],然后单击[继续](图 4.22)。

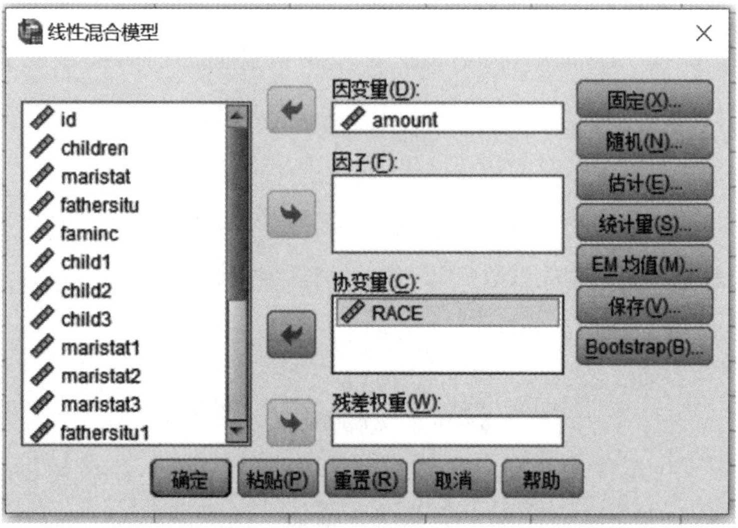

图 4.21　SPSS 操作示意图：指定因变量和协变量（模型二）

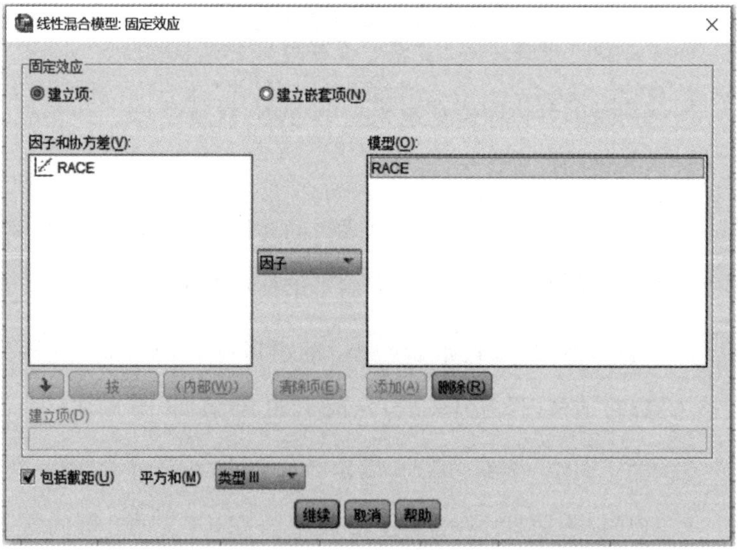

图 4.22　SPSS 操作示意图：固定效应（模型二）

④单击［随机］按钮，进入［随机效果］对话框，在［协方差类

型]框选择[未结构化],是对协方差矩阵不设定任何约束,然后勾选[包括截距],完成后单击[继续](图 4.23)。为方便解读,本分析中设定回归线斜率固定,因此没有把任何变量放入[模型]框中。

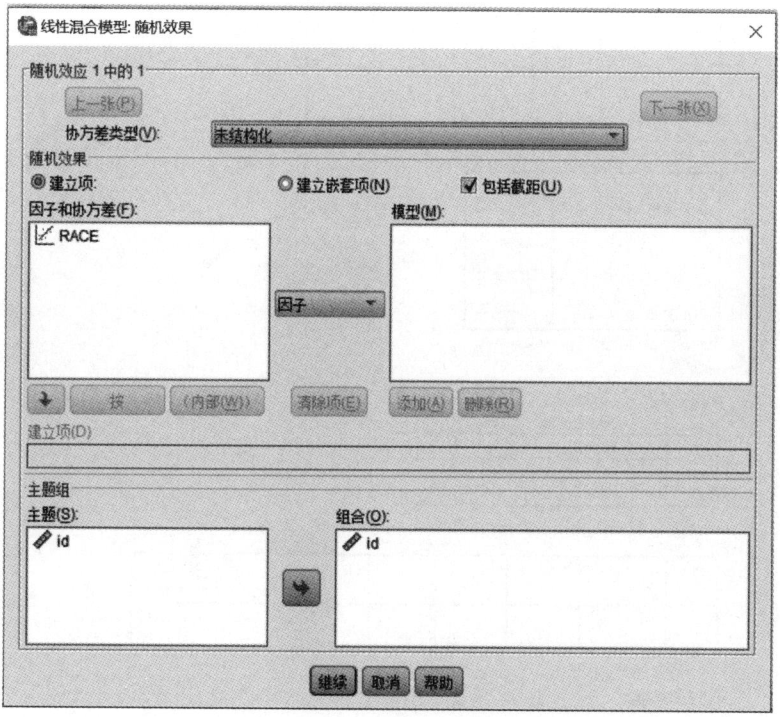

图 4.23　SPSS 操作示意图:随机效果(模型二)

⑤单击[统计量]按钮,进入[统计量]对话框,勾选[参数估计]和[协方差参数检验](同图 4.19),然后单击[继续]。

⑥回到[线性混合模型]的窗口,单击[确定],SPSS 开始运行并输出分析结果。

查看 SPSS 关于模型的输出结果(图 4.24),可以看到模型维度中显示此模型指定了 4 个参数，比空模型多了 RACE 的固定效应参数。新模型的拟合优度指标中有约束的-2LL 值为 113305.001，比空模型的(113362.230)降低约 57，拟合优度略有改善。

模型维数ᵃ

		水平数	协方差结构	参数的数目	个体变量
固定效应	截距	1		1	
	RACE	1		1	
随机效应	截距	1	标识	1	id
残差				1	
合计		3		4	

a. 因变量：amount。

信息条件ᵃ

-2 受约束的对数似然值	113305.001
Akaike 的信息条件 (AIC)	113309.001
Hurvich 和 Tsai 的条件 (AICC)	113309.003
Bozdogan 的条件 (CAIC)	113325.331
Schwarz 的 Bayesian 条件 (BIC)	113323.331

以“较少为较好”的格式显示信息条件。

a. 因变量：amount。

固定效应

固定效应的检验类型 IIIᵃ

源	分子 df	分母 df	F	显著性
截距	1	1376.465	2904.124	.000
RACE	1	1376.743	52.802	.000

a. 因变量：amount。

固定效应估计ᵃ

参数	估计	标准误差	df	t	显著性	95% 置信区间	
						下限	上限
截距	292.528688	5.428263	1376.465	53.890	.000	281.880125	303.177252
RACE	-42.725077	5.879748	1376.743	-7.266	.000	-54.259311	-31.190844

a. 因变量：amount。

协方差参数

协方差参数估计ᵃ

参数		估计	标准误差	Wald Z	显著性	95% 置信区间	
						下限	上限
残差		6306.382510	98.658216	63.922	.000	6115.950397	6502.744100
截距 [个体 = id]	方差	5092.903945	229.484531	22.193	.000	4662.411823	5563.144480

a. 因变量：amount。

图 4.24　SPSS 输出结果(模型二)

固定效应表格中报告 RACE 变量回归系数的 F 检验值为 52.802，p 值小于 0.001，意味着受访者性别对于因变量有显著影响。RACE 固定效应的估计值为-42.725,T 检验结果也是显著。在协方差参数表格中,应答者之间在因变量上的方差的估计值由空模型的 5319.26 减少到 5092.904,说明 RACE 作为预测变量解释了应答者之间的一些变异。但应答者之间和应答者自身在因变量上的方差仍然显著,说明因变量的变异还有待更多变量的解释。

加入虚拟案例中的维度变量,考察是否对因变量有影响

在上一模型的基础上,继续放入虚拟案例层面的维度变量。在 SPSS 上需要在以下对话框中设置。

①在[线性混合模型]的窗口除了将 amount 送入[因变量]对话框,将 RACE 放入[协变量]对话框,还需要将转换成二分变量的维度变量送入[因子]对话框(图 4.25),注意为避免多重共线,每个维度的二分变量需要保留一个类别不进入模型。

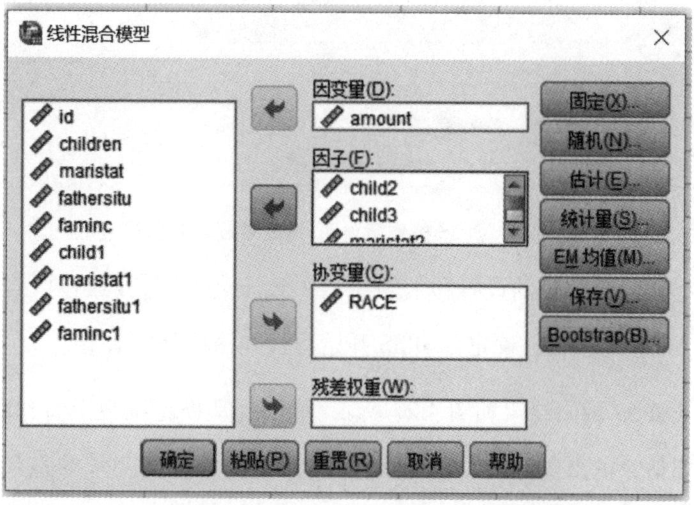

图 4.25　SPSS 操作示意图:指定因变量、因子和协变量(模型三)

②单击[固定]按钮，进入[固定效应]对话框。虚拟案例的维度采用正交设计，在分析中仅需考虑各维度变量的主效应，于是在两个对话框中间的下拉选项中选择[主效应]，然后将各维度的二分变量和应答者层面的 RACE 变量送入[模型]对话框，勾选[包括截距]，在[平方和]框内选择[类型Ⅲ]，然后单击[继续]（图 4.26）。

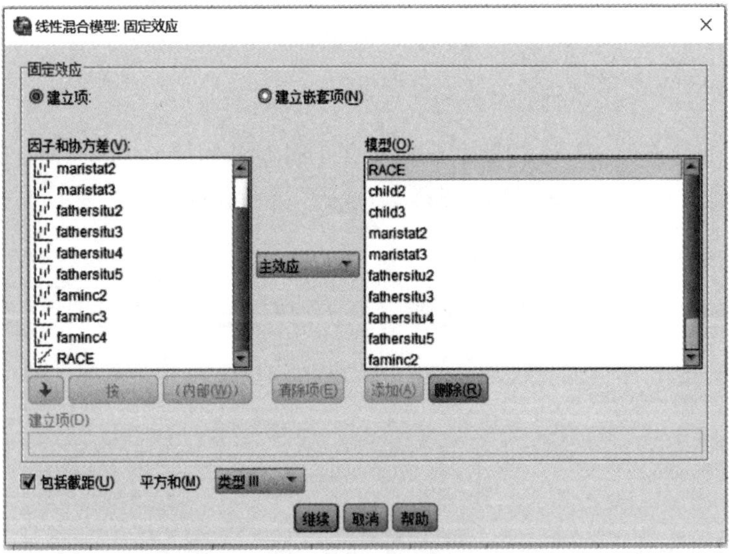

图 4.26　SPSS 操作示意图：固定效应（模型三）

③其余部分的设置和上一模型一致。最后回到[线性混合模型]的窗口，单击[确定]，SPSS 开始运行并输出分析结果。

SPSS 输出结果如图 4.27 所示。首先，从模型维数上看，此模型要估计的参数达 15 个，增加了虚拟案例各维度变量的系数估计。拟合优度指标中有约束的-2LL 值为 110952.091，与上一模型（113305.001）相比，拟合优度改善约 2353。

模型维数[a]

		水平数	协方差结构	参数的数目	个体变量
固定效应	截距	1		1	
	RACE	1		1	
	child2	2		1	
	child3	2		1	
	maristat2	2		1	
	maristat3	2		1	
	fathersitu2	2		1	
	fathersitu3	2		1	
	fathersitu4	2		1	
	fathersitu5	2		1	
	faminc2	2		1	
	faminc3	2		1	
	faminc4	2		1	
随机效应	截距	1	标识	1	id
残差				1	
合计		25		15	

a. 因变量：amount。

信息条件[a]

-2 受约束的对数似然值	110952.091
Akaike 的信息条件 (AIC)	110956.091
Hurvich 和 Tsai 的条件 (AICC)	110956.092
Bozdogan 的条件 (CAIC)	110972.418
Schwarz 的 Bayesian 条件 (BIC)	110970.418

以“较少为较好”的格式显示信息条件。

a. 因变量：amount。

固定效应

固定效应的检验类型 III[a]

源	分子 df	分母 df	F	显著性
截距	1	2355.170	3145.447	.000
RACE	1	1377.913	56.324	.000
child2	1	8469.424	56.264	.000
child3	1	8465.002	397.973	.000
maristat2	1	8494.806	1.369	.242
maristat3	1	8470.709	9.626	.002
fathersitu2	1	8478.126	15.700	.000
fathersitu3	1	8480.495	10.496	.001
fathersitu4	1	8476.926	4.272	.039
fathersitu5	1	8482.153	124.864	.000
faminc2	1	8490.611	25.336	.000
faminc3	1	8474.734	307.693	.000
faminc4	1	8499.045	1308.854	.000

a. 因变量：amount。

固定效应估计[a]

参数	估计	标准误差	df	t	显著性	95% 置信区间	
						下限	上限
截距	454.073383	10.412554	8421.833	43.608	.000	433.662218	474.484548
RACE	-42.961929	5.724509	1377.913	-7.505	.000	-54.191623	-31.732234
[child2=0]	-13.835242	1.844477	8469.424	-7.501	.000	-17.450867	-10.219617
[child2=1]	0[b]	0	.	.	.	.	.
[child3=0]	-36.922739	1.850833	8465.002	-19.949	.000	-40.550824	-33.294655
[child3=1]	0[b]	0	.	.	.	.	.
[maristat2=0]	2.191031	1.872709	8494.806	1.170	.242	-1.479933	5.861996
[maristat2=1]	0[b]	0	.	.	.	.	.
[maristat3=0]	5.734054	1.848164	8470.709	3.103	.002	2.111202	9.356906
[maristat3=1]	0[b]	0	.	.	.	.	.
[fathersitu2=0]	-9.614295	2.426430	8478.126	-3.962	.000	-14.370689	-4.857900
[fathersitu2=1]	0[b]	0	.	.	.	.	.
[fathersitu3=0]	7.783841	2.402608	8480.495	3.240	.001	3.074145	12.493538
[fathersitu3=1]	0[b]	0	.	.	.	.	.
[fathersitu4=0]	-4.971802	2.405510	8476.926	-2.067	.039	-9.687187	-.256416
[fathersitu4=1]	0[b]	0	.	.	.	.	.
[fathersitu5=0]	-27.198700	2.434055	8482.153	-11.174	.000	-31.970040	-22.427360
[fathersitu5=1]	0[b]	0	.	.	.	.	.
[faminc2=0]	-12.799472	2.542877	8490.611	-5.033	.000	-17.784129	-7.814815
[faminc2=1]	0[b]	0	.	.	.	.	.
[faminc3=0]	-44.120192	2.515234	8474.734	-17.541	.000	-49.050663	-39.189720
[faminc3=1]	0[b]	0	.	.	.	.	.
[faminc4=0]	-91.397925	2.526334	8499.045	-36.178	.000	-96.350153	-86.445696
[faminc4=1]	0[b]	0	.	.	.	.	.

a. 因变量：amount。

b. 因为此参数冗余，所以将其设为零。

协方差参数

协方差参数估计[a]

参数		估计	标准误差	Wald Z	显著性	95% 置信区间	
						下限	上限
残差		4798.556320	75.116631	63.881	.000	4653.566047	4948.064029
截距 [个体 = id]	方差	4998.574043	217.312516	23.002	.000	4590.291081	5443.171691

a. 因变量：amount。

图 4.27　SPSS 输出结果（模型三）

对自变量固定效应的检验，除了 maristat2 变量外其他均为统计显著。SPSS 对各自变量固定效应估计值的报告容易造成读者的困惑。在这个表格的第一列，虚拟案例层面的维度变量都列出了水平值，第二列中报告的是当维度变量为 0 时的系数估计值，也就是说把维度变量为 1 作为参考值，这和常规的回归分析的自变量系数报告方法有所不同，如果还按照常规方法解读，就需要转变系数的正负号。如 child2 = 0 的估计值为 -13.835，应解读为："排除模型中其他因素的影响，受访者认为有两个孩子的家庭的每周收入比仅有一个孩子的家庭要多 13.84 元。"对于其他维度二分变量的解读也是如此。

最后查看协方差参数，应答者之间在因变量上的方差的估计值为 4998.57，再次降低了 94，而应答者自身在因变量上的方差则由于维度变量的解释，由空模型的 6306.25 减少到 4798.56。然而应答者之间和应答者自身在因变量上的方差仍然显著，说明模型还有待完善。

4.2.3　STATA 软件

STATA13 中增加了 mixed 命令用于多水平线性模型分析，代替了原有的 xtreg 命令。此命令的格式为：

```
    mixed depvar fe_equation [|| re_equation] [|| re_equation ...] [, options]

where the syntax of fe_equation is

        [indepvars] [if] [in] [weight] [, fe_options]

and the syntax of re_equation is one of the following:

    for random coefficients and intercepts

        levelvar: [varlist] [, re_options]

    for a random effect among the values of a factor variable

        levelvar: R.varname [, re_options]
```

语句设置方法如下：

depvar	因变量
fe_equation	自变量列表
re_equation	"："前放入分层变量，后放入随机效应的变量列表
options	常用的有 reml（有约束的最大似然法），cov(un)（非结构化的随机效应协方差矩阵）

下面使用STATA对本例中的数据估计空模型和多水平混合模型。

空模型

STATA命令为：

```
mixed amount || id:, reml
```

其中amount为因变量，双竖线隔开后是分层变量（受访者代码）。因为是空模型，没有加入任何自变量。估计方法采用有约束的最大似然法。

STATA输出结果为：

```
. mixed amount || id:, reml

Performing EM optimization:

Performing gradient-based optimization:

Iteration 0:   log restricted-likelihood = -56681.115
Iteration 1:   log restricted-likelihood = -56681.115

Computing standard errors:

Mixed-effects REML regression                   Number of obs      =      9555
Group variable: id                              Number of groups   =      1383

                                                Obs per group: min =         1
                                                               avg =       6.9
                                                               max =         7


                                                Wald chi2(0)       =         .
Log restricted-likelihood = -56681.115          Prob > chi2        =         .

------------------------------------------------------------------------------
      amount |      Coef.   Std. Err.      z    P>|z|     [95% Conf. Interval]
-------------+----------------------------------------------------------------
       _cons |   256.1164   2.124916   120.53   0.000     251.9516    260.2812
------------------------------------------------------------------------------

------------------------------------------------------------------------------
  Random-effects Parameters  |   Estimate   Std. Err.     [95% Conf. Interval]
-----------------------------+------------------------------------------------
id: Identity                 |
                  var(_cons) |   5319.263   237.9839      4872.689    5806.764
-----------------------------+------------------------------------------------
               var(Residual) |   6306.248   98.65473      6115.823    6502.603
------------------------------------------------------------------------------
LR test vs. linear regression: chibar2(01) =  3180.83 Prob >= chibar2 = 0.0000
```

应答者之间在因变量上的方差（指 var(_cons) 5319.263）

应答者自身在因变量上的方差（指 var(Residual) 6306.248）

和 SPSS 输出不同的是,STATA 的输出没有直接给出拟合优度指标 - 2LL,而是给出了有约束的 LL 统计值,在本模型中为 -56681.115,在这个数值上乘以-2,即是-2LL。

在随机效应系数的表格中,var(_cons)是回归线截距的方差,也就是应答者之间在因变量上的方差;var(Residual)是应答者自身在因变量上的方差。对其的解读和 SPSS 输出相同。

加入应答者种族变量

STATA 命令为:

```
mixed amount RACE || id:, reml
```

在因变量 amount 后加入应答者层面的特征变量 RACE。同样,为解读方便,此模型没有考虑斜率随机的情形,因此在层变量 id:后没有加入任何变量。输出结果如下:

加入虚拟案例中的维度变量

STATA 命令为:

```
mixed amount RACE child2 child3 maristat2 maristat3 ///
fathersitu2 fathersitu3 fathersitu4 fathersitu5 ///
faminc2 faminc3 faminc4 || id:, reml
```

在此模型中加入四个维度变量重新编码生成的 11 个二分变量,放在因变量的后面。仍然假定斜率固定,id:后面没有变量名。输出结果如下:

```
. mixed amount RACE || id: , reml

Performing EM optimization:

Performing gradient-based optimization:

Iteration 0:   log restricted-likelihood = -56652.501
Iteration 1:   log restricted-likelihood = -56652.501

Computing standard errors:

Mixed-effects REML regression                   Number of obs      =      9555
Group variable: id                              Number of groups   =      1383

                                                Obs per group: min =         1
                                                               avg =       6.9
                                                               max =         7


                                                Wald chi2(1)       =     52.80
Log restricted-likelihood = -56652.501          Prob > chi2        =    0.0000

------------------------------------------------------------------------------
      amount |      Coef.   Std. Err.      z    P>|z|     [95% Conf. Interval]
-------------+----------------------------------------------------------------
        RACE |  -42.72508   5.879746    -7.27   0.000    -54.24917   -31.20099
       _cons |   292.5287   5.428261    53.89   0.000     281.8895    303.1679
------------------------------------------------------------------------------

------------------------------------------------------------------------------
  Random-effects Parameters  |   Estimate   Std. Err.     [95% Conf. Interval]
-----------------------------+------------------------------------------------
id: Identity                 |
                   var(_cons) |     5092.9   229.4844      4662.409     5563.14
-----------------------------+------------------------------------------------
                var(Residual) |   6306.383   98.65823      6115.951    6502.745
------------------------------------------------------------------------------
LR test vs. linear regression: chibar2(01) =  3041.96 Prob >= chibar2 = 0.0000
```

STATA 对于自变量系数估计的报告比较符合惯例。和 SPSS 输出对照比较，可以发现相同变量系数的符号正好相反，具体原因前文已做解释。对于模型的解读也不再赘言。

4.3 列举调查-实验的多元回归分析

列举调查-实验数据的分析可以采用常规的均值差的分析方法，通过比较实验组和控制组选择条目数均值的差异来判断选择敏感条目的人数比例。为了在分析中能考虑应答者的特征等变量的影响,学者们研发了复杂的统计分析方法,并且以 R 统计包的形式共享。本部分将介绍如何使用名为 list 的 R 统计包对列举调查使用数据进行多元回归分析。

4.3.1　数据介绍

用于此部分演示的数据来自 1991 年美国种族与政治调查(National Race and Politics Survey)中的一个列举调查-实验。该实验的控制条目问题为:

> 现在我要读出三件事,这三件事有时会让人感到气愤或不安。当我读完所有三件事后,请告诉我有多少件事情让你感到不安。(我不想知道具体哪件事情,只需要知道有多少件。)
>
> 1.联邦政府提高了汽油税
>
> 2.职业运动员得到百万美元以上的工资
>
> 3.大企业集团污染环境
>
> 这些事中有几件事会让你感到不安?

实验组增添的敏感条目问题为:

> 4.一个黑人家庭搬到你家隔壁

数据集命名为 Race,从全国调查数据集中整理提取出来,共包括 6 个变量,1213 个观测,具体变量描述见表 4.5,数据集中 y 为结果变量,treat 为处理变量。

表 4.5　Race 数据集中的变量

变量名称	变量描述	取值范围
y	让受访者感到不安的事件个数	0~4
south	受访者是否住在美国南部各州	0~1
male	受访者是否为男性	0~1
college	受访者是否有大学学历	0~1
age	受访者的年龄(除以 10)	0~10
treat	受访者是否在实验组	0~1

4.3.2　程序包介绍

用于列举实验数据分析的程序包名称为 list，是由普林斯顿大学的政治学者 Graeme Blair 和 Kosuke Imai 的研究团队于 2010 年首次开发，最新版本是 2015 年更新的 8.0 版本。程序包的分析方法是基于 Imai（2011），Blair and Imai（2012）等多篇文章，主要功能包括采用贝叶斯 MCMC 方法实施的对于列举实验数据的多元回归分析模型，基于多元回归模型的预测值计算，对于列举实验设计效应的检测，结合列举实验和直接提问来估计敏感行为的发生比例等。

此程序包不是 R 软件的预设包，需要使用者通过输入 R 命令下载并安装在本地电脑，而且在每次使用这些程序包之前都需要将其载入，具体 R 命令如下：

```
install.packages("list")    # 安装程序包
library(list)               # 载入程序包
```

软件包中用于分析多元回归模型的函数为 ictreg,其语句格式为:

```
ictreg(formula, data = parent.frame(), treat = "treat", J, method = "ml",
weights, overdispersed = FALSE, constrained = TRUE, floor = FALSE,
ceiling = FALSE, ceiling.fit = "glm", floor.fit = "glm",
ceiling.formula = ~ 1, floor.formula = ~ 1, fit.start = "lm",
fit.nonsensitive = "nls", multi.condition = "none",
maxIter = 5000, verbose = FALSE, ...)
```

其中一些常用的设定有:

formula	模型的表达公式
data	用来建模的数据集名称
treat	列举调查-实验中的处理变量
J	列举调查-实验中控制条目的数目
method	回归分析的方法,可设定 ml(最大似然估计),lm(线性模型估计),或 nls(非线性最小平方估计)
overdispersed	出现超散布性的指示变量。可设定 TRUE 或 FALSE。如果设定前者,将使用 beta 二项分布模型,如果设定后者,则使用二项分布模型。不适用于 nls 或 lm 估计方法
constrained	逻辑值,指明控制组的参数是否要限定相等。不适用于 nls 或 lm 估计方法

4.3.3　应用示例

Race 数据集是该程序包内的示例数据集,在分析数据之前首先要将其导入:

```
data(race)                       # 导入程序包中的 race 数据集
attach(race)                     # 将数据集添加到内存中方便查看
```

数据集中 y，即让受访者感到不安的事件个数，为因变量，处理变量为 treat。2.4 节中介绍，当模型中不包括任何自变量时，得到的分析结果就是均值差。因此在模型的公式上设定为 y～1，该调查-实验的控制题目有 3 个，所以 J＝3，估计方法采用线性模型。具体 R 程序如下：

```
# 计算均值差
diff.in.means.results <- ictreg(y ~ 1, data = race,
                                 treat = "treat", J=3, method = "lm")
summary(diff.in.means.results)
```

输出结果为：

```
Item Count Technique Regression

Call: ictreg(formula = y ~ 1, data = race, treat = "treat", J = 3,
    method = "lm")

Sensitive item
              Est.    S.E.
(Intercept) 0.0678 0.04962

Control items
               Est.    S.E.
(Intercept) 2.13413 0.03317

Residual standard error: 0.866365 with 1211 degrees of freedom

Number of control items J set to 3. Treatment groups were indicated by
" and "   and the control group by ".
```

以上结果显示，控制组的受访者平均选取的条目数为 2.13413，标准误是 0.03317。实验组的受访者选取的条目数比控制组的受访者平均多选取 0.0678 条，标准误为 0.04962。由此可以推算对敏感事件,即"一个黑人家庭搬到你家隔壁",感到不安的人数比例为 6.78%,根据标准误得出该比例在 0.05 水平上统计不显著,也就是说总体来看两组受访者的应答均值没有显著差异。

研究者希望进一步发现美国南方白人和北方白人在这一列举调查-实验中的应答均值是否有显著差异,并且这些差异不是因为他们的人口特征造成。于是在模型中引入 south 作为自变量,age, male 和 college 作为控制变量。采用线性模型(LM)、非线性模型(NLS)和最大似然模型(ML)方法的命令语句分别如下:

```
# 拟合 LM 模型
lm.results <- ictreg(y ~ south + age + male + college, data = race,
        treat = "treat", J=3, method = "lm")
summary(lm.results)

# 拟合 NLS 模型
nls.results <- ictreg(y ~ south + age + male + college, data = race,
        treat = "treat", J=3, method = "nls")
summary(nls.results)

# 拟合有限制的 ML 模型
ml.constrained.results <- ictreg(y ~ south + age + male + college,
data = race,
        treat = "treat", J=3, method = "ml", overdispersed = FALSE,
constrained = TRUE) summary(ml.constrained.results)

# 拟合无限制的 ML 模型
ml.unconstrained.results <- ictreg(y ~ south + age + male + college,
        data = race, treat = "treat", J=3, method = "ml", overdisper-
        sed = FALSE, constrained = FALSE)
summary(ml.unconstrained.results)
```

前面提到,ML 估计值有更好的统计功效,而 NLS 估计值则在稳健性上略有优势。下面重点展示 ML 和 NLS 模型分析的输出结果。

NLS 模型分析的输出结果为:

```
Item Count Technique Regression

Call: ictreg(formula = y ~ south + age + male + college, data = race,
    treat = "treat", J = 3, method = "nls")

Sensitive item
                   Est.    S.E.
(Intercept) -7.08431 3.66927
south        2.48984 1.26819
age          0.26094 0.31467
male         3.09687 2.82923
college      0.61232 1.02951

Control items
                   Est.    S.E.
(Intercept)  1.38811 0.18683
south       -0.27655 0.11617
age          0.03307 0.03503
male        -0.33223 0.10702
college     -0.66175 0.11314

Residual standard error: 0.900805 with 619 degrees of freedom

Number of control items J set to 3. Treatment groups were indicated by
"and "   and the control group by ".
```

有限制的 ML 模型分析的输出结果为：

```
Item Count Technique Regression

Call: ictreg(formula = y ~ south + age + male + college, data = race,
    treat = "treat", J = 3, method = "ml", overdispersed = FALSE,
    constrained = TRUE)

Sensitive item
                   Est.    S.E.
(Intercept) -5.50833 1.02112
south        1.67564 0.55855
age          0.63587 0.16334
male         0.84647 0.49375
college     -0.31527 0.47360
```

```
Control items
                Est.    S.E.
(Intercept)  1.19141 0.14369
south       -0.29204 0.09692
age          0.03322 0.02768
male        -0.25060 0.08194
college     -0.51641 0.08368

Log-likelihood: -1444.394

Number of control items J set to 3. Treatment groups were indicated by
'1' and the control group by '0'.
```

在两个输出结果的敏感条目中，south 变量的估计系数均为正值，并且在 5%的置信水平上统计显著，说明在排除年龄、性别和受教育程度的影响之后，平均来说美国南方白人比北方白人更容易因为“一个黑人家庭搬到隔壁”而感到不安。分析结果也确实显示出 ML 估计的标准误要小于 NLS 的估计值，从而有更好的统计功效。

然而基于 NLS 或 ML 模型的系数很难解释自变量和因变量直接的具体关系，常用的一个办法就是借助模型的预测值作图来说明。在 list 软件包中的函数 predict.icteg 和 plot.predict.ictreg 可以根据列举调查-实验的多元回归模型计算预测的差异值及其置信区间，并且以图形方式展现出来。具体操作步骤如下：

①在原数据集 race 的基础上生成两个新的数据集，一个数据集中的 south 变量全部取值为 1，命名为 race.south；另一个数据集中的 south 变量全部取值为 0，命名为 race.nonsouth。数据集的制作命令如下：

```
race.south <- race.nonsouth <- race
race.south[, "south"] <- 1
race.nonsouth[, "south"] <- 0
```

②基于原有 race 数据集使用 ictreg 函数拟合有限制的 ML 模型。

```
# 拟合有限制的 ML 模型
ml.constrained.results <- ictreg(y ~ south + age + male + college,
      data = race, treat = " treat ", J = 3, method = " ml ",
      overdispersed = FALSE, constrained = TRUE)
```

③根据模型结果，使用 predict 函数计算南方白人和北方白人在敏感条目上应答比例的预测值及其 95%的置信区间。predict 的语句格式为：

```
predict(object, newdata, newdata.diff, direct.glm, se.fit = FALSE,
    interval = c("none","confidence"), level = .95, avg = FALSE, sen-
    sitive.item, ...)
```

其中一些常用的设定为：

object	从上一步继承来的 ictreg 的分析结果
newdata	用来预测的数据框
newdata.diff	用来和 newdata 设定的数据框比较的数据框
interval	区间计算的类型：设为"none"表示不计算，"confidence"表示计算置信区间
level	置信区间的显著性水平，默认值为 95%
avg	设为"FALSE"表示计算每一个观测的预测值；设为"TRUE"表示计算所有观测的均值预测值及相关统计值

在本例中，首先分别预测南方白人和北方白人在敏感条目上的应答比例及其 95%的置信区间，于是将 newdata 设定为 race.south 或 race.nonsouth，同时将 interval 设定为"confidence"，将 avg 设定为"TRUE"，具体命令语句如下：

```
# 预测南方白人和北方白人在敏感条目上的应答比例及其 95% 的置信区间
avg.pred.south.mle <- predict(ml.constrained.results, newdata =
      race.south, avg = TRUE, interval = "confidence")
avg.pred.nonsouth.mle <- predict(ml.constrained.results, newdata =
      race.nonsouth, avg = TRUE, interval = "confidence")
```

也可以直接比较南方白人和北方白人在敏感条目上应答比例预测值的差异。这时需要补充 newdata.diff 选项，将其设定为和 newdata 对应的要比较的数据框，如：

```
# 预测南方白人和北方白人在敏感条目上的应答比例的差异及其 95% 的置信区间
avg.pred.diff.mle <- predict(ml.constrained.results, newdata = race.
       south, newdata.diff = race.nonsouth, avg = TRUE, interval =
       "confidence")
```

④根据上一步获取的预测值，使用 plot 函数绘制预测值及其置信区间示意图。plot 的命令格式为：

```
plot (x, labels = NA, axes.ict = TRUE, xlim = NULL, ylim = NULL, xlab =
     NULL, ylab = "Estimated Proportion", axes = F, pch = 19, xvec =
     NULL, ...)
```

一般只需对 x 和 labels 进行设定，其他选项可以使用默认值。如将南方白人和北方白人的预测比例和 95%的置信区间绘制在同一张图上的命令为：

```
# 绘制南方白人和北方白人的预测比例和 95% 的置信区间
plot (c (avg. pred. south. mle, avg. pred. nonsouth. mle), labels =
     c("South", "Non-South"))
```

输出结果如图 4.28 所示。其中线段中心的点代表预测的比例，线段代表 95%的置信区间的位置及宽度。可以直观地看出，在控制住年龄、性别和教育程度的影响下，美国南方白人在敏感条目上的应答比例预测值超过 30%(0.318)，而北方白人的比例仅略高于 10%(0.106)，并且预测值的 95%的置信区间没有包括数值“0”，意味着这些应答比例为 0 的可能性非常小。

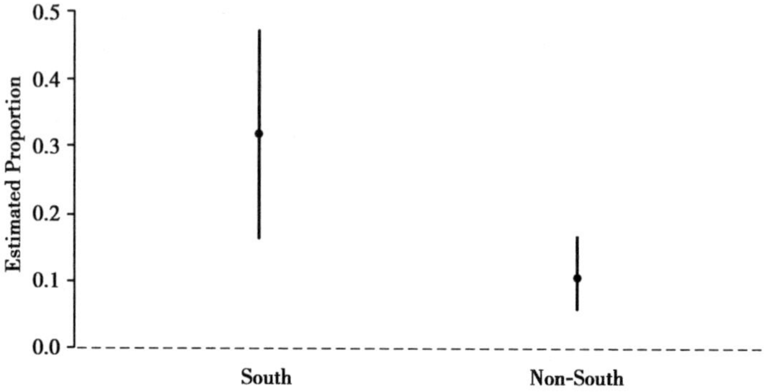

图 4.28 R 绘图一（列举调查-实验多元数据分析）

如果还想在图上表示出南方白人和北方白人在敏感条目上应答比例的差异及其检验结果，只需用如下命令：

```
# 绘制南方白人和北方白人的预测比例差异和 95% 的置信区间
plot(avg.pred.diff.mle, labels = c("South", "Non-South", "Differ-
    ence"))
```

如图 4.29 所示，二者之间的差异及其 95%的置信区间也展示在图上。同理，预测比例的差异是 0.212，在 5%的水平上统计显著，说明美国南方白人与北方白人相比，会有更多的人因为黑人家庭做邻居的事情而感到不安。

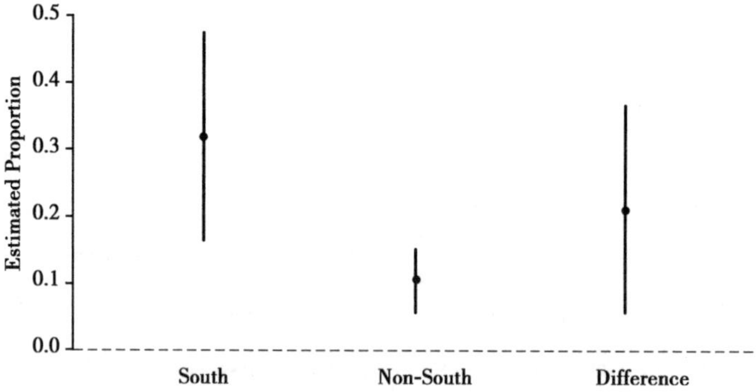

图 4.29 R 绘图二（列举调查-实验多元数据分析）

在 list 软件包里,还包含了其他函数用来检验列举调查-实验条目的设计效应和天花板/地板效应,感兴趣的读者可以参考软件包里的介绍文档。

参考文献

陈然,于朔,2014.支持还是反对军事冲突?——日本与邻国争端中民意的调查-实验分析[J].国际安全研究,(05):138-154.

陈晓平,2003.休谟问题评析——兼评“归纳问题”与“因果问题”之争[J].学术研究,(01):20-26.

陈晓平,2008.密尔的排除归纳法辨析[J].科学技术与辩证法,(04):1-8.

孟天广,杨平,苏政,2015.转型中国的公民意见与地方财政决策——基于对地方政府的调查-实验[J].公共管理学报,(03):57-68.

彭玉生,2011.社会科学中的因果分析[J].社会学研究,(03):1-32.

任莉颖,严洁,2014.并行数据与社会调查质量探讨[J].统计与决策,(06):27-32.

斯考切波,2007.国家与社会革命:对法国、俄国和中国的比较分析[M].何俊志,王学东,译.上海:上海人民出版社.

谢宇,2010.认识中国的不平等[J].社会,(03):1-20.

严洁,邱泽奇,任莉颖,等,2012. 社会调查质量研究:访员臆答与干预效果.社会学研究,(02):168-181.

Abul-Ela, Abdel-Latif A., and Bernard G. Greenberg, 1967. A Multi-Proportions Randomized Response Model[J]. Journal of the American Statistical Association, 62(319): 990-1008.

Alferes, Valentim R. 2012. *Methods of Randomization in Experimental Design*[M]. Los Angeles: SAGE.

Astrom, Therese, Ulla Jergeby, and Anna-Karin Andershed, et al, 2013. "Social workers" assessments of needs and interventions for adolescents with substance misuse problems, criminal behaviour and mental health difficulties: a vignette study[J]. European Journal of Social Work, 16(5): 635-650.

Atzmueller, Christiane, and Peter M. Steiner, 2010. Experimental Vignette Studies in Survey Research[J]. Methodology-European Journal of Research Methods for the Behavioral and Social Sciences, 6(3): 128-138.

Barabas, Jason, and Jennifer Jerit, 2010. Are Survey Experiments Externally Valid? [J]. The American Political Science Review, 104(2): 226-242.

Biemer, Paul P., Robert M. Groves, and Lars E. Lyberg, et al, 2011. Measurement errors in surveys[J]. (173): John Wiley & Sons.

Bishop, George F., and Robert W. Oldendick, 1982. Effects of Presenting One Versus Two Sides of an Issue in Survey Questions[J]. The Public Opinion Quarterly, 46(1): 69-85.

Blair, Graeme, and Kosuke Imai, 2012. Statistical Analysis of List Experiments[J]. Political Analysis, 20(1): 47-77.

Blom-Hansen, Jens, Rebecca Morton, and Soren Serritzlew, 2015. Experiments in Public Management Research[J]. International Public Management Journal, 18(2SI): 151-170.

Boruch, Robert F., and Joe S. Cecil, 1979. Assuring the Confidentiality of Social Science Research Data[M]. Philadelphia: University of Pennsylvaniz Press.

Bositis, David A., and Douglas Steinel, 1987. A Synoptic History and Typology of Experimental Research in Political Science[J]. Political Behavior, 9(3): 263-284.

Bozeman, Barry, 1992. Experimental Design in Public Policy and Management Research: Introduction[J]. Journal of Public Administration Research and Theory: J-Part, 2(4): 440-442.

Bozeman, Barry, and Patrick Scott, 1992. Laboratory Experiments in Public Policy and Management[J]. Journal of Public Administration Research and Theory: J-Part, 2(3): 293-313.

Brady, H. E, 2000. Contributions of survey research to political science[J]. Ps-Political Science & Politics, 33(1): 47-57.

Brenner, Maria, 2013. Development of a factorial survey to explore restricting a child's movement for a clinical procedure[J]. Nurse researcher, 21(2): 40-48.

Cantril, Hadley, and S. S. Wilks, 1940. Problems and Techniques[J]. The Public Opinion Quarterly, 4(2): 330-338.

Cassino, Dan, and Cengiz Erisen, 2010. Priming Bush and Iraq in 2008: A Survey Experiment[J]. American Politics Research, 38(2SI): 372-394.

Cotter, Patrick R., and Jeffrey Cohen, et al, 1982. Race-of-Interviewer Effects in Telephone Interviews[J]. The Public Opinion Quarterly, 46(2): 278-284.

Couper, Mick P., and Frederick G. Conrad, et al, 2007. Visual context effects in web surveys[J]. Public Opinion Quarterly, 71(4): 623-634.

Couper, Mick, and Lars Lyberg, 2005. The Use of Paradata in Survey Research[J]. In Proceedings of the 55th Session of the International Statistical Institute.

Cruces, Guillermo, and Ricardo Perez-Truglia, et al, 2013. Biased perceptions of income distribution and preferences for redistribution: Evidence from a survey experiment[J]. Journal of Public Economics, 98: 100-112.

Davis, Rachel, M. Savvopoulou, et al, 2014. Predictors of healthcare professionals' attitudes towards family involvement in safety-relevant behaviours: a cross-sectional factorial survey study[J]. BMJ Open, 4(e0055499).

Droitcour, Judith, Rachel A. Caspar, and Michael L. Hubbard, et al, 1991. The Item Count Technique as a Method of Indirect Questioning: A Review of Its Development and a Case Study Application[J]. In Measurement errors in surveys, ed. P. P. Biemer, R. M. Groves, L. E. Lyberg, N. A. Mathiowetz and S. Sudman: John Wiley & Sons, Inc.

Druckman, James N., and Donald P. Green, et al, 2006. The growth and development of experimental research in political science[J]. American Political Science Review, 100(4): 627-635.

Edgell, Stephen E., Samuel Himmelfarb, and Karen L, et al, 1982. Validity of Forced Responses in a Randomized Response Model[J]. Sociological Methods & Research, 11 (1): 89-100.

Emerson, Michael O., and Karen J. Chai, et al, 2001. Does Race Matter in Residential Segregation? Exploring the Preferences of White Americans[J]. American Sociological Review, 66(6): 922-935.

Folsom, Ralph E., Bernard G. Greenberg, and Daniel G. Horvitz, et al, 1973. The Two Alternate Questions Randomized Response Model for Human Surveys[J]. Journal of the American Statistical Association, 68(343): 525-530.

Fox, James Alan, and Paul E. Tracy, 1986. Randomized response: a method for sensitive surveys[J]. 07(058). Beverly Hills: Sage Publications.

Fumagalli, Laura, Heather Laurie, and Peter Lynn, 2013. Experiments with methods to reduce attrition in longitudinal surveys[J]. Journal of the Royal Statistical Society Series A-Statistics in Society, 176(2): 499-519.

Gaines, Brian J., James H. Kuklinski, and Paul J. Quirk, 2007. The logic of the survey experiment reexamined[J]. Political Analysis, 15(1): 1-20.

Gerring, John, Rose McDermott, 2007. An Experimental Template for Case Study Research[J]. American Journal of Political Science, 51(3): 688-701.

Glynn, Adam N, 2013. What Can We Learn With Statistical Truth Serum? Design and Analysis of The List Experiment[J]. Public Opinion Quarterly, 771(SI): 159-172.

Greenberg, Bernard G., Abdel-Latif A. Abul-Ela, Walt R. Simmons, and Daniel G. Horvitz, 1969. The Unrelated Question Randomized Response Model: Theoretical Framework[J]. Journal of the American Statistical Association, 64(326): 520-539.

Groves, Robert M, 2009. Survey methodology[J]. Vol. 2nd. Hoboken, N.J: Wiley.

Hainmueller, Jens, and Michael J. Hiscox, 2010. Attitudes toward Highly Skilled and Low-skilled Immigration: Evidence from a Survey Experiment[J]. American Political Science Review, 104(1): 61-84.

Hans, Jason D., and Claire Kimberly, 2014. Abortion attitudes in context: A multidimensional vignette approach[J]. Social Science Research , 48: 145-156.

Harmon, Thomas, Charles F. Turner, Susan M. Rogers, Elizabeth Eggleston, Anthony M. Roman, Maria A. Villarroel, James R. Chromy, Laxminarayana Ganapathi, and Sheping Li, 2009. Impact of T-ACASI on Survey Measurements of Subjective Phenomena[J]. Public Opinion Quarterly, 73(2): 255-280.

Hedges, B. M, 1979. Question Wording Effects: Presenting One or Both Sides of a Case[J]. Journal of the Royal Statistical Society. Series D (The Statistician), 28(2): 83-99.

Holbrook, Allyson L., and Jon A. Krosnick, 2010. Social desirability bias in voter turnout reports[J]. Public Opinion Quarterly, 74(1): 37-67.

Horiuchi, Yusaku, Kosuke Imai, and Naoko Taniguchi, 2007a. Designing and Analyzing Randomized Experiments: Application to a Japanese Election Survey Experiment[J]. American Journal of Political Science, 51(3): 669-687.

Horiuchi, Yusaku, Kosuke Imai, and Naoko Taniguchi, 2007b. Designing and analyzing randomized experiments: Application to a Japanese election survey experiment[J]. American Journal of Political Science, 51(3): 669-687.

Hox, Joop J., Igg Kreft, and Plj Hermkens, 1991. The Analysis of Factorial Surveys[J]. Sociological Methods & Research, 19(4): 493-510.

Imai, Kosuke, 2009. Statistical Analysis of Randomized Experiments with Non-Ignorable Missing Binary Outcomes: An Application to a Voting Experiment[J]. Journal of the Royal Statistical Society. Series C (Applied Statistics), 58(1): 83-104.

Imai, Kosuke, 2011. Multivariate Regression Analysis for the Item Count Technique[J]. Journal of the American Statistical Association, 106(494): 407-416.

Imai, Kosuke, Bethany Park, and Kenneth F. Greene, 2015. Using the Predicted Responses from List Experiments as Explanatory Variables in Regression Models[J]. Political Analysis, 23(2): 180-196.

Imai, Kosuke, Gary King, and Olivia Lau, 2008. Toward a Common Framework for Statistical Analysis and Development[J]. Journal of Computational and Graphical Statistics, 17(4): 892-913.

Imbens, Guido W., and Donald B. Rubin, 1997. Bayesian inference for causal effects in randomized experiments with noncompliance [J]. Annals of Statistics, 25(1): 305-327.

Jackson, Michelle, and D. R. Cox, 2013a. The Principles of Experimental Design and Their Application in Sociology[J]. Annual Review of Sociology, 39: 27-49.

Jann, Ben, Julia Jerke, and Ivar Krumpal, 2012. Asking Sensitive Questions Using the Crosswise Model[J]. Public Opinion Quarterly, 76(1): 32-49.

Jaros, Dean, and Gene L. Mason, 1969. Party Choice and Support for Demagogues: An Experimental Examination[J]. The American Political Science Review, 63(1): 100-110.

Jasso, Guillermina, 1978. On the Justice of Earnings: A New Specification of the Justice Evaluation Function[J]. American Journal of Sociology, 83(6): 1398-1419.

Jasso, Guillermina, 2006. Factorial survey methods for studying beliefs and judgments[J]. Sociological Methods & Research, 34(3): 334-423.

Jasso, Guillermina, and Karl-Dieter Opp, 1997. Probing the Character of Norms: A Factorial Survey Analysis of the Norms of Political Action[J]. American Sociological Review, 62(6): 947-964.

Jasso, Guillermina, and Peter H. Rossi, 1977. Distributive Justice and Earned Income[J]. American Sociological Review, 42(4): 639-651.

Kamin, Leon J, 1958. Ethnic and party affiliations of candidates as determinants of voting[J]. Canadian journal of psychology, 12(4): 205-212.

Killick, Campbell, and Brian J. Taylor, 2012. Judgements of Social Care Professionals on Elder Abuse Referrals: A Factorial Survey[J]. British Journal of Social Work, 42(5): 814-832.

Kuk, Anthong Y.C., 1990. Asking Sensitive Questions Indirectly[J]. Biometrika, 77(2): 436-438.

Kuklinski, James H., and Michael D. Cobb, et al, 1997. Racial Attitudes and the "New South"[J]. The Journal of Politics, 59(2): 323-349.

Laguilles, Jerold S., and Elizabeth A. Williams, et al, 2011. Can Lottery Incentives Boost Web Survey Response Rates? Findings from Four Experiments[J]. Research in Higher Education, 52(5): 537-553.

Landsheer, Johannes A., and Peter Van Der Heijden, et al, 1999. Trust and Understanding, Two Psychological Aspects of Randomized Response[J]. Quality and Quantity, 33(1): 1-12.

Lauder, William, P. Anne Scott, and Anne Whyte, 2001. Nurses' judgements of self-neglect: a factorial survey[J]. International Journal of Nursing Studies, 38(5): 601-608.

Locander, William B., and John P. Burton, 1976. The Effect of Question Form on Gathering Income Data by Telephone[J]. Journal of Marketing Research, 13(2): 189-192.

Luiten, Annemieke, and Barry Schouten, 2013. Tailored fieldwork design to increase representative household survey response: an experiment in the Survey of Consumer Satisfaction[J]. Journal of the Royal Statistical Society Series A Statistics in Society, 176(1): 169-189.

Margetts, Helen Z, 2011. Experiments for Public Management Research [J]. Public Management Review, 13(PII 9340398232SI): 189-208.

Marsden, Peter V., and James D. Wright, 2010. Handbook of survey research[J]. Vol. 2nd, Bingley: Emerald.

McDermott, Rose, 2013. The Ten Commandments of Experiments[J]. Ps-Political Science & Politics, 46(3): 605-610.

Meng, Tianguang, Jennifer Pan, and Ping Yang, 2014. Conditional Receptivity to Citizen Participation: Evidence From a Survey Experiment in China[J]. Comparative Political Studies, 50(4): 399-433.

Millar, Morgan M., and Don A. Dillman, 2011. Improving Response to Web and Mixed-Mode Surveys[J]. Public Opinion Quarterly, 75(2): 249-269.

Moors, J. J. A, 1971. Optimization of the Unrelated Question Randomized Response Model[J]. Journal of the American Statistical Association, 66 (335): 627-629.

Morton, Rebecca B., and Kenneth C. Williams, 2010. Experimental political science and the study of causality: From nature to the lab[M]: Cambridge University Press.

Mueller-Engelmann, Meike, and Norbert Donner-Banzhoff, et al, 2013. When Decisions Should Be Shared: A Study of Social Norms in Medical Decision Making Using a Factorial Survey Approach[J]. Medical Decision Making, 33 (1SI): 37-47.

Mutz, Diana C, 2011. Population-based survey experiments[M]: Princeton University Press.

Nock, Steven L., and Paul W. Kingston, et al, 2008. The Distribution of Obligations[J]. In Intergenerational Caregiving, ed. A. Booth, A. C. Crouters, S. M. Bianchi and J. A. Seltzer. Washington, DC: The Urban Institute Press.

Nock, Steven L., and Peter H. Rossi, 1979. Household Types and Social Standing[J]. Social Forces, 57(4): 1325-1345.

Nock, Steven L., and Thomas M. Guterbock, 2010. An anatomy of survey-based experiments[J]. In Handbook of Survey Research, ed. P. V. Marsden and J. D. Wright: Bingley: Emerald.

Oakley, A, 1998. Experimentation and social interventions: a forgotten but important history[J]. British Medical Journal, 317(7167): 1239-1242.

Pforr, Klaus, and Michael Blohm, et al, 2015. Are Incentive Effects on Response Rates and Nonresponse Bias in Large-Scale, Face-to-Face Surveys Generalizable to Germany? Evidence from Ten Experiments[J]. Public Opinion Quarterly, 79(3): 740-768.

Presser, Stanley, and Howard Schuman, 1980. The Measurement of a Middle Position in Attitude Surveys[J]. The Public Opinion Quarterly, 44(1): 70-85.

Rattray, Janice E., and William Lauder, et al, 2011. Indicators of acute deterioration in adult patients nursed in acute wards: a factorial survey[J]. Journal of Clinical Nursing, 20(5-6): 723-732.

Reinmuth, James E., and Michael D. Geurts, 1975. The Collection of Sensitive Information Using a Two-Stage, Randomized Response Model[J]. Journal of

Marketing Research,12(4): 402-407.

Revilla, Melanie, 2015. Comparison of the quality estimates in a mixed-mode and a unimode design: an experiment from the European Social Survey [J]. Quality & Quantity, 49(3): 1219-1238.

Rosen, Corey M, 1973. A Test of Presidential Leadership of Public Opinion: The Split-Ballot Technique[J]. Polity, 6(2): 282-290.

Rossi, Peter H., and William A. Sampson, et al, 1974. Measuring household social standing[J]. Social Science Research, 3(3): 169-190.

Rossi, Peter Henry, and Steven L. Nock, 1982. Measuring social judgements: the factorial survey approach[M]. Beverly Hills: Sage Publications.

Schuman, Howard, and Stanley Presser, et al, 1981. Context Effects on Survey Responses to Questions About Abortion[J]. The Public Opinion Quarterly, 45 (2): 216-223.

Schuman, Howard, and Stanley Presser, 1979a. The Open and Closed Question[J]. American Sociological Review, 44(4): 692.

Schuman, Howard, and Stanley Presser, 1979b. The Assessment of "No Opinion" in Attitude Surveys[J]. Sociological Methodology, 10: 241-275.

Schuman, Howard, and Stanley Presser, 1980. Public Opinion and Public Ignorance: The Fine Line between Attitudes and Nonattitudes[J]. American Journal of Sociology, 85(2): 1214.

Schwappach, David L. B., and Olga Frank, et al, 2013. A vignette study to examine health care professionals' attitudes towards patient involvement in error prevention[J]. Journal of Evaluation in Clinical Practice, 19(5): 840-848.

Shadish, William R., and Thomas D. Cook, et al, 2002. Statistical Conclusion Validity and Internal Validity[J]. In Experimental and Quasi Experimental Designs for Generilized Causal Inference, ed. W. R. Shadish, T. D. Cook and D. T. Campbell. Boston: Houghton Mifflin.

Singer, Eleanor, John Van Hoewyk, and Mary P. Maher, 2000. Experiments with incentives in telephone surveys [J]. Public Opinion Quarterly, 64 (2): 171-188.

Sniderman, Paul M, 2011. The Logic and Design of the Survey Experiment: An Autobiography of a Methodological Innovation[J]. In Cambridge Handbook of Experimental Political Science, ed. J. N. Druckman, D. P. Green, J. H. Kuklinski and A. Lupia. Cambridge, UK: Cambridge University Press.

Sniderman, Paul M., and Edward G, et al, 1996. Beyond Race: Social Justice as a Race Neutral Idea[J]. American Journal of Political Science, 40(1): 33.

Sniderman, Paul M., and Douglas B. Grob, 1996. Innovations in Experimental Design in Attitude Surveys[J]. Annual Review of Sociology, 22(1): 377-399.

Sniderman, Paul M., and Edward G. Carmines, 1997. Reaching beyond race[M]. Cambridge, Mass: Harvard University Press.

Sniderman, Paul M., and Thomas Piazza, 1993. The Scar of Race[M]. Cambridge, MA: Harvard Unversity Press.

Stokes, Jacqueline, and Glen Schmidt, 2012. Child Protection Decision Making: A Factorial Analysis Using Case Vignettes[J]. Social Work, 57(1): 83-90.

Streb, Matthew J., Barbara Burrell, and Brian Frederick, et al, 2008. Social Desirability Effects and Support for a Female American President[J]. The Public Opinion Quarterly, 72(1): 76-89.

Tai, Qiuqing, and Rory Truex, 2015. Public Opinion towards Return Migration: A Survey Experiment of Chinese Netizens[J]. China Quarterly, 223: 770-786.

Takahasi, Koiti, and Hirotaka Sakasegawa, 1977. A randomized response technique without making use of any randomizing device[J]. Annals of the Institute of Statistical Mathematics, 29(1): 1-8.

Taylor, Brian J, 2006. Factorial surveys: Using vignettes to study professional judgement[J]. British Journal of Social Work, 36(7): 1187-1207.

Tolsma, Jochem, and Joris Blaauw, et al, 2012. When do people report crime to the police? Results from a factorial survey design in the Netherlands, 2010[J]. Journal of Experimental Criminology, 8(2): 117-134.

Tourangeau, R., and T. W. Smith, 1996. Asking sensitive questions —The impact of data collection mode, question format, and question context[J]. Public Opinion Quarterly, 60(2): 275-304.

Tourangeau, Roger, and Mick P. Couper, et al, 2004. Spacing, Position, and Order: Interpretive Heuristics for Visual Features of Survey Questions[J]. The Public Opinion Quarterly, 68(3): 368-393.

Tourangeau, Roger, and Mick P. Couper, et al, 2007. Color, labels, and interpretive heuristics for response scales[J]. Public Opinion Quarterly, 71(1): 91-112.

Transue, John E., and Daniel J. Lee, et al, 2009. Treatment Spillover Effects across Survey Experiments[J]. Political Analysis, 17(2): 143-161.

Trappmann, Mark, and Ivar Krumpal, et al, 2014. Item Sum: A New Technique for Asking Quantitative Sensitive Questions[J]. Journal of Survey Statistics and Methodology, 2(1): 58-77.

Tsuchiya, Takahiro, and Yoko Hirai, et al, 2007. A Study of the Properties of the Item Count Technique[J]. The Public Opinion Quarterly, 71(2): 253-272.

Villarroel, Maria A., and Charles F. Turner, et al, 2006. Same-Gender Sex in the United States: Impact of T-ACASI on Prevalence Estimates[J]. The Public Opinion Quarterly, 70(2): 166-196.

Wagner, James, and Jennifer Arrieta, et al, 2014. Does Sequence Matter in Multimode Surveys Results from an Experiment[J]. Field Methods, 26(2): 141-155.

Wallander, Lisa, 2009a. 25 years of factorial surveys in sociology: A review[J]. Social Science Research, 38(3): 505-520.

Wallander, Lisa, 2009b. 25 years of factorial surveys in sociology: A review[J]. Social Science Research, 38(3): 505-520.

Wallander, Lisa, 2012. Measuring social workers' judgements: Why and how to use the factorial survey approach in the study of professional judgements[J]. Journal of Social Work, 12(4): 364-384.

Warner, Stanley L, 1965. Randomized Response: A Survey Technique for Eliminating Evasive Answer Bias[J]. Journal of the American Statistical Association, 60(309): 63-69.

Warner, Stanley L, 1971. The Linear Randomized Response Model[J]. Journal of the American Statistical Association, 66(336): 884-888.

Warriner, Keith, and John Goyder, et al, 1996. Charities, No; Lotteries, No; Cash, Yes: Main Effects and Interactions in a Canadian Incentives Experiment[J]. The Public Opinion Quarterly, 60(4): 542-562.

Wetzels, Willem, and Hans Schmeets, et al, 2008. Impact of Prepaid Incentives in Face-to-Face Surveys: A Large-Scale Experiment with Postage Stamps[J]. International Journal of Public Opinion Research, 20(4): 507-516.

Yu, Jun-Wu, Guo-Liang Tian, and Man-Lai Tang, 2008. Two new models for survey sampling with sensitive characteristic: design and analysis[J]. Metrika, 67(3): 251-263.

Zagorsky, Jay L., and Patricia Rhoton, 2008. The effects of promised monetary incentives on attrition in a long-term panel survey[J]. Public Opinion Quarterly, 72(3): 502-513.